CYBER WAR IN PERSPECTIVE:
RUSSIAN AGGRESSION AGAINST UKRAINE

CYBER WAR
IN PERSPECTIVE:

*Russian Aggression
against Ukraine*

Edited by
KENNETH GEERS

CCDCOE NATO Cooperative Cyber Defence
Centre of Excellence Tallinn, Estonia

NATO CCD COE Publications
Filtri tee 12, 10132 Tallinn, Estonia
Phone: +372 717 6800 Fax: +372 717 6308
E-mail: publications@ccdcoe.org
Web: www.ccdcoe.org

LEGAL NOTICE

Print: EVG Print
Cover design & content layout: Villu Koskaru

ISBN 978-9949-9544-4-5 (print)
ISBN 978-9949-9544-5-2 (pdf)

NATO Cooperative Cyber Defence Centre of Excellence

The Tallinn-based NATO Cooperative Cyber Defence Centre of Excellence (NATO CCD COE) is a NATO-accredited knowledge hub, think-tank and training facility. The international military organisation focuses on interdisciplinary applied research and development, as well as consultations, trainings and exercises in the field of cyber security. The Centre's mission is to enhance capability, cooperation and information-sharing between NATO, Allies and partners in cyber defence.

Membership of the Centre is open to all Allies. The Czech Republic, Estonia, France, Germany, Hungary, Italy, Latvia, Lithuania, Greece, the Netherlands, Poland, Slovakia, Spain, Turkey, the United Kingdom and the USA have signed on as sponsoring nations. Austria and Finland have joined the Centre as contributing participants. The Centre is funded and staffed by these member nations.

 CCDCOE

NATO Cooperative Cyber Defence
Centre of Excellence Tallinn, Estonia

CONTENTS

Foreword

Director, NATO Cooperative Cyber Defence Centre of Excellence

In mid-January 2014, the Ukrainian Rada passed tough anti-protest regulations that seemed to be designed to nip the emerging anti-government mood in the bud. Over the next months, in the harsh Ukrainian winter, opposition protests escalated and turned bloody. The ensuing turmoil included a runaway President, Russian occupation of Crimea and an armed conflict in Eastern Ukraine.

The world held its breath and many expected to see a full-fledged 'cyber war'. However, although an increase in typical cyber skirmishes was reported throughout the crisis, prominent cyber operations with destructive effects have not yet occurred. The possible reasons for this seemingly low-level employment of cyber attacks in Ukraine characterise the particular role of cyber operations in modern conflicts.

The case of Ukraine proves that the use of cyber operations has to be understood in the wider strategic context. In Ukraine we saw – in line with national doctrine – that Russian information warfare both included and relied upon cyber elements. Reported cyber incidents such as defacements, information leaks or DDoS attacks against media or governmental organisations were predominantly in support of the intense Russian information operation against Ukraine and the West.

Furthermore, due to the historical interconnectedness of networks and sophisticated spyware tools applied by APT groups, it is widely presumed that Russia is actively leveraging the intelligence provided by its effective cyber espionage campaigns for strategic gain. As cyberspace functions as the main medium for disseminating and gathering information, destructive cyber operations hindering information flows in Ukraine would have been unreasonable from the Russian point of view.

Another strategic consideration affecting Russian use of cyber attacks is the relative effectiveness of traditional kinetic operations. If we look at the Russian actions in Crimea and the Donbass, there was no practical need to engage in destructive

8

offensive cyber operations to achieve the military objectives. For instance, one of the first targets during the occupation of Crimea was an Internet Exchange Point, which was taken over by Russian special forces in order to assure information superiority by disrupting cable connections with the mainland. In short, the case indicates that kinetic actions might in some circumstances be more effective and less costly than sophisticated cyber operations. This factor is even more relevant in Ukraine, where the infrastructure is often outdated and not highly IT-dependent.

Even though highly visible and destructive attacks have not been reported, information-oriented cyber operations in Ukraine have nevertheless functioned as an essential strategic element of Russian whole spectrum warfare.

In brief, the book reflects several mutually reinforcing reasons why we did not witness large-scale or massive cyber attacks with destructive effects:

- Espionage and information campaigns conducted through cyberspace trumped other considerations for the Russian side;
- It is reasonable to achieve results with less resources and effort involved, i.e. if a cable can be cut physically, there is no need to use sophisticated cyber attacks;
- Both sides in the conflict have shown a considerable ability to control the escalation of the conflict. The cyber domain did not witness large-scale warfighting, but neither did the domain of air after the tragedy of MH17;
- Ukraine did not offer very lucrative targets for destructive cyber attacks.

To put these points into perspective: modern war is a messy affair, not a clean and glittery Hollywood movie. The emergence of cyber as a separate domain of warfighting does not necessarily offer magic solutions and miraculous short-cuts to achieve strategic goals. As of November 2015, the case has shown that destructive cyber operations are not (yet) a silver bullet in the arsenal of states which still operate below certain thresholds due to legal and political considerations and uncertainties over escalation. Nevertheless, we have to keep in mind that the conflict in Ukraine is not yet over – the level and nature of cyber attacks can change rapidly, as the political-military environment in Ukraine remains unstable and unpredictable.

Against the backdrop of the often unclear debate on so-called 'hybrid warfare' and its cyber elements, this publication offers a 'reality check' for policy-makers, scholars and the media to understand the 'haze' of cyber war. This is done by applying an interdisciplinary approach as our book involves 17 subject-matter experts analysing the strategic, policy, legal and technical aspects of the case.

The NATO Cooperative Cyber Defence Centre of Excellence would like to thank all of the book's authors, and especially the editor, Centre Ambassador Kenneth Geers, for their contributions to the project.

Key Events

Timeframe	Geopolitical Events
2013–2014	
November 2013 – February 2014	Ukrainian President Yanukovych's cabinet rejects the Ukraine-EU Association Agreement, igniting anti-government protests in Kyiv. Demonstrations gather pace in January and February of 2014 and culminate when clashes between protesters and government turn deadly. As a result, Yanukovich flees to Russia and the Parliament names Turchynov as interim President.
27 February – 16 March	On February 27, pro-Russian gunmen in combat uniforms – dubbed 'little green men' – occupy Crimea and seize strategic sites. On March 16, 97% of voters reportedly back Crimea's unrecognised referendum to join Russia. The EU and US agree on a first round of sanctions against Russia; several rounds follow as the crisis progresses.
April – May	Armed conflict begins in eastern Ukraine. The first casualties between pro-Russian separatists and Ukrainian government forces are reported on April 17. Unrecognised referendums are held. Separatists declare independence in Donetsk and Luhansk on May 11.
25 May	Petro Poroshenko is elected President of Ukraine.
17 June	Malaysia Airlines flight MH17 from Amsterdam to Kuala Lumpur is shot down over eastern Ukraine, leaving nearly 300 dead. Shortly after the crash, the Security Service (SBU) of Ukraine releases an intercepted phone call purportedly between separatists in eastern Ukraine, discussing the fact that they shot down the plane.
September	The Minsk Protocol is signed by representatives of Ukraine, the Russian Federation, the Donetsk People's Republic, and the Lugansk People's Republic. A ceasefire agreement fails to stop fighting in Donbass as fierce fighting for Donetsk's airport erupts.
26 October	Parliamentary elections are held: Poroshenko's Bloc wins and pro-western parties dominate the new political landscape.
2015	
January – February	The Minsk Protocol ceasefire fails as heavy fighting continues. After weeks of fighting, on 22 January, Ukrainian forces withdraw from the main terminal of the strategically important Donetsk airport.
	On February 11, new talks start in Minsk to achieve a new peace deal. Parties agree to a pull-out of heavy weaponry, but sporadic clashes continue. After heavy fighting in Debaltseve, Ukrainian forces retreat on 18 February.
March	The UN reports that an estimated 6,000 people have been killed in eastern Ukraine since 2014.
August – September	The most recent ceasefire, agreed by the contact group in late August, appears to be holding, as fighting is at its lowest point since the beginning of the conflict.

Sporadic cyber skirmishes, including **distributed denial of service (DDoS) attacks** and website **defacements,** accompany events throughout the crisis. Prominent examples include *Russia Today*'s (RT) altered headlines with the word 'Nazi' added and DDoS attacks against the NATO and NATO CCD COE websites, which are briefly taken offline during the Euromaidan protests.

> Private sector reports announce that **advanced persistent threat (APT) cyber espionage tools** have been discovered in Ukraine and in NATO countries. Malware analysis suggests that the campaigns are based in Russia. New and more menacing forms of malware include Turla/Uroburos/Snake, RedOctober, MiniDuke, and NetTraveler.

Anonymous users or **hacktivist groups** such as CyberBerkut continuously **leak** stolen, **sensitive information.** For example, on February 4 2014, a phone call between the US Assistant Secretary of State and the US Ambassador to Ukraine, which includes derisive comments regarding the EU, is uploaded to YouTube.

> At the Euromaidan street demonstrations, there are physical and cyber attacks against opposition servers, smartphones, websites, and Internet accounts; the most serious incidents coincide with the lethal shooting of protestors.

During the occupation of Crimea, Russian special forces seize an Internet Exchange Point (IXP) and sever Internet cables. According to Ukrainian intelligence, an 'IP-telephonic' attack originating from Crimea targets the mobile devices of Ukrainian parliament members. Hackers also leak stolen data, including a bugged phone call between the Estonian Ministry of Foreign Affairs and the EU, which fuels conspiracy theories and appears to support the Russian narrative regarding sniper shootings at Euromaidan.

> Ukrainian officials report a sophisticated cyber attack against the Ukrainian Central Election Commission on May 21-25 2014. DDoS attacks impede information exchange. A computer virus is launched to undermine the credibility of the elections and presents false election results to the official election website. Specialists contain the virus, but the Russian TV station Channel One nonetheless airs the fake results.

Media reports describe **a 'troll factory'** in St. Petersburg, Russia, where hundreds of people are allegedly **creating pro-Russian government content for both domestic and international social media.** This analysis highlights the active use of social media as a prominent threat vector for information operations.

> A private sector report claims that a Russian cyber espionage campaign has targeted the MH17 investigation being conducted by Dutch, Malaysian, Australian, Belgian, and Ukrainian authorities.

In eastern Ukraine, signals intelligence **(SIGINT) operations make use of Internet data** (e.g. location data from mobile phones and Wi-Fi networks) to locate and target Ukrainian military forces. Hacktivists on both sides continue to leak sensitive or compromising data to support their cause. In one case, hackers access public CCTV cameras in eastern Ukraine. The region has been isolated from the rest of Ukraine via Internet censorship and regular forensics checks on citizens' computers and mobile devices.

---

1   This event overview is not exhaustive and includes prominent incidents;
     it is based on open source reports and information provided by this book's authors.

CHAPTER 1

INTRODUCTION: CYBER WAR IN PERSPECTIVE

KENNETH GEERS

NATO CCD COE[1] / Atlantic Council /
Taras Shevchenko National University of Kyiv

Cyber war is a hot topic. Armed forces, intelligence, and law enforcement agencies have made computer security – from defence to offence – a top priority for investment and recruitment. In fact, current efforts to take the higher ground in cyberspace are so intense that many governments will overreach, with unfortunate ramifications for democracy and human rights around the world.

The current Russo-Ukrainian conflict appears to have all the necessary ingredients for cyber war. Moscow and Kyiv, and indeed the entire NATO Alliance, are playing for the highest geopolitical stakes. Russia has already annexed Crimea, and there is an ongoing military standoff in eastern Ukraine. Both countries possess a high level of expertise in science, technology, engineering and mathematics (STEM), which has naturally led to an aptitude for, and experience with, computer hacking.

Despite these factors, there are still many sceptics over cyber war, and more questions than answers. Although malicious code has served criminals and spies very well, can cyber attacks offer soldiers more than a temporary,

> *Can cyber attacks offer soldiers more than a temporary, tactical edge on the battlefield?*

tactical edge on the battlefield? Can it have a strategic effect? What norms should be established in international relations to govern nation-state hacking in peacetime and in war?

---

1   Dr Kenneth Geers was a Scientist at NATO CCD COE in 2007–2011 and now holds the position of Centre Ambassador.

This book serves as a benchmark in the early history of Internet-era warfare. For world leaders and system administrators alike, the 'cyber dimension' of the Ukraine crisis offers many lessons and sheds light on whether cyber war is still closer to science fiction than reality. The research is divided into five sections: Strategic Framework, Tactical Viewpoints, Information Warfare, Policy and Law, and The Future. Each chapter has been written by a leading expert in national security, network security, or both. It has been a pleasure and an honour to work with all of them. Many thanks to the North Atlantic Treaty Organisation Cooperative Cyber Defence Centre of Excellence (NATO CCD COE) for sponsoring this research.

Cyber War in Perspective: Russian Aggression against Ukraine opens with a chapter by Russia scholar **Keir Giles** of the Conflict Studies Research Centre in Oxford, UK. Keir offers deep insight into the background to this crisis, and explains why it may not be resolved any time soon. Russia and the West are said to have two distinct views of the world. Moscow is unlikely to tolerate true independence and sovereignty for its former Soviet satellite states, and remains vehemently opposed to Western support for them. It has many strategies and tactics – traditional and cyber – that it can employ against Ukraine and its other neighbours, while the West is both hesitant and divided.

In Chapter 3, **James J. Wirtz**, Dean of the Naval Postgraduate School in California, describes the global context surrounding these events. Today, nation-states are integrating cyber tactics into their political and military strategies. Professor Wirtz posits that when it comes to the use of cyber, 'national styles' might be emerging as states attempt to use cyber capabilities to achieve strategic objectives. He suggests that it is wrong to treat cyber attacks as a silver bullet, and that it is better to consider how a sort of combined arms approach will prevail. On a positive note, the need for legal and bureaucratic integration of policies and programmes should produce national idiosyncrasies on the cyber battlefield that can help with the vexing challenge of attribution.

James Andrew Lewis of the Centre for Strategic and International Studies (CSIS) analyses the geopolitical effects of cyber attacks in Chapter 4. He discusses two metrics: strategic effects that diminish an opponent's will or capacity to fight (e.g. influencing public opinion) and tactical effects that degrade military power (e.g. confusing troops, or denying service to weapons). Success is premised upon observable, real-world effects. In Ukraine, Russian cyber operations had no strategic effect and only a limited, short-term political effect.

In Chapter 5, RAND's **Martin Libicki** takes one of this book's strongest stances. He asks why, despite the existence of a hot military conflict and ample hacker talent, there is *no cyber war* in Ukraine. There have been hacktivist outbursts, web defacements, distributed denial-of-service (DDoS) attacks, and cyber espionage, but everything we have seen so far falls well short of how national security thinkers – and Hollywood – have portrayed cyber war. Libicki explores several possible reasons. Does Ukraine not possess cyber-enabled critical infrastructures? Are Russia and Ukraine wary of taking (or escalating) their conflict into the cyber domain? Or are our notions of cyber war simply overrated?

Nikolay Koval, head of Ukraine's Computer Emergency Response Team (CERT-UA) during the revolution, describes in Chapter 6 how cyber attacks rose in parallel with ongoing political events, in both number and severity. In 2012, hackers 'defaced' Ukrainian government websites with politically motivated digital graffiti. In 2013, network defenders discovered new and more menacing forms of malware, such as RedOctober, MiniDuke, and NetTraveler. In 2014, hacktivist groups such as *CyberBerkut* published stolen Ukrainian Government documents. Koval analyses in detail the most technically advanced attack investigated by CERT-UA: the May 2014 compromise of Ukraine's Central Election Commission (CEC). He closes by appealing to the Ukrainian Government to allocate greater funds to hire and retain qualified personnel.

In Chapter 7, ISACA Kyiv researcher **Glib Pakharenko** has written a first-hand account of cyber attacks during the revolution in Ukraine. At the *EuroMaidan* street demonstrations, there were physical and logical attacks against opposition servers, smartphones, websites, and Internet accounts; the most serious incidents coincided with the lethal shooting of protestors. In Crimea, attacks ranged from severing network cables to commandeering satellites to wholesale changes in *Wikipedia*. In eastern Ukraine, cyber espionage such as the use of location data from mobile phones and Wi-Fi networks has aided in targeting Ukrainian army units; the region has also been isolated from the rest of Ukraine by Internet censorship and regular forensics checks on citizens' computers and mobile devices. Pakharenko ends this chapter by providing the Ukrainian Government with a significant 'to do' list of best practices in network security.

FireEye's **Jen Weedon**, in Chapter 8, discusses Russia's strategic use of computer network exploitation (i.e. cyber espionage). Today, via the Internet, intelligence agencies can gather information on an industrial scale, which can be used for any purpose, including tactical support to military operations. From a targeting perspective, Weedon discusses strategies for creating a decisive information advantage, 'prepping' a battlefield through denial and deception, and how hackers might even cause real-world physical destruction; and details the technical aspects of suspected Russian cyber operations, including malware samples, hacker tactics, and compromised infrastructure.

In Chapter 9, **Tim Maurer** of the New America Foundation explores the role that non-state, 'proxy' cyber actors have played in the Ukraine crisis. In both Russia and Ukraine, there is ample private sector computer hacking expertise which each government would theoretically have an incentive to exploit for efficacy and plausible deniability. However, throughout this crisis, there has counterintuitively been very limited proxy use. There have been a few dubious 'hacktivist' attacks, but expert volunteers and cyber criminals do not appear to have been politicised or mobilised to any significant degree in support of geopolitical cyber campaigns. Criminal behaviour remains largely profit-driven. In particular, the Ukrainian Government has not shown a capacity to harness volunteer cyber expertise, as Russia is thought to have done during its previous crises with Estonia and Georgia.

Swedish Defence University researcher **Margarita Levin Jaitner** highlights current Russian Information Warfare (IW) theory in Chapter 10. She contends that Moscow has an inherent belief in the power of information control to advance its political and military goals. In Russian doctrine, cyber security is subordinate to information security, and cyberspace is only one part of the 'information space'. National security planners are concerned with both 'technical' and 'cognitive' attacks, and recognise that achieving information superiority involves everything from propaganda to hacking to kinetic military operations. Margarita Jaitner argues that the annexation of Crimea was a textbook case in information superiority.

> *Moscow has an inherent belief in the power of information control.*

In Chapter 11, **Liisa Past**, a NATO CCD COE expert on strategic communications, analyses leadership discourse. Liisa Past reveals that Russian President Vladimir Putin and Ukrainian President Petro Poroshenko have employed similar rhetorical strategies, including the development of an 'us vs. them' dichotomy in which the in-group is portrayed as constructive and solution-oriented, while the out-group is illegitimate and dangerous. In their current conflict, neither Russia nor Ukraine denies that cyberspace is a domain of warfare, but neither has stressed its importance. Russian political discourse has mostly overlooked cyber issues (which is in line with Russian military doctrine), while Ukraine has framed them within the larger concept of 'hybrid warfare'. The most notable difference in political rhetoric is Kyiv's clear orientation to the West and NATO, while Moscow is keenly focused on Russian national interests.

Elina Lange-Ionatamishvili and **Sanda Svetoka** of the NATO Strategic Communications Centre of Excellence in Latvia, in Chapter 12, discuss the role of social media in this conflict. In the Internet era, the battle for hearts and minds has never been more important. Social media is a trust-based network that provides fertile soil for intelligence collection, propaganda dissemination, and psychological operations (PSYOPS) to influence public opinion – or to lead adversaries into harm's way. 'Soft' cyber attacks can be as severe as any attack on critical infrastructure. In Ukraine, they have generated fear, uncertainty, and doubt about the economic, cultural, and national security of Ukraine, while promoting positive messages about Russia's role in Crimea and eastern Ukraine. The authors provide recommendations for defence against such attacks, including how to identify them, challenge them, and how to develop a resilient political narrative to withstand false propaganda.

In Chapter 13, University of Michigan doctoral student **Nadiya Kostyuk** reviews Ukraine's cyber security policy – past, present, and future. She analyses numerous historical factors that make Ukraine a cyber safe haven: a strong science, technology, engineering, and mathematics (STEM) education, underwhelming economic performance since the fall of the Soviet Union in 1991, and social norms which dictate that stealing from the West is not a bad thing. The icing on the cake is that there are currently few cyber security regulations in Ukraine. All of these factors shed light on the vexing challenge of containing cyber crime in the region. Looking toward the future, Nadiya Kostyuk argues that Ukraine's political, military, and economic crises will inhibit the stabilisation of Ukrainian cyberspace for some time.

Lt Col **Jan Stinissen** of the NATO CCD COE, in Chapter 14, offers a legal framework for cyber operations in Ukraine. He explains that international law applies to cyberspace, and the law of armed conflict applies to all relevant cyber operations. Jan discusses the legal definitions of 'war' and 'cyberwar', as well as the concepts of 'armed conflict', 'armed attack', and 'use of force'. Typically, cyber attacks do not come in isolation, but rather as one element of a larger military operation; the wider context will determine the legal framework for its cyber component. There are many qualifying factors including state vs. non-state actor, and armed conflict vs. law enforcement. In the Ukraine crisis, operations in Crimea (which has already been annexed by Russia) may be viewed differently from those in eastern Ukraine. Stinissen asserts that, globally, most known cyber attacks have simply not been serious enough to be governed by the law of armed conflict, but that this is likely to change in the future.

In Chapter 15, NATO CCD COE researcher **Henry Rõigas** discusses the impact of known cyber attacks in Ukraine on proposed political cyber 'norms', the rules of state behaviour in international relations. On the positive side, the absence of attacks against critical infrastructure could be a boon to future international security and stability, especially if it is a result of intentional restraint on the part of Moscow and Kyiv. This case challenges the prevailing perception that a loose normative framework currently allows states to employ cyber attacks as a tool for coercion. On the negative side, the examples of computer network operations we have seen appear to violate the information security norms promoted by Russia and the Shanghai Cooperation Organisation (SCO), as they seem to constitute a war on information itself, that is a dedicated effort to alter public opinion through deceptive propaganda.

Finnish Professor **Jarno Limnéll**, in Chapter 16, discusses the ramifications of the Ukraine war, and its cyber component, for Russia's neighbours. Moscow's aggressive behaviour in Ukraine has forced many countries to re-evaluate their political and military relationships, especially with NATO. For historical reasons, Finland and Estonia are well positioned to analyse Russia's use of hybrid warfare, including information operations. Today, these countries are actively pursuing ways to bolster their national defences against Russia's military strategies and tactics in Ukraine. The NATO Alliance should take concrete measures to reassure its member states, such as the creation of a common cyber defence framework.

In Chapter 17, **Jason Healey** and **Michelle Cantos** of Columbia University imagine four potential cyber conflict scenarios in this crisis. First, even if the hot war cools off, Russia can still raise the temperature in cyberspace, and cause serious network disruptions in Ukraine. Second, Russia could selectively target the West, adding a new vector to its already increased volume of threats, military exercises, submarine deployments, and nuclear warnings. Third, Vladimir Putin could mirror the 'frozen conflict' dynamic in cyberspace by threatening prolonged disruptions of the global Internet. And fourth, if the Ukraine conflict spins out of control, Russia, in desperation, might even have the power to take down the Internet entirely.

> *Hostile nation-state cyber operations are a long-term, dynamic, multidimensional threat.*

To close our book, in Chapter 18, Brookings Institution Nonresident Senior Fellow **Richard Bejtlich** offers essential advice not only for Ukraine, but for any nation or organisation wishing to improve its cyber security posture. Bejtlich draws from the deep well of classic military doctrine, arguing that hostile nation-state cyber operations are not a single event but a long-term, dynamic, multidimensional threat. The only hope that Ukraine or any other nation has for building an effective defence against professional network attacks is to incorporate strategic thinking into its defensive architecture, personnel, and operations.

CHAPTER 2

Russia and Its Neighbours: Old Attitudes, New Capabilities

Keir Giles

Conflict Studies Research Centre

1   The View from Moscow

The crisis around Ukraine is part of a wider confrontation between Russia and the West, which has persisted at varying degrees of intensity since the fall of the Soviet Union despite periods when the West as a whole refused to recognise that any conflict of strategic interest with Russia existed. After a period where this confrontation lay relatively dormant, the conflict in Ukraine results from the culmination of two important trends in the Russian view of itself and the world: first, a greater and more urgent perception of threat, whether real or imagined, to Russia's own security; and second, a recognition that Russia itself has regained sufficient strength, military and otherwise, to assert itself.

The notion that Russia is faced with an existential threat – even when that threat is imperceptible from outside Russia – has multiple and complex origins. Some of these are permanent and persistent; for example, the idea of vulnerability of Russia's borders, which leads to the conviction that in order to protect its borders Russia must exert control far beyond them. In the last century this was one of the drivers for Soviet ultimatums to the Baltic states and Finland which eventually led to their invasion in 1939. This continuing perception feeds into the current portrayal by Russia of NATO enlargement, including to those same Baltic states, as a threat. Regardless of NATO's intent, it presents a menace simply by 'approaching Russia's borders'.[1]

---

1   As expressed in a wide range of Russian security policy documents, including the December 2014 'Military Doctrine of the Russian Federation' and its predecessors.

Other, more recent developments have heightened the sense of urgency for Russian security planners. The fear that the West is considering bringing about regime change in Russia does not stand up to objective scrutiny, but appears deep-rooted among a broad sector of the Russian security elite. It has been accentuated in the past decade by, as Moscow sees it, further unrestrained and irresponsible interventions by the West with the intention of regime change, leaving chaos and disorder in their wake. Western action in Libya and support for anti-government rebels in Syria provide prime examples.

> *Recent developments have heightened the sense of urgency for Russian security planners.*

Thus the prospect of destabilisation closer to home in Ukraine would have been of even more acute and direct concern in Moscow. Even without the accompanying disorder, the threat of the 'loss' of Ukraine to the West posed an immediate military problem: it appears to have been considered plausible in Moscow that this presented an immediate danger of losing the Black Sea Fleet's base in Sevastopol, together with the often-overlooked supporting infrastructure scattered across the Crimean peninsula, to NATO. According to Secretary of the Russian Security Council Nikolay Patrushev, the consequences could be even more far-reaching: 'Americans are trying to involve the Russian Federation in interstate military conflict, to facilitate the change of power by way of using the events in Ukraine, and ultimately to carve up our country.'[2] Whether this view is sincerely held by the Russian leadership or not, it is the one that is consistently presented to the Russian public, and to its Armed Forces, as explaining the roots of the current conflict.

The fact that Russia was able to use large numbers of Special Operations Forces (SOF) swiftly and effectively to seize control of Crimea, and subsequently to wage an ongoing low-level campaign in eastern Ukraine involving long-term mobilisation of its conventional forces, is a pointer to the other key element of the new Russian approach to confrontation; the recognition that Russia is now in a position to exercise a much more assertive foreign policy than in the recent past.

One element of this is the unprecedented and expensive overhaul and rearmament of Russia's Armed Forces which began after the armed conflict with Georgia in 2008 and continues today. The fact that the Russian troops at work in Ukraine are entirely unrecognisable from the forces which entered Georgia just seven years earlier caused surprise and consternation among those Western defence communities that had not been paying attention. But the Ukraine campaign overall is far more than a military operation. Successful coordination of military movements and action with other measures in the political, economic and especially information domains, are the result of strenuous efforts by the

---

2   Interview with Security Council Secretary Nikolay Patrushev, *Rossiyskaya gazeta*, 11 February 2015.

Putin administration over preceding years to harness other levers of state power to act in a coordinated manner.[3]

The results of this coordination has left the unprepared West scrambling for a response, and struggling even to define the phenomenon, as witness the tortuous attempts by NATO and Western governments to decide what precisely constitutes 'hybrid warfare'. But the notion of hybridity as applied to the current concept meets little understanding in Moscow. Instead, Russia can be said simply to be attempting to implement grand strategy in the classical sense. Russia's attempt at this whole of government approach to managing conflict is embodied in the National Defence Control Centre in central Moscow, where a wide range of different government ministries and agencies including those responsible for energy, the economy, ecology and more are brought together under the leadership of the General Staff.[4]

Intensive militarisation, sometimes referred to directly as mobilisation, is also now pervading Russian society, stoked by unending leadership rhetoric of war, confrontation and threat, and blanket military coverage on TV. According to Estonian Ambassador to the Russian Federation Jüri Luik, the Russian narrative of war is 'instrumentalising the population and putting it on a mental war footing', not only by tapping into the traditional Russian narrative of victimhood over centuries, but also by engendering 'a heroic feeling that now is the time of risk'.[5] Furthermore, analysis of Russian security thinking shows not only this asymmetry of threat perception, but also a complete divergence with the West in terms of notions of how and when the military should be used to counter those threats.

The notion of hybridity meets little understanding in Moscow.

As so often, there is no single explanation for a given course of action by Russia, and direct intervention in Crimea and Ukraine has also been parsed as a response to the threat posed to Russian business interests by closer integration with the European Union (EU). The EU model of open markets and rules-based dealings runs directly counter to the Russian way of doing business in the near abroad, reinforcing the growing Russian perception of the EU as a problem rather than an opportunity; but few analysts would have predicted that it would be the prospect of an EU Association Agreement for Ukraine, rather than any involvement with NATO, which would eventually lead to military intervention by Russia.

The ambivalent attitude to Ukraine as a sovereign nation with a right to choose its own foreign policy direction has its roots in an entirely different view of the end

---

3   Andrew Monaghan. 'Defibrillating the Vertikal', Chatham House, October 2014, http://www.chathamhouse.org/publication/defibrillating-vertikal-putin-and-russian-grand-strategy.
4   'Начальник российского Генштаба рассказал журналистам о задачах и роли Национального центра по управлению обороной РФ', Russian Ministry of Defence website, 1 November 2014, http://function.mil.ru/news_page/country/more.htm?id=11998309@egNews.
5   Speaking at the Lennart Meri Conference, Tallinn, 24 April 2015.

of the Soviet Union. That view holds that the former Soviet republics, including Ukraine and the Baltic States, in effect belong to Russia. According to President Putin, in 1991 'Russia voluntarily – I emphasise – voluntarily and consciously made absolutely historic concessions in giving up its own territory'.[6] This persistent view is not limited to President Putin. According to veteran scholar of Russia Paul Goble:

> 'The Russian elite is sincerely convinced that the preservation of influence on the former Soviet republics surrounding it is the status quo and a natural right given by history,' even though 'for the entire rest of the world such an approach is incomprehensible and unnatural'.

What this means is that Moscow acts 'as if the Soviet Union had not fallen apart, as if it had only been reformatted, but relations between sovereign and vassal have remained as before'.[7] It is plain that at least in some sectors of society, these aspirations by Russia to regain imperial dominion over its surroundings enjoy broad support. The now-celebrated Prosecutor General of Crimea, Natalya Poklonskaya, in an interview at the time of annexation declared her ambition to 'start again in a great state, a great power, an *empire*, like Russia'.[8]

This approach to Russia's inheritance of domination over its neighbourhood appears consistent over time. In 1953, an assessment of recent history that had led to Soviet domination over Eastern Europe concluded that in the Russian view:

Informed analysis pointed to Ukraine as the next target for Russian action.

> 'Stalin was no more than reasserting Russian authority over territories which had long recognised Tsarist rule, and which had been torn away from Russia at the time of her revolutionary weakness after the First World War'.[9]

The effect of these long-standing assumptions is a mind-set that leads to casual references by Russian generals to '*nashi bvvshiye strany*' ('our former countries'), statements that even Finland and Poland were 'parts of Russia', and that all major powers have a non-threatening sanitary zone ('*sanitarnaya zona*') around them.[10] Russia's attempts to maintain, or reassert, this buffer zone are a major contributor to the current stand-off.

Since 1991, Moscow has employed a wide range of coercive tools in attempts –

---

6   Ksenija Kirillova. 'Путин фактически назвал Украину территорией России', *Novyy Region 2*, 28 April 2015, http://nr2.com.ua/blogs/Ksenija_Kirillova/Putin-fakticheski-nazval-Ukrainu-territoriey-Rossii-95566.html.

7   Paul A. Goble. 'Putin Gives the World His Geography Lesson: 'All the Former USSR is Russia', *The Interpreter*, 28 April 2015, http://www.interpretermag.com/putingivestheworldhisgeographylessonalltheformerussrisrussia/.

8   Russian television interview available at https://www.youtube.com/watch?v=XX4JCQViRKg (at 2'40").

9   William Hardy McNeill. 'America, Britain and Russia: Their Co-operation and Conflict 1941-1946', (Oxford University Press 1953).

10   Private conversations with author in late 2014.

often unsuccessful – to maintain influence and leverage over its Western neighbours.[11] From the mid-2000s, Russia benefited from a sudden influx of revenue thanks to higher oil prices and began to review its perception of its own strengths accordingly. From the earliest stages, this was reflected in huge budget increases for the Armed Forces,[12] and an intensified pattern of testing levers of influence against Western neighbours.[13] High-profile incidents during this stage included gas cut-offs for Ukraine in 2006, the crude cyber offensive against Estonia in May 2007, and ultimately the use of military force against Georgia in 2008. In each case, the results validated this approach for Russia: the Georgian conflict in particular demonstrated the validity of use of armed force as a foreign policy tool bringing swift and effective results, with only limited and temporary economic and reputational costs to bear.

It was in this context that a range of informed analysis pointed to Ukraine as the next target for assertive Russian action. A UK parliamentary report in 2009 noted that:

> '*Many of our witnesses stressed that Russia poses a military threat to other former Soviet states, particularly in light of its actions in Georgia... Some witnesses argued that Russia posed a military threat to Ukraine... one scenario was that Putin could send in military forces to secure the Russian military base at Sevastopol*'.[14]

2   Is This Cyber Warfare?

As noted above, the levers of power which Russia is bringing to bear in Ukraine are wide-ranging. This study looks in detail at the specific cyber conflict aspect of the Ukraine crisis, but even this concept is impressively broad thanks to the holistic and inclusive Russian approach to what constitutes information warfare, of which cyber is an integral part.

Opinions are divided as to whether what is taking place in and around Ukraine can or should be called cyber war. As Jan Stinissen argues in Chapter 14, current cyber operations do not meet a strict legal definition of a state of war. But at the same time, according to one analysis, operations in Ukraine undoubtedly constitute cyber warfare. The conflict:

> '*meets the generally accepted standard for the following reasons: the cyber warfare component is overt, meaning the perpetrators make little effort to hide either their identities or their allegiances. The two countries*

---

11   For a recent overview of the unfriendly means Russia adopts to influence its neighbours, see 'Russia's Toolkit' in 'The Russian Challenge', Chatham House, June 2015, http://www.chathamhouse.org/publication/russian-challenge-authoritarian-nationalism.

12   Keir Giles. 'Military Service in Russia: No New Model Army', Conflict Studies Research Centre, May 2007.

13   Jakob Hedenskog and Robert L. Larsson. 'Russian Leverage on the CIS and the Baltic States', FOI, June 2007, available at www.foi.se/ReportFiles/foir_2280.pdf.

14   'Russia: a new confrontation?', House of Commons Defence Committee, Tenth Report of Session 2008-09, 10 July 2009.

are in open, hostile and declared conflict with each other. Both sides have stated military and political objectives'.[15]

As if to emphasise the point, intensive cyber attacks reportedly cease during the occasional observance of ceasefires.[16]

Other elements of the cyber conflict also confound definition. Operations to date represent an evolution in Russian tactics compared to previous campaigns. Both cyber and traditional elements of conflict are present, but they are both less overt and more difficult to understand and defend against.

In part, this is due to Ukraine's very different cyber terrain. Comparisons to Russia's rudimentary cyber efforts at the time of the Georgian conflict in 2008 are of limited value. Unlike Georgia, Ukraine's more interconnected nature makes it impossible to restrict access to the internet overall, except in the very special case of the Crimean peninsula. But in addition, there is no reason why Russia should try, especially given the integrated nature of Ukrainian and Russian information space. Since Russia already enjoyed domination of Ukrainian cyberspace, including telecommunications companies, infrastructure, and overlapping networks, there was little incentive to disrupt it. In short, Russia had no need to attack that which it already owned.[17] To give one simplistic but indicative example, little offensive cyber effort is needed for Russia to access sensitive Ukrainian e-mail traffic when so many Ukrainians, including government officials, use Russian mail services and therefore provide automatic access to the Russian security and intelligence services.[18]

A distinctive aspect of information operations in Ukraine itself, and one with important implications for how cyber war may be waged in future, is the way Russian activity in the cyber domain facilitates broader information warfare aims. This manifests itself not only in straightforward spearphishing of Ukrainian officials[19] for exploitation, but also in specific uses of malware in the conflict.[20] A particular example is the redirection of malware originally intended for cybercrime to manipulating viewer figures to promote pro-Russian video clips.[21] But potentially even more significant for the nature of future cyber operations is the new interface

---

15 Tony Martin-Vegue. 'Are we witnessing a cyber war between Russia and Ukraine? Don't blink – you might miss it', *CSO*, 24 April 2015, http://www.csoonline.com/article/2913743/cyber-attacks-espionage/are-we-witnessing-a-cyber-war-between-russia-and-ukraine-dont-blink-you-might-miss-it.html.

16 Aarti Shahani. 'Report: To Aid Combat, Russia Wages Cyberwar Against Ukraine', *NPR*, 28 April 2015, http://www.npr.org/blogs/alltechconsidered/2015/04/28/402678116/report-to-aid-combat-russia-wages-cyberwar-against-ukraine.

17 Patrick Tucker. 'Why Ukraine Has Already Lost The Cyberwar, Too', *Defense One*, 28 April 2014, http://www.defenseone.com/technology/2014/04/why-ukraine-has-already-lost-cyberwar-too/83350/print/.

18 Anna Poludenko-Young. 'Ukrainian Officials, Russian Security Services Thank You for Your Cooperation!', *GlobalVoices*, 23 May 2015, http://globalvoicesonline.org/2015/05/23/ukrainian-officials-russian-security-services-thank-you-for-your-cooperation/.

19 Undated PowerPoint presentation by SBU (Security Service of Ukraine), entitled 'В умовах військової агресії з боку Російської Федерації, війна ведеться не лише на землі, в повітрі та в дипломатичних колах, вперше в історії війн застосовані нові форми ведення агресії – гібридна війна з використанням кіберпростору України'.

20 Kenneth Geers. 'Strategic Analysis: As Russia-Ukraine Conflict Continues, Malware Activity Rises', *FireEye*, 28 May 2014, https://www.fireeye.com/blog/threat-research/2014/05/strategic-analysis-as-russia-ukraine-conflict-continues-malware-activity-rises.html.

21 Rami Kogan. 'Bedep trojan malware spread by the Angler exploit kit gets political', *Trustwave*, 29 April 2015, https://www.trustwave.com/Resources/SpiderLabs-Blog/Bedep-trojan-malware-spread-by-the-Angler-exploit-kit-gets-political/.

between cyber and kinetic operations. When Russia wished to isolate Crimea from news from the outside world, no sophisticated cyber exploits were required. Instead, SOF detachments simply took over the Simferopol IXP and selectively disrupted cable connections to the mainland.[22] In short, complex and expensive information weapons are entirely unnecessary in situations where the adversary can gain physical control of infrastructure.

> *Russian activity in the cyber domain facilitates broader information warfare aims.*

The circumstances of Crimea were unique, and not only because of the peninsula's distinctive internet geography; but Russian planners will have noted this striking success and will be looking for where it can be applied elsewhere. There are two important implications for planning for future crises with Russia. First, both civil and military contingency planning should include scenarios where friendly access to the internet is degraded or absent; and second, civilian internet infrastructure needs at least as much defence and protection as other strategic assets.

In any case, the course of the conflict so far has seen no visible full-scale cyber hostilities of the kind envisaged by theorists, a theme examined in more detail by Martin Libicki in Chapter 5. The tactics, techniques and procedures which have been used at various stages of the conflict are the subject of two separate detailed examinations by Nikolay Koval and Glib Pakharenko in Chapters 6 and 7.

3 REACTIONS AND RESPONSES

Information campaigning, facilitated by cyber activities, contributed powerfully to Russia's ability to prosecute operations against Ukraine in the early stages of the conflict with little coordinated opposition from the West. The fact that for almost a year the EU was unable to refer publicly to the presence of Russian troops in Ukraine[23] denotes a broader inability to challenge the Russian version of events without which a meaningful response is difficult or impossible. Early media coverage of the conflict made it 'apparent … that some interlocutors had swallowed whole some of the cruder falsifications of Russian propaganda.'[24]

As the realisation of the nature of the Russian information campaign began to filter through Western media and policy-making circles, this gave way to a dangerous optimism about the effectiveness of Russian measures, and a widespread assumption that Russian disinformation was failing because of its lack of plausibil-

---

22 'Кримські регіональні підрозділи ПАТ «Укртелеком» офіційно повідомляють про блокування невідомими декількох вузлів зв'язку на півострові', Ukrtelekom, 28 February 2014, http://www.ukrtelecom.ua/presscenter/news/official?id=120327.

23 Andrew Rettman,. 'EU breaks taboo on 'Russian forces in Ukraine'', *EU Observer*, 16 February 2015, https://euobserver.com/foreign/127667.

24 John Besemeres. 'Russian disinformation and Western misconceptions', *Inside Story*, 23 September 2014, http://insidestory.org.au/russian-disinformation-and-western-misconceptions.

ity. Supposedly, Russian lies were ineffective because they were so obvious that they did not confuse senior and intelligent individuals in the West. But this was to under-estimate the effects of layered messaging, subtly screened and concealed by more obvious fabrications, continued saturation, and in particular the pernicious effect of the 'filter bubble' on online reading habits – the way personalised search results driven by advertising models can effectively isolate internet users from alternative information and viewpoints.[25]

Russian official sources continue to disseminate lies which are easily detected and discredited in the West, as with the striking example of the 'discovery' of sup-posed US MANPADS in Donetsk in late July 2015.[26] But the implausibility is irrel-evant for Russian objectives: the story has been planted and will continue to be dis-seminated via the internet, and will not be contradicted in mainstream sources within Russia. Instead of convincing Western readers that the disinformation is true, Rus-sian success is defined in two other ways: isolating the domestic audience from non-approved information so that Russian state actions are permissible; and influencing foreign decision making by supply-ing polluted information, exploiting the fact that Western elected representatives receive and are sensitive to the same information flows as their voters. When Rus-sian disinformation delivered in this manner is part of the framework for decisions, this constitutes success for Moscow, because a key element of the long-standing Soviet and Russian approach of reflexive control is in place.

> *Implausibility is irrelevant for Russian objectives.*

Crucially, it must be remembered that Russian disinformation campaigns aimed at the West are conducted not only in NATO languages, but also in Arabic and Russian targeting minorities across Europe. This itself has major implications for managing future confrontations between Russia and other front-line states, which must involve finding a means to respond to Russian information operations when the initiative necessarily lies with Russia. As put pithily by journalist and author Peter Pomerantsev, 'they will always win the narrative war, because they can make stuff up'.[27]

For the time being, much of the Western response appears focused on find-ing a label for the newly-demonstrated Russian way of warfare. A range of early contenders, such as 'non-linear war', 'ambiguous war' and others have largely been abandoned in favour of 'hybrid warfare', a concept originally designed for describing insurgency rather than warfighting by an aspiring regional power, but now applied to a totally new situation. Nevertheless many of the components now being used to define hybridity are nothing new in Russian practice. One argument

25 'How to Burst the 'Filter Bubble' that Protects Us from Opposing Views', *MIT Technology Review*, 29 November 2013, http://www.technologyreview.com/view/522111/how-to-burst-the-filter-bubble-that-protects-us-from-opposing-views/.

26 Brian Ashcraft. 'Pro-Tip: Don't Copy Battlefield 3 Stingers', 23 July 2015, *Kotaku.com*, http://kotaku.com/pro-tip-dont-copy-battlefield-3-stingers-1719695507.

27 Speaking at the Lennart Meri Conference, Tallinn. 24 April 2015.

holds that a previous round of expansionism by Russia in 1939-40 shared sufficient characteristics with current operations around Ukraine, including intimidation, spurious legitimacy, and information campaigns backed with the prospect of full-scale invasion, to also be called hybrid warfare.[28] Russia's clinging to the attitudes and approaches of a former age holds other dangers too: Russian military, and in particular nuclear, messaging is baffling to its Western audience because the post-nationalist West has moved on from the Cold War mind-set in which it is rooted. The result is a dangerous situation where the messages from Russia are received, but not understood.

4   OUTLOOK

At the time of writing the situation around Ukraine remains fluid and unpredictable. While Russia shows no signs of pushing for greater territorial control of Ukraine, moves toward conciliation by the West give rise to fears of appeasement and the danger of a repeat of the disastrous resolution to the Georgia conflict seven years before.[29] But one undeniable achievement by Russia is the transformation of the security environment in Central and Eastern Europe. Faced with a challenge that is no longer deniable, Europe has overcome its 'strategic inertia'.[30] NATO in particular has been revitalised: the NATO agenda has shifted radically from contemplation of a future role after withdrawal from Afghanistan, now that the Alliance has a clear motivation to return to its core purpose. Poland and the Baltic states, long cast as irresponsible trouble-makers for warning of the implications of a resurgent Russia, are now fully vindicated and benefiting from the overall NATO and unilateral US military response to the crisis. Each is at present supporting these front-line states with very small increments of conventional military forces, while considering how to respond to the broader threat of a more assertive Russia.[31]

The Ukraine conflict has the potential to bring about a transformative effect specifically within cyber doctrine. Unlike Russia, the siloed Western approach to cyber has typically focused on technical responses to technical threats, largely disregarding the interface with information warfare in the broad sense. This approach is entirely apt for persistent or background threats, but probably insufficient for when a national security crisis emerges, since at that point there will be no such thing as a 'pure cyber' confrontation. In other words, the West may have been well prepared

---

28 Vitalii Usenko and Dmytro Usenko. 'Russian hybrid warfare: what are effects-based network operations and how to counteract them', *Euromaidan Press*, 17 January 2015, http://euromaidanpress.com/2015/01/17/russian-hybrid-warfare-what-are-effect-based-network-operations-and-how-to-counteract-them/.

29 Karoun Demirjian. 'Visits by top U.S officials give Russia something to crow about', *The Washington Post*, 18 May 2015, http://www.washingtonpost.com/world/europe/visits-by-top-us-offi...about/2015/05/18/3c562a94-fd6b-11e4-8c77-bf274685e1df_story.html.

30 Andrew A. Michta. 'Europe's Moment of Blinding Strategic Clarity', *The American Interest*, 24 October 2014, http://www.the-american-interest.com/2014/10/24/europes-moment-of-blinding-strategic-clarity/.

31 Daniel Schearf. 'Russia Concerns Driving Neighbors to NATO', *Voice of America*, 5 August 2015, http://www.voanews.com/content/russia-concerns-driving-neighbors-to-nato/2903033.html.

for cyber war, but events in Ukraine show that it also needs to be prepared for information war when cyber operations are used as a facilitator or attack vector.

More broadly, Russia has clearly demonstrated an improved capability to coordinate its levers of state power in order to achieve strategic objectives in contrast to the West's apparent deficit of grand strategy. In his chapter 'Strategic Defence in Cyberspace: Beyond Tools and Tactics', Richard Bejtlich calls for strategic thought in cyber policy, but this approach needs to be mirrored across all domains in order to successfully counter the broad-based Russian approach to modern warfare.

The crisis around Ukraine has brought Europe closer to recognition that its values and interests are incompatible with those of Russia, and that if the West wishes to support Russia's neighbours in asserting their sovereignty and choosing their own destiny, confrontation with Russia is the inevitable result.[32] This also implies recognition that 2014–15 is not an aberration in relations between Russia and the West; rather, it is the previous 25 years of relative quiescence that were the exception to the rule. European nations have now been prompted by events to once more take an interest in their own defence. But while concentrating on countering and forestalling Russia's next unacceptable act of force, they must also be prepared for a sustained period of difficult and expensive tension.[33] In Russia's neighbourhood, the new normal is a return to old ways.

> *2014–15 is not an aberration in relations between Russia and the West.*

---

32 A theme explored in greater detail in 'The Russian Challenge', op. cit.
33 Keir Giles. 'Staring down a grizzly Russia', *The World Today*, Volume 70, Number 2, April–May 2014.

CHAPTER 3

CYBER WAR AND STRATEGIC CULTURE: THE RUSSIAN INTEGRATION OF CYBER POWER INTO GRAND STRATEGY

JAMES J. WIRTZ

Naval Postgraduate School

Discussion of the cyber domain in general, and specific considerations of cyber attacks, cyber war and cyber power, often seem oddly detached from a broader strategic and geopolitical context.[1] Several reasons can be suggested for why the cyber dimension of conflict seems to be considered in isolation from the *physical and political* goals that states and non-state actors attempt to achieve through their activities in the virtual world of cyberspace. Offensive and defensive cyber capabilities are highly classified by all parties; it is impossible to say with certainty what capabilities are wielded, making it difficult to assess 'cyber orders of battle' and 'cyber balances of power'. Newspaper reports, anecdotes, and rumours of capabilities offer clues, but it is difficult to link rumours to grand strategic objectives. Cyber warfare is an exquisitely technical subject dominated by engineers, mathematicians, and computer scientists – individuals who can be forgiven for focusing on the latest patch needed in some software program, and for not thinking about the connection between technical exploitation and grand political strategy. In a sense, issues related to cyber warfare are often treated, not just as something technically new on the military landscape, but as something that is unprecedented in military affairs.

If one turns a strategist's eye toward the cyber domain, key questions immediately emerge. How will states integrate their cyber capabilities into an overall strat-

---

1 The opinions here are not those of the U.S. Navy, U.S. Government or the North Atlantic Treaty Organisation.

egy to achieve military and political goals? In other words, no matter how brilliant the algorithm, no matter how devious the penetration, how can cyber power be integrated into a 'combined arms' or even a 'whole of government' approach leading to battlefield success or to a grand strategy that creates a political *fait accompli*? Unless one embraces the dubious proposition that cyber really constitutes the ultimate silver bullet in political and military conflict, it is unlikely to be employed independently as a war-winning weapon. Moreover, given the need for integration, issues of political and strategic culture, to say nothing of bureaucratic preferences and peacetime legal restraints, can be expected to produce national styles and preferences when it comes to conflict in cyberspace.[2]

> *Political and strategic culture produce national styles and preferences in cyberspace.*

Although attribution of known cyber attacks remains a hotly contested and much denied issue (given the very limited evidence available), there is some indication that strategic culture and organisational preferences shape the way the United States, China and Russia use their cyber power. According to press reports, the United States was behind the Stuxnet malware attack on centrifuges at Iran's Natanz enrichment facility.[3] Many analysts suggested at the time that the Stuxnet attack was noteworthy as the first example of the use of a cyber weapon to cause physical damage, but it also reflected the long-standing American tradition of long-range precision bombardment and the preference for targeting key nodes in an opponent's infrastructure to produce maximum damage with minimal effort.[4] By contrast, the recent Office of Personnel Management hack, which press reporting attributes to the People's Republic of China, seems to reflect a Chinese preoccupation with guarding its own citizens from nefarious outside influences, while going to great lengths to gather information that is locked behind others' defensive barriers.[5]

Russian cyber activities, especially those associated with the recent conflict in Ukraine and the annexation of Crimea, probably offer the best example of the employment of cyber attacks to shape the overall political course of a dispute. According to David J. Smith:

---

2   According to Colin Gray, 'The political context of strategy is exceedingly broad. It includes the domestic political and bureaucratic processes by which strategy is made and amended…all strategies are contrived and executed by people and institutions that must be considered encultured by the societies that bred them'. Colin Gray. *The Strategy Bridge: Theory for Practice* (Oxford: Oxford University Press, 2010). pp. 39-40.

3   Ellen Nakashima and Joby Warrick. 'Stuxnet was work of U.S. and Israeli experts, officials say,' *Washington Post*, June 2, 2012. https://www.washingtonpost.com/world/national-security/stuxnet-was-work-of-us-and-israeli-experts-officials-say/2012/06/01/gJQAlnEy6U_story.html; David E. Sanger. 'Obama Ordered Sped Up Wave of Cyberattacks Against Iran,' *The New York Times*, June 1, 2012, p. A1. http://www.nytimes.com/2012/06/01/world/middleeast/obama-ordered-wave-of-cyber-attacks-against-iran.html.

4   Lawrence Freedman. *The Evolution of Nuclear Strategy,* (3rd edition, New York: Palgrave MacMillan, 2003), pp. 11-12; Michael E. Brown, *Flying Blind: The Politics of the U.S. Strategic Bomber Program* (Ithaca: Cornell University Press, 1992), pp. 29-67.

5   Sean Lyngaas. 'Exclusive: The OPM breach details you haven't seen,' *Federal Computer Week* August 21, 2015. http://fcw.com/articles/2015/08/21/opm-breach-timeline.aspx; Jon R. Lindsay. 'The Impact of China on Cybersecurity: Fact and Friction,' *International Security*, Vol. 39, No. 3 (Winter 2014/2015), pp, 7-47.

Russia holds a broad concept of information warfare, which includes intelligence, counterintelligence, deceit, disinformation, electronic warfare, debilitation of communications, degradation of navigation support, psychological pressure, degradation of information systems and propaganda. Computers are among the many tools of Russian information warfare, which is carried out 24 hours a day, seven days a week, in war and peace. Seen this way, distributed denial of services attacks (DDoS), advanced exploitation techniques and Russia Today television are all related tools of information warfare.[6]

Russia, more than any other nascent actor on the cyber stage, seems to have devised a way to integrate cyber warfare into a grand strategy capable of achieving political objectives.

The remainder of this essay explains what it is about Russian strategic culture that enables it to wield cyber power in a strategically effective manner. It begins with a brief discussion of Russian strate-

> *Russia seems to have devised a way to integrate cyber warfare into grand strategy.*

gic culture, especially how it manifested in past debates the impact of technology on warfare. It then describes how Russia has employed its cyber power to defeat US and NATO deterrence strategies, effectively delivering a strategic defeat to the alliance at the outset of its 'hybrid' war against Ukraine. The essay concludes by offering some observations about the strategic nature of cyber warfare.

1   RUSSIAN STRATEGIC CULTURE AND TECHNOLOGY

Often, states or individuals who initially invent or master some new technology fail to understand, not only its strategic implications, but also how best to employ it in a tactical or operational setting. Historically, Russia, including its Soviet manifestation, has not been at the forefront of scientific or technical innovation. As one recent history explained, Soviet Cold War espionage was largely dedicated to stealing scientific, technical, and military information from the West in a desperate and ultimately failed effort to keep pace with more sophisticated and innovative opponents.[7] Nevertheless, while the Russians may lack in technological prowess and innovative drive, they tend to excel in their ability to foresee the broad impact of technology on the battlespace. Several sources can be suggested as the basis of this talent. As Robert Bathhurst explained decades ago, the Russians tend to be 'dreamers', allowing

---

6   David J. Smith. 'How Russia Harnesses Cyberwarfare,' *Defense Dossier*, Issue 4, August 2012, pp. 7-8.

7   According to Michael Warner, 'Soviet spies were crucial to keeping the USSR alive and competitive for two reasons: they stole enough industrial secrets to substitute for innovation in some sectors, and they kept Moscow apprised of where the West was reading Soviet secrets,' Michael Warner. *The Rise and Fall of Intelligence: An International Security History* (Washington, D.C.: Georgetown University Press, 2014), p. 161.

their imaginations to run wild and envision the implications of technology.[8] In the 1920s, for instance, Soviet writers were thinking about supersonic dogfights on the fringes of space – something that has not occurred nearly a century later. During the Cold War, visions of a fully functioning Star Wars missile defence system shook the Kremlin to its foundations, despite the fact that even proponents of Reagan-era missile defence recognised that many of the components of the system were at the outer fringes of technical feasibility. In other words, while America focuses on issues of technology and systems integration, Russia tends to leap immediately to considerations of the strategic implications of emerging weapons systems.

> *America focuses on technology, Russia tends to leap to the strategic implications of weapons systems.*

A second influence that shapes Russian views of emerging technology is the fact that, in their hearts, they are good Clausewitzians. In other words, they understand the paramount nature of politics in war. War is a political act. Its purpose is to alter the political judgments of opponents to better suit our own interests. Thus, to have a strategic effect, cyber power must be used in a way that will shape the political outcome of war. Russians are thus quick to think through the links between technology, military operations, strategy, and ultimately political outcomes, despite their lack of technological dexterity. Soviet estimates of the military balance, for example, reflected a broad assessment of the so-called 'correlation of forces', which incorporated political and economic trends, not just force ratios based on 'bean counts' of military units. Soviet alarm over NATO's 1983 Able Archer exercise, for instance, was greatly influenced by the political rhetoric emanating from the Reagan White House, not by some fundamental shift in the military balance in Europe. The Russian officer corps, especially in Soviet days, was also encouraged to think through the strategic implications of new technologies. Today, the Russian Army provides senior officers with multiple venues to debate not only doctrine, but theory. By contrast, US officers, who tend to focus on operational matters, generally lack similar venues to assess the strategic and political implications of new technology.[9] In fact, many analysts point to a 2013 article signed by the Chief of the Russian General Staff, *The Value of Science in Anticipating* as laying out the Russian way of cyber warfare.[10]

A fine illustration of these phenomena is the emergence of the concept of 'Military-Technical Revolution,' more commonly referred to by Western analysts as the

---

8   Robert B. Bathurst. *Intelligence and the Mirror* (London: Sage, 1993).

9   For a recent discussion of how operational considerations, for instance, take centre stage in what is purportedly Naval strategy see Peter D. Haynes. *Toward a New Maritime Strategy: American Naval Thinking in the Post-Cold War Era* (Annapolis: Naval Institute Press, 2015).

10 Valery Gerasimov. 'The Value of Science in Anticipating [in Russian], Military-Industrial Courier, February 27, 2013, quoted in Matthew Rojansky and Michael Kofman. 'A Closer look at Russia's 'Hybrid War', *Wilson Centre Kennan Cable* , No 7, April 2015, p. 3.

'Revolution in Military Affairs.'[11] By the mid-1970s, NATO defence planners recognised that they confronted a serious challenge along the Central Front. If war broke out in Europe, NATO would do well against first-echelon Warsaw Pact formations, but the Alliance could only slowly bring reinforcements across the Atlantic. Soviet third-echelon forces – units made up mostly of inactive reservists in peacetime – would probably defeat NATO because they would reach the battle before reinforcements streaming across the Atlantic. The United States and its allies had to prevent the third-echelon of the Red Army from reaching the Forward Edge of the Battle Area (FEBA). The solution to the third-echelon threat was found in several new technologies that would allow NATO to conduct precision strikes against Warsaw Pact staging areas, depots, transportation hubs, and armoured formations hundreds of miles behind the FEBA. By the mid-1980s, US programmes known as Assault Breaker and Smart Weapons Program, and NATO initiatives called Emerging Technologies and Follow on Forces Attack, were integrated into a new US Army Air-Land Battle doctrine, creating a nascent reconnaissance-strike complex. US planners adopted a rather nonstrategic and apolitical view of these new technologies – they simply saw them as a way to stop Soviet third-echelon forces from reaching the Central Front.

By contrast, the Soviets now anticipated a 'Military-Technical Revolution', predicting that the emerging reconnaissance-strike complex would transform conventional combat, producing truly strategic and political effects. Soviet strategists believed that long-range precision strikes could destroy forces and critical supply, communication, and command nodes deep within the enemy's rear, creating conditions for a catastrophic theatre-wide collapse. Put somewhat differently, the system of systems possessed by the Americans and their NATO allies would rob the Warsaw Pact of its ability to mass and manoeuvre forces, or even to conduct combined arms operations. Soviet officers estimated that the nature of war was about to change: conventional, not nuclear, munitions might soon become the weapon of choice against massed armoured and infantry formations. They saw the potential impact that this emerging system of systems could have on strategy, war, and international politics; there was a real possibility that the Warsaw Pact could be rendered militarily and politically ineffective by these emerging weapons and ways of war.

Ironically, Soviet predictions of a Military-Technical Revolution set off alarm bells in the West, as analysts scrambled to detect the new secret Soviet weapon that would produce these revolutionary developments in war. Americans were slow to realise that the Soviets were in fact writing about American weapons, and the nascent precision-strike complex, which was in fact possessed exclusively by the United States and the NATO alliance. As a result, many of the key concepts related to the application of information-age technologies in warfare were produced by Soviets thinking about the weapons systems being deployed by their opponents, and not by the more technically competent Americans.

---

11   Dima Adamsky. *The Culture of Military Innovation: The Impact of Cultural Factors on the Revolution in Military Affairs in Russia, the US and Israel* (Stanford: Stanford University Press, 2010).

Today, how is this Clausewitzian-inspired Russian strategic imagination being applied to the use of cyber power? The answer can be found by first exploring the strategic challenge they apparently believe they face: the NATO alliance. NATO is based on the concept of collective defence that enhances its strategy of deterrence. Through formal agreements and long-standing and extensive collaboration, NATO sends a strong signal that member states will stand together in the face of threats to collectively deter aggression against its members. The objective of this deterrent policy is to preserve the peace. This is a key observation. The goal of NATO's deterrent strategy is to reduce or even eliminate the possibility of war by ensuring that aggressors understand *ex ante* that an attack against one of its members is an attack against the entire Alliance. Especially today, NATO primarily exists to prevent war, not to develop enhanced strategies or capabilities to prosecute war or to wield forces to achieve ancillary objectives. In a sense, NATO exists to preserve the peace and to make sure that changes to the status quo in Europe occur through political processes that lead to the spread of democracy, the rule of law, and adherence to international norms. The *raison d'être* of NATO is to preserve the peace; the purpose behind its strategy is to deter war.

To achieve its objective – rapid change of the European status quo to better fit their Russia-centric, not democratically-cantered, interests and preferences – Russia opted to pick a course of action not to defeat NATO, but to defeat NATO's *strategy*. By presenting the Western alliance with a *fait accompli* through actions that produce minimal death and destruction, Russia attempted to shift the onus of escalation onto NATO, thereby inflicting a strategic defeat on the Alliance at the outset of hostilities or even in the event of non-democratic changes to the status quo. Russia is banking on the hope that NATO will either be incapable or unwilling to transform this strategic defeat into active conventional combat, which would further undermine NATO's goal of preserving the peace. In effect, the Russians seem to have realised that by defeating NATO's strategy at the outset of a confrontation, they can actually alter political perceptions within the Alliance in a way that suits their objectives. Put somewhat differently, the risk of a forceful NATO response to some provocation is minimised by keeping the death and destruction associated with any *fait accompli* to an absolute minimum. NATO is especially vulnerable to cyberattacks and information warfare because Russia can undermine NATO's deterrent strategy without causing casualties. NATO has the option of reversing the *fait accompli*, but the required level of death and destruction simply highlights the failure of its deterrent strategy.

> *Russia opted to pick a course of action not to defeat NATO, but NATO's strategy.*

Cyber power, as a key facet of hybrid warfare, is an important enabler in an attack on NATO's deterrent strategy.[12] Cyber attacks are not specifically targeted to eliminate key nodes, but to intensify the fog of war by sowing confusion within command and control networks and NATO polities. For instance, according to press reports, Russian movement into the Ukraine was accompanied by myriad cyber attacks, including Distributed Denial of Service (DDoS) tactics against

> *Cyber power is an important enabler in an attack on NATO's deterrent strategy.*

computers in Kyiv, Poland, the European Parliament, and the European Commission.[13] If local political and military leaders cannot develop an accurate estimate of quickly developing events, critical hours or even days can be gained with which Russia can create facts on the ground that can only be reversed at great effort. A little bit of 'sand in the works', so to speak, is enough to further delay the relatively slow pace of decision-making in the West.[14]

The annexation of Crimea also began with a series of covert operations that used a disinformation campaign to create ambiguity and delay Ukraine's response, effectively extending the element of surprise achieved by the Russian gambit. According to Michael Kofman and Matthew Rohansky:

> *'Russia's use of broadcast tools for propaganda and psychological operations, part of a broader information campaign to support the Crimean annexation, caught both the Ukraine and the West by surprise. Moscow amped up the alarmist content of its broadcasting … stoking fear and confusion in Crimea'.*[15]

Admittedly, the annexation was completed using more traditional operations involving conventional units, but the cyber-enabled opening moves not only allowed Russia to test the Western response, but to buy the time needed to create a *fait accompli* through conventional means.

Western analysts have noted that even though the Crimea crisis surprised the West, the Russian effort to integrate television and the internet, especially various

---

12 As Michael Kofman and Matthew Rojansky note, 'hybrid warfare,' including the Russian variations used against the Ukraine is not unique. The point here, however, is that Russia is particularly adept as using cyber power in the practice of hybrid warfare; see Kofman and Rojansky, (*op cit*) p. 2. Other analysts have noted how the Crimea annexation and the additional actions against Ukraine were dependant on capabilities long under development that were especially crafted not to trigger a NATO response; Aleksandr Golts and Heidi Reisinger. 'Russia's Hybrid Warfare: Waging War below the Radar of Traditional Collective Defence', Research Paper No 105 (Research Division – NATO Defence College Rome) November 2014.

13 Owen Matthews. 'BIG READ: Russia leading the way in the cyber arms race,' *Irish Examiner*, Saturday June 13, 2015. www.irishexaminer.com'lifestyle'feature'big-read-russia-leading-the-way-in-the-cyber-arms-race-336675.html.

14 The key point is that information denial or dominance does not have to be absolute, it just needs to foster delay and uncertainty in Western political and military decision-making. According to Paul Saunders, 'Russia's seizure of Crimea happened very quickly. U.S. and European decision-making processes just don't move at that speed, particularly when facing ambiguity. Once a Crimea-style operation has begun, it will be extremely difficult if not impossible for Western decision-makers to be sufficiently confident about the other side's intent to take consequential action before it's too late'; Saunders, P. 'Why America Can't Stop Russia's Hybrid Warfare,' *The National Interest* June 23, 2015. www.nationalinterest.org/feature/shy-america-can't-stop-russias-hybrid-warfare-13166.

15 Kofman and Rojansky, p. 4.

types of social media, into its effort to shape opponents' political perspectives, has been ongoing for quite some time. In a sense, Russia has worked hard to use the internet to shape the political environment of conflict: it has (1) developed internally and externally focused media with a significant online presence; (2) used social media to guarantee that Russian narratives reach the broadest possible audience; and (3) polished their content in terms of language and presentation so that it rings true in various cultural settings.[16] These activities have recently been given their own moniker – trolling – the practice of creating cyber actors with false identities to communicate tailored messages to an unsuspecting audience.[17] According to Keir Giles:

> 'Russian assessments of current events makes it clear that Russia considers itself to be engaged in full-scale information warfare, involving not only offensive but defensive operations – whether or not its notional adversaries have actually noticed this is happening'.[18]

What most analysts fail to realise, however, is that Moscow has shaped this cyber-enabled information warfare in a very strategic manner. Cyber power is being wielded as a strategic weapon to create facts on the ground with the minimal use of kinetic force.

3   Conclusion

Because of its rather inchoate nature, the cyber domain is a milieu in which various strategic cultures can be manifest. Russian strategic culture focuses on war as a political activity; for cyber power to have a truly strategic effect, Russia believes that it must contribute directly to shaping political outcomes by altering the political perceptions of their opponents to better suit their interests. If one also accepts the idea that Russians are especially adept at understanding the political and strategic impact of new technologies, it is possible that they have grasped the real strategic opportunities created by the information revolution – opportunities that might be given short shrift by analysts shaped by different strategic cultures.

The true test of strategy, however, is found in a specific geopolitical and military context. In terms of Crimea and Ukraine, the Russians have developed an exquisite strategic application of cyber power not to defeat NATO's military capabilities, but to defeat NATO's strategy by creating a *fait accompli* while sidestepping NATO's deterrent. By using cyber power to create 'facts on the ground' with minimal casual-

---

16   Keir Giles. 'Working Paper: Russia's Hybrid Warfare: a Success in Propaganda,' European Security and Defence College, 18 February 2015. www.baks.bund.de'de'aktuelles/working-paper-russias-hybrid-warfe-a-success-in propaganda
17   Adrian Chen. 'The Agency,' *New York Times Magazine*, June 2, 2015. p. 57.
18   Giles.

ties, they shifted the onus of escalation onto NATO to reverse the *fait accompli*. In a sense, they created a situation in which NATO leaders must choose between suffering a harsh strategic defeat (the eruption of war in Europe) and the accommodation of the Russian annexation of Crimea and ongoing pressure against Ukraine. Cyber power, either in the form of direct attacks or a concerted information campaign, was used to create this dilemma for NATO by delaying a Western response until these stark choices emerged. The lesson is clear: if one can defeat an opponent's strategy, then it is possible to achieve one's objectives without defeating an opponent's forces or triggering execution of a deterrent threat.

CHAPTER 4

'COMPELLING OPPONENTS TO OUR WILL': THE ROLE OF CYBER WARFARE IN UKRAINE

JAMES ANDREW LEWIS

Centre for Strategic and International Studies (CSIS)

1   METRIC FOR CYBER ATTACK

The conflict in Ukraine has challenged fundamental elements of Western alliance strategy. Russian efforts exploit a general reluctance by the West – natural in democracies – to risk war. The West has been unable to deter Russia from its adventure.

Cyber warfare has played only a limited role in this. The concepts of strategic and military effect provide us with two metrics for assessing the effect of cyber attacks generally, and for Russian cyber activities in Ukraine. Strategic effect would be to diminish the opponent's will or capacity to resist. This can include politically coercive cyber actions such as were used against Estonia. Military effect would be degradation in the performance of commanders, troops, and weapons, demonstrated by U.S. actions in its Middle Eastern conflicts or as part of the 2007 Israeli airstrike in Syria[1].

Cyber attacks that produce strategic or military effect can include the manipulation of software, data, knowledge, and opinion to degrade performance and produce political or psychological effect. Introducing uncertainty into the minds of opposing commanders or political leaders is a worthy military objective. Manipulating public opinion to damage an opponent's legitimacy and authority in both domestic and international audiences is also valuable. Some actions may provide only symbolic effect aimed at a domestic audience, but this too is valuable for a nation in conflict.

---

1   David Makovsky. 'The Silent Strike: How Israel bombed a Syrian nuclear installation and kept it secret,' *The New Yorker*, 17 September 2012, http://www.newyorker.com/magazine/2012/09/17/the-silent-strike.

To assess non-kinetic effect as a contributor for strategic or military advantage, we must look for observable effects in three categories: creating confusion, shaping opinion, and inflicting damage to data or services. Using these metrics, we can conclude that Russian cyber efforts in Ukraine produced an early tactical effect that has since tapered off and, since they are limited to actions that do not produce physical or disruptive consequences, have largely failed to achieve strategic or military effect.

2   STRATEGIC AND MILITARY EFFECT

The Ukraine conflict has been described as hybrid warfare; a mixture of unconventional tactics and strategies, irregular forces, covert action, cyber operations, and political manipulation to achieve strategic goals. In essence, hybrid warfare is a collection of tactics designed to circumvent deterrence and avoid military retaliation by skirting the threshold of what could be considered state use of armed force. In this new style of conflict, non-kinetic actions can be as important as kinetic attacks. Hybrid warfare highlights the central problem for our understanding and management of interstate conflict; conventional warfare is now only part of a larger range of coercive actions available to nations.

Cyber operations – the ability to remotely manipulate computer networks – have created a capability that is well suited to this new political-military environment. Cyber capabilities create an operational space in which nations can conduct offensive action with less political risk, given the grey area in international law which cyber war inhabits, and where opponents can find it difficult to respond. Advanced cyber action can create physical effects equivalent to kinetic attack, but we should not interpret cyber capabilities solely from the perspective of physical effect.

> *Cyber capabilities create an operational space in which nations can conduct offensive action with less political risk.*

While cyber attacks can produce effects similar to kinetic weapons, there is an informational aspect involving the manipulation of opinion and decision-making that is equally important and much more frequently used. Cyber attack can produce results equivalent to kinetic attack, but this is not its primary effect, which (at least for now) is to manipulate data, knowledge, and opinion to produce political or psychological effect rather than physical damage. Introducing uncertainty into the minds of opposing commanders or political leaders is a worthwhile military goal, as it will cause them to make mistakes or to become hesitant, providing the attacker with dominance of the battle space and the advantage of putting the defender in a reactive posture. Cyber actions that manipulate public opinion to affect an opponent's legitimacy and authority are also valuable in conflict among states.

Cyber attack creates an operational space for coercive action that avoids many of the political risks of kinetic warfare. Cyber attacks are attractive in that they offer varying degrees of covertness and their treatment under international law remains ambiguous in regard to whether they qualify as an 'armed attack' that would legitimise retaliation. Although cyber tools and techniques can be used in harmful ways, they are not weapons *per se*, which can make it difficult to decide when a cyber incident can be considered an armed attack or a use of force.

An initial effort to define how a cyber incident could qualify as a use of force or armed attack would be to consider that an effect of the cyber action was the equivalent of an attack using conventional weapons producing physical destruction or casualties. A cyber incident that produced injury or death to persons and the destruction of or damage to property would certainly be considered as a use of force or armed attack. A cyber attack that produced intangible effects of such scope, intensity, and duration that they are judged to have consequences or harmful effects of sufficient scale and gravity could also be considered an armed attack.

No Russian action in Ukraine rises to this level. Overall, the use of offensive cyber capabilities for kinetic effect has been minimal, with only a few known incidents. Russia is one of the most skilled among the nations who have developed cyber capabilities, but we have not seen extensive use of actual attacks against Ukraine. Neither critical infrastructure nor Ukrainian weapons have been damaged or disrupted. Russia has used its cyber capabilities primarily for political coercion, opinion-shaping, and intelligence gathering, and these cyber operations fall below the threshold set in Article V of the North Atlantic Treaty. Operations in Estonia, Georgia, and now Ukraine suggest that NATO may need to adjust its thinking about how opponents will use cyber attacks.

Russia has been relatively careful in the overt use of its own forces – especially compared to its actions against Georgia where the Russian Ministry of Defence confirmed that Russian armoured units were engaged in combat for 'peace enforcement'. The Russian army occupied Georgian territory and Russian aircraft bombed targets including the capital.[2] Russian actions in Ukraine took a different course. The current caution may reflect lessons learned in Georgia or a desire to preserve some degree of deniability, and manoeuvring to avoid an overt violation of international law.

Cyber attack does not require 'an act of violence to compel our opponent to fulfil our will'.[3] Violence through cyber means is possible, but that is not the only or even primary use of cyber attack. Its effects are more often intangible and

---

2   Library of Congress, *Russian Federation: Legal Aspects of War in Georgia*, http://www.loc.gov/law/help/russian-georgia-war.php.
3   Clausewitz's definition of war.

informational, and are intended to manipulate data, create uncertainty, and shape opinion. An emphasis on kinetic effect can obscure important operational distinctions in the use of cyber techniques and complicates efforts to develop norms for cyber conflict.

3   NORMS AND THE APPLICATION OF INTERNATIONAL LAW[4]

Russia's activities in Ukraine have implications for both cyber warfare and for cyber norms. Russian actions have carved new contours for conflict that do not map perfectly to existing concepts and rules for warfare and defence. Existing norms and laws for armed attack were based on the use or threat of use of physical violence and force. These must be adjusted, if not amended, for cyber conflict.

Efforts to redefine violence and force to include the full range of possible cyber actions (such as Russian and Chinese efforts in the United Nations (UN) to define information as a weapon[5]) have so far introduced more ambiguity than clarity. Information is clearly not a weapon, but a minimalist definition that emphasises kinetic effect is also inadequate in capturing the full range of cyber effects.

> *The 'rules' for cyber conflict pose a challenge to existing international law.*

As such, the 'rules' for cyber conflict pose a challenge to existing international law. Currently, there is no agreement among leading nations, and it is interesting to note that with the 2015 Group of Governmental Experts (GGE), which was tasked to look at the application of international law to cyber conflict,[6] this topic proved to be the most difficult. Disagreements over the application of international law between Russia, China and a few others on one hand, and NATO nations on the other, almost derailed the talks.

The crux of the disagreement was over the application of specific provisions of the UN Charter, (the general applicability of the Charter had been agreed to in earlier GGEs), and in particular the applicability of Article 2/4 (renouncing the use of force) and Article 51 (the inherent right to self-defence). One question for the development of further norms for cyber conflict becomes whether it is possible to move beyond the norms embedded in the UN Charter and the international agreements governing the conduct of warfare and armed conflict, to address this new aspect of warfare and to create norms that govern non-ki-

---

4   The author was rapporteur to the UN Group of Governmental Experts in 2010, 2013 and 2015.

5   See, for example, SCO, *Agreement between the Governments of the Member States of the Shanghai Cooperation Organisation on Cooperation in the Field of International Information Security*, 2009, https://ccdcoe.org/sites/default/files/documents/SCO-090616-IISAgreementRussian.pdf [in Russian].

6   Along with norms and confidence building measures, see *Group of Governmental Experts Report on Developments in the Field of Information and Telecommunications in the Context of International Security*, A/70/174, 22 July 2015, UNODA, http://www.un.org/ga/search/view_doc.asp?symbol=A/70/174.

netic action. One possible avenue for progress would be to expand the Charter commitment to avoid actions that threaten the territorial integrity or political independence of a state (found in Articles 2/4 and 51) to explicitly include cyber actions.

Continued ambiguity over the application of these UN Charter articles serves the interests of Russia and China by not creating grounds for or legitimising retaliation for cyber actions.[7] This includes a general rejection of Western efforts to define 'use of force' and 'armed attack' using the concepts of equivalence and effect. These ambiguities, however, are not unique to cyber conflict, date from the signing of the Charter, and reflect conflicting desires to renounce the use of force while preserving the right to use force in self-defence. The Russian and Chinese goal, similar to other actions in arms control negotiations by these countries, is to constrain the U.S. and its allies.

Intentional ambiguity may define the emerging strategic conflict between Russia and the West for the foreseeable future. Russian cyber tactics accentuate and expand ambiguity. The Russian concept of cyber warfare blends elements of what would be considered information warfare in the West. It is well known that the Russians prefer to use the phrase 'information conflict' to 'cyber conflict' on the grounds that cyber is too narrow and technical. Unsurprisingly, this preference reflects their use and understanding of cyber techniques.

The norms before the UN General Assembly for approval at its 70th session will reiterate the rule of international law and the UN Charter, although how these are to be applied is a matter of intense dispute. They call for states not to attack critical infrastructure in peacetime, and to take note of the principles of humanity, necessity, proportionality, and distinction whey they exercise their inherent rights recognised by the UN Charter, including the right of self-defence. They do not address the use of cyber tools for political coercion, and it is interesting and indicative to note that Russia, which has made the most frequent use of cyber coercion, is the leading proponent for such norms.

State practice suggests that there is an implicit threshold among states to avoid cyber actions against each other that could be interpreted as the use of force or an armed attack. This creates implicit norms for state behaviour derived from international practice that constrain malicious cyber actions, but these implicit norms are inadequate for this new form of conflict. The kind of cyber conflict we have seen in Ukraine poses a challenge not only to existing Western strategy (which is based on international law and UN Charter commitments) but also for the development of norms. If the trend in warfare is to circumvent direct confrontation between conventional forces (particularly the conventional forces of the U.S. and its allies), and if cyber conflict will often not involve kinetic effect or territorial intrusions, existing norms and rules for conflict will have limited application.

---

7   According to conversations between the author and GGE representatives from many countries.

We can place cyber norms into four categories:

- Those that call for observation of existing international law regarding state responsibility, especially the laws of armed conflict;
- Those that seek to exempt from cyber attack infrastructures where an attack could have an indiscriminate effect such as critical infrastructures, including the infrastructure of the global internet;
- Norms on state responsibilities to assist other states that are the victim of cyber attacks; and
- Norms on the proliferation of cyber technologies that could be used for malevolent purposes (which is still nascent and suffers from definitional problems).

None of these norms can be easily extended to the new modes of coercion created by cyber capabilities. The stricture that comes closest is the Article 2/4 commitment to refrain from the use of force against the political independence of another state, but cyber actions such as we have seen in Ukraine cannot be considered a use of force.

Cyber actions that do not have physical effect and which are taken outside the context of formal conflict do not fit well with the existing structure of international practice. Nations appear to observe an implicit threshold for their use of cyber tools and with very few exceptions, have avoided actions that could be considered under international law as a use of force or an armed attack. Attempts to expand these implicit understandings or to redefine the use of force to include coercive or politically manipulative cyber actions immediately run into problems. The central problem is access to information, because several countries would happily support a norm that restricts access to information.

> *Nations appear to observe an implicit threshold for their use of cyber tools.*

Russia, in particular, is quick to label any criticism of its behaviour as disinformation, information warfare, or propaganda. Russian negotiating behaviour, shaped in good measure by Soviet precedent, is often defensive, seeking to constrain the U.S. and its allies in areas where the West has a technological advantage, or to limit the political risks the internet creates. This defensive orientation creates a negotiating agenda that conflicts with Western countries when it comes to norms.

4   COMPARING UKRAINE TO ESTONIA AND GEORGIA

Contrasting Russian cyber activities in Ukraine with Estonia and Georgia is helpful in assessing their use and value, as well as in considering what new norms might look like. The cyber attacks in Estonia[8], composed of service disruptions and denial

---

8   Eneken Tikk, Kadri Kaska and Liis Vihul. *International Cyber Incidents: Legal Considerations* (Tallinn, Estonia: NATO Cooperative Cyber Defence of Excellence, 2010).

of service incidents, could best be compared to the online equivalent of a noisy protest in front of government buildings and banks. They had little tangible effect, but they created uncertainty and fear among Estonian leaders as they were considered a potential precursor to armed Russian intervention. In Georgia[9], cyber attacks were closely coordinated with Russian military operations.

The effects of the cyber attacks in Estonia and Georgia deserve more careful study. The attacks did not cripple or bring Estonia to its knees, and NATO's decision not to invoke Article V reflects this fact. They were frightening not because of the cyber effect, but because of Estonian concerns about Russian intentions, NATO's reliability, and their internal Russian-speaking minority. Similarly, cyber attacks on Georgia were largely symbolic. The most visible incident was the defacement of the Georgian President's website by Russian hackers, who drew moustaches on his photograph. The most interesting part of the Georgia episode was the close operational coordination between the hackers and the Russian military. The Russians continue to experiment with cyber tools to support their political objectives.

If the Russian goal in Ukraine is to shape global public opinion, there were some early successes in painting the Ukrainians as 'fascists' (a favoured communist insult) guilty of human rights violations. But no one believes that anymore, and the tide of public opinion has turned heavily against Russia. A recent Pew Research survey on global opinion captures the change and is entitled 'Russia, Putin, Held in Low Esteem around the World'.[10] In this, the current Russian regime has not done as well as its communist predecessors, who could at least cloak their actions in the rhetoric of Marxism. Russia's current effort to hire hundreds of internet trolls[11] to insert pro-Russian opinions in the Western press has proven to be feckless. Perhaps the benefit is domestic, persuading the Russian population of the righteousness of Russia's course of action,[12] but as a tool of coercion, the absence of informational disruption (as in the case of Sony or Aramco) or physical effects (as with Stuxnet) makes Russian cyber operations annoying, but ultimately inconsequential.

> *If the Russian goal is to shape global public opinion, there were early successes in painting the Ukrainians as 'fascists'.*

The most successful Russian tactics were creating or supporting pro-Russian separatist groups in areas with significant Russian-speaking minorities and then using Russian special and ultimately conventional forces to stiffen and protect these groups from the Ukrainian response. Cyber attack was largely irrelevant.

---

9   *Ibid.*

10   Bruce Stokes. 'Russia, Putin, Held in Low Esteem around the World,' *Pew Research Centre*, 5 August 2015, http://www.pew-global.org/2015/08/05/russia-putin-held-in-low-regard-around-the-world/.

11   See, for example, Dmitry Volchek and Daisy Sindelar, 'One Professional Russian Troll Tells All,' *RadioFreeEurope/RadioLiberty*, 25 March 2015, sec. Russia, http://www.rferl.org/content/how-to-guide-russian-trolling-trolls/26919999.html.

12   Katie Simmons, Bruce Strokes and Jacob Poushter. 'NATO Publics Blame Russia for Ukrainian Crisis, but Reluctant to Provide Military Aid,' *Pew Research Centre*, 15 July 2015, http://www.pewglobal.org/2015/06/10/2-russian-public-opinion-putin-praised-west-panned/.

Both Western and Russian analysts may have drawn the wrong lessons from Estonia and Georgia. States (especially states with a fondness for Lenin) will use cyber attacks for politically coercive purposes and might use them for military purposes, to disrupt data or services. But the incidents in Ukraine did not disrupt command and control, deny access to information, or have any noticeable military effect.

This means that we (and the Russians) may overestimate the coercive effect of cyber attacks and that their real military value is achieved when there is physical effect or disruption of data and critical services, something that most denial of service attacks cannot produce. Cyber attacks are a support weapon and will shape the battlefield, but by themselves they will not produce victory. Cyber attacks support other weapons and operations, as in the 2007 Israeli attack against Syrian air defence. This is still a subject of intense debate, but experience suggests that it is easy to exaggerate the effect of cyber attack. A more accurate assessment would rank cyber activities into three categories: espionage, operational, and political. However, note that the benefits of the former are clear, while the latter are open to question.

To provide strategic or military effect, cyber actions must produce destructive effect and be integrated into existing military structures, doctrine, planning, and operations. Estonia and Georgia can be contrasted with two known attacks that did have military effect. The Israeli air strike against a Syrian nuclear facility is reported to have used cyber means to disrupt Syrian air defence radars, allowing the aircraft to fly undetected across much of the country.[13] In this case, there was no physical damage but a vital service was disrupted. With Stuxnet, there was

> *If cyber is the weaponisation of signals intelligence, there must be physical damage.*

physical damage, albeit inflicted covertly, that could be duplicated in overt warfare, noting that a degree of caution is warranted to predict the effect of cyber attacks on civilian infrastructure.[14] We should also note the reported use of cyber techniques by the U.S. to disrupt or confuse Taliban command and control, often with lethal results for the insurgents.[15] If cyber is the weaponisation of signals intelligence, it appears that to have actual military effect, there must be physical damage.

This is a consideration of cyber as a tool of military action and does not consider either traditional methods of electronic warfare, which Russia has used extensively in Ukraine,[16] nor the intelligence value of Russian cyber espionage. We do not know the role cyber espionage played in these efforts, but if Russian successes against the United States are any guide, we can assume cyber spying made a positive contribu-

---

13   David Makovsky. 'The Silent Strike: How Israel bombed a Syrian nuclear installation and kept it secret,' *The New Yorker*, 17 September 2012, http://www.newyorker.com/magazine/2012/09/17/the-silent-strike.

14   Kim Zetter. 'An Unprecedented Look At Stuxnet, The World's First Digital Weapon,' *Wired*, 3 November 2014, http://www.wired.com/2014/11/countdown-to-zero-day-stuxnet/.

15   Interviews with US military officials.

16   Joe Gould. 'Electronic Warfare: What US Army Can Learn From Ukraine,' *Defense News*, 4 August 2015, http://www.defense-news.com/story/defense/policy-budget/warfare/2015/08/02/us-army-ukraine-russia-electronic-warfare/30913397/.

tion. That Russia has completely penetrated Ukrainian communication networks and has unparalleled access to Ukrainian communications is likely to provide considerable value for Russian tactics and planning, but cyber as a tool of coercion has proven to be of limited utility.

This is certainly not the cyber war as it is often depicted in public media, but it does not mean that cyber attack is overrated and militaries can deemphasise it. That would be a rash conclusion. It means that the Russians, for whatever reason, chose not to use the most damaging forms of cyber attack against Ukraine, Georgia, or Estonia. If allegations that Russia were responsible for damaging cyber attacks on a German steel mill[17] and a Turkish pipeline[18] are correct, these would demonstrate that Russia has the capability necessary for cyber attacks that would create physical damage and qualify as a use of force. Russia's 2008 exploit in penetrating Central Command's classified networks[19] was an early demonstration of its ability to implant malware on an opponent's networks that could erase data and disrupt command and control, but the Russians chose not to do this.

In Ukraine, Russia has experimented with how best to produce military and political benefits from cyber operations. Political context and alliance relationships have a powerful influence in constraining the use of force, including cyber attacks. Its cyber actions appear to reflect a decision not to engage the full range of Russian cyber capabilities. Other potential opponents, including NATO, should not assume that in the event of conflict, the Russians will make the same decision.

---

17   'Hack attack causes 'massive damage' at steel works,' *BBC*, 22 December 2014, http://www.bbc.com/news/technology-30575104.
18   Ariel Bogle. 'A Cyber Attack May Have Caused a Turkish Oil Pipeline to Catch Fire in 2008,' *Slate*, 11 December 2014, http://www.slate.com/blogs/future_tense/2014/12/11/bloomberg_reports_a_cyber_attack_may_have_made_a_turkish_oil_pipe-line_catch.html.
19   Phil Stewart and Jim Wolf. 'Old worm won't die after 2008 attack on military,' *Reuters*, 16 June 2011, http://www.reuters.com/article/2011/06/17/us-usa-cybersecurity-worm-idUSTRE75F5TB20110617.

Chapter 5

The Cyber War that Wasn't

Martin Libicki

RAND

1 Introduction: Isn't It Time for Cyber War?

For the last twenty years, with the advent of serious thinking about 'cyber war', most analysts – and even the more sceptical thinkers – have been convinced that all future kinetic wars between modern countries would have a clear cyber component. However, the current Russo-Ukrainian conflict is challenging this widely held notion.

Coinciding with this assumption, however, it must be said that within the past generation there have been few conflicts in which both sides appeared both capable of and vulnerable to cyber attack. Either one party to the conflict – usually the United States – held all the cyber cards, or neither did. For cyber war to take place, at least one side must have enough digitised networked equipment to make much difference. In some past conflicts, the US may have abstained from firing digital weapons because the other side simply lacked appropriate targets.

> *Analysts have been convinced that future kinetic wars would have a clear cyber component.*

Many analysts have speculated that the US, and now other highly networked societies, may hesitate to use cyber tactics because of their own inherent vulnerabilities in this domain.

Apart from Stuxnet, the most frequently cited example of cyber war in action came during an alleged Israel Air Force strike against Syrian nuclear facilities in 2007. Integrated air-defence systems (IADS) have been considered ripe targets for cyber warfare, but it was understood that there would be a cost-benefit analysis relative to dispatching them using more familiar tools such as electronic warfare or missiles. There were rumours, for example, that the US employed cyberwar techniques against Serbian IADS in 1999, but these rumours were never substantiated. Even the Syrian story may be a fairy tale, as the details are classified and subject to much speculation. It is possible that the tactics were in fact more conventional, such as traditional jamming.[1]

2   UNIQUE ASPECTS OF THE RUSSO-UKRAINIAN CONFLICT

The current Russo-Ukrainian conflict, however, is a different case, and it should help us to understand if cyber war is, in 2015, more myth or reality. According to the prevailing assumption, this war should have seen serious and open cyber war strategies and tactics. Both countries have technologically advanced societies and weaponry that at least came up to 1990 standards of modernity. Both countries have a strong information technology (IT) base, and hackers a-plenty, although many of them are engaged in organised crime rather than working for the state.[2] Russia's state-sponsored hackers are widely believed to be on par with, or very close to, NSA-level standards.

The most notable thing about the war in Ukraine, however, is the near-complete absence of any perceptible cyber war. There has been vigorous cyber espionage,[3] the targeting of cell phones by Russian electronic warfare, and the use of old-fashioned bolt-cutters to sever lines of communication in Crimea.[4] Patriotic hacktivists on both sides have conducted harassing but small cyber attacks against each other,[5] both sides have conducted Distributed Denial-of-Service (DDoS) attacks (e.g., by Russia against Ukraine's parliament),[6] and

---

1   As Richard Clarke and Robert Knake maintain in *Cyberwar, The Next Threat to National Security and What to do About It*, New York NY: HarperCollins, 2010; see also David Makovsky. 'The Silent Strike: How Israel bombed a Syrian nuclear installation and kept it secret,' *The New Yorker,* 17 September 2012, http://www.newyorker.com/magazine/2012/09/17/the-silent-strike.

2   Ukraine's hackers do not make as much news but consider Dan Goodin. 'Strange snafu hijacks UK nuke maker's traffic, routes it through Ukraine,' *ARS Technica UK,* 13 March 2015, http://arstechnica.com/security/2015/03/mysterious-snafu-hijacks-uk-nukes-makers-traffic-through-ukraine/.

3   Apparently, the Russians have developed some powerful malware for that purpose against Ukraine: cyber-snake (aka Ouroboros). See Sam Jones. 'Cyber Snake plagues Ukraine networks,' *FT Online,* 7 March 2014, in http://www.ft.com/cms/s/0/615c-29ba-a614-11e3-8a2a-00144feab7de.html or David Sanger and Steven Erlanger, 'Suspicion Falls on Russia as 'Snake' Cyberattacks Target Ukraine's Government' *NY Times Online,* 8 March 2014, http://www.nytimes.com/2014/03/09/world/europe/suspicion-falls-on-russia-as-snake-cyberattacks-target-ukraines-government.html.

4   Sam Jones. 'Kremlin alleged to wage cyber warfare on Kiev,' *FT Online,* 5 June 2014, http://www.ft.com/intl/cms/s/0/e504e278-e29d-11e3-a829-00144feabdc0.html#axzz3b4c6egXI. See also the claim of General Breedlove, EUCOM's Commander: 'They disconnected the Ukrainian forces in Crimea from their command and control,' from Michael Gordon. 'NATO Commander Says He Sees Potent Threat From Russia,' *NY Time Online,* 2 April 2014, http://www.nytimes.com/2014/04/03/world/europe/nato-general-says-russian-force-poised-to-invade-ukraine.html.

5   "Cyber Berkut' Hackers Target Major Ukrainian Bank,' *The Moscow Times,* 4 June 2014, http://www.themoscowtimes.com/business/article/cyber-berkut-hackers-target-major-ukrainian-bank/502992.html of July 4, 2014.

6   Nicole Perloth. 'Cyberattacks Rise as Ukraine Crisis Spills to Internet,' *New York Times Bits,* 4 March 2014, http://bits.blogs.nytimes.com/2014/03/04/cyberattacks-rise-as-ukraine-crisis-spills-on-the-internet/.

a (fruitless) campaign to corrupt voting processes in Ukraine.[7] However, we have seen nothing comparable to the cyber attacks carried out against Estonia in 2007 or Georgia in 2008.

On the other hand, the information and propaganda war in the social media domain (particularly from the Russian side) has been relentless. In this regard, Moscow has a competitive advantage over Kyiv. The two countries share a common language, Russian (the use of the Ukrainian language is growing fast, but that language is Slavic), and most Russian-language-friendly sites such as *VKontakte* (the Russian Facebook) are headquartered in Russia. That said, little if any of the conflict taking place in social media requires subverting computers through the discovery of vulnerabilities or the engagement of exploits.

In particular, there are two major forms of cyber attack that have not taken place in the Russo-Ukrainian conflict: attacks on critical infrastructure and attacks on defence systems. It is possible that, in the future, we may learn that there have been such attacks, but that they were simply subtle enough to slip under the radar. With Stuxnet, Iran's centrifuge plant at Natanz was infected for six months, with centrifuges failing at unexpected rates, before Iranian engineers understood

> *Two major forms of cyber attack have not taken place: on critical infrastructure and on defence systems.*

why. Successful cyber attacks could indefinitely be ascribed to incompetent management before a complete picture is understood. And as for military systems, credible stories of their successful attacks may emerge years later, when people are freer to talk about what happened in the war.

Even with all of that in mind, in the Internet era it has become difficult to keep secrets for long periods of time, and the growing absence of cyber attack evidence is turning into the evidence of absence.

3   POSSIBLE REASONS FOR THE ABSENCE OF CYBER CONFLICT

So, based on what we know now, why has this kinetic conflict seen so little cyber conflict? Here are some possible answers to that question.

Ukraine does not have the requisite hackers. Russian hackers need no introduction. They work for the state, for cyber crime syndicates, and for themselves as patriotic hacktivist defenders of Mother Russia. However, on the Ukrainian side (a much smaller nation to begin with), it is possible that a large percentage of the hacker talent is of Russian descent and may have divided loyalties in this conflict. That said,

---

7   Mark Clayton. 'Ukraine election narrowly avoided 'wanton destruction' from hackers,' *Christian Science Monitor,* 17 June 2014, http://www.csmonitor.com/World/Passcode/2014/0617/Ukraine-election-narrowly-avoided-wanton-destruction-from-hackers-video.

many small countries have made large contributions in cyberspace, including Estonia, Iceland, Lebanon[8] and Israel.

Neither Russia nor Ukraine has valid targets. This gets closer to the truth. Although the Soviet Union of 1990 had sophisticated weapons, their long suits were in metallurgy and radio-frequency devices. When the Soviet Union collapsed, it was significantly behind the West in terms of electronics and software. In the last five years, there has been a modest recapitalisation in Russia, but close to none in Ukraine. Since the end of the Cold War, the United States has for the most part maintained its substantial lead over Russia in digitisation and networking. Thus, US fears about its systems falling prey to hackers are currently not shared by the majority of nation-states, who feel that they are not particularly vulnerable. However, the truth probably lies somewhere in the middle: for example, no one is buying analogue telecommunications systems anymore, not even in the developing world. New equipment is digital and networked, not only because it is more powerful, but because it is cheaper over the long run. Therefore, even in Russia and Ukraine, the level of digitisation is likely high enough to engender real concerns about their societies' vulnerability to cyber attack. Their militaries may be antiquated, but due to the close relationship between the IT of modern civilian and military domains, there is probably still plenty for hackers to target.

There is no need – The Russians already own Ukraine: Much of Ukraine's infrastructure – notably the phone system – dates from the Soviet era. It is logical, therefore, that the Russians have already wired the phone system for interception and, it would hardly be in their interest to take it down.[9] This explanation does not explain anything the Ukrainian side has or has not done, nor does it explain the lack of attacks on other systems such as power, natural gas distribution or finance. However, it may help to understand a lack of attacks on telecommunications, given that a cyber attack could disrupt a lucrative cyber espionage operation by alerting defenders that their systems have been penetrated and forcing a system scrub. Such action may not only knock out existing implants but also make the reinsertion of malware more difficult. The effects of cyber attack tend to be short term, while stealthy cyber exploitation can persist for years. Therefore, for strategic purposes, attacks such as Denial-of-Service (DoS) can be counterproductive. Well-designed technologies like Skype, however, which have end-to-end encryption, could lessen the value of cyber espionage over time (but not by much, because encryption does not protect if computers on one or both ends of the conversation are compromised), and increase the likelihood of denial-of-service attacks.

Neither Russia nor Ukraine wants such an escalation: In theory, the Russo-Ukrainian conflict is not a war between two states, but an insurgency and count-

---

8   Kelly Jackson Higgins. 'Lebanon Believed behind Newly Uncovered Cyber Espionage Operation,' *Information Week,* 31 March 2015, http://www.darkreading.com/attacks-breaches/lebanon-believed-behind-newly-uncovered-cyber-espionage-operation/d/d-id/1319695.

9   Jeffrey Carr, quoted in Patrick Tucker. 'Why Ukraine Has Already Lost The Cyberwar, Too,' *Defence One,* 28 April 2014, http://www.defenseone.com/technology/2014/04/why-ukraine-has-already-lost-cyberwar-too/83350/.

er-insurgency campaign over territory in eastern Ukraine. According to the Russian Government, Russian forces are not even in the fight, and thus far, neither country's infrastructure (outside the battle zone) has been touched. In this context, if Russia were to attack Ukraine's infrastructure or vice versa it would be hard to ascribe the attack to separatists, who likely would not possess the requisite advanced hacker skills among their 'patriotic hacker' ranks. Organised crime syndicates may have the technical expertise, but may lack the trust or the intelligence-informed approach required. Still, given that both of these groups enjoy some state protection in Russia, such an operation is not out of the question. The more important point here is that any such escalation could change the narrative of the conflict from an inter-ethnic squabble to an interstate war. An obvious attack by Russia against Ukraine's infrastructure may conflict with its current political narrative. A Ukrainian attack against Russia could be a warning signal to Moscow that it will have to pay a price for its actions (a sporty move indeed), as well as a sign that it cannot do better in a conventional fight with the Russian military. A wild card here is that cyber war techniques in 2015 may be viewed in and of themselves as unduly escalatory, but this fear likely does not apply to cyber attacks precisely focused on enemy military targets in theatre where their use ought to seem no more alarming than the use of, say, electronic warfare. Finally, it is important to remember that two nuclear states may easily prefer fighting without resorting to nuclear weapons; in cyber warfare, many analysts have noted that any two sides are likely riddled with exploitable vulnerabilities.[10]

Cyber war is not a 'silver bullet'. Proponents of cyber war argue that attacks are cheap, asymmetric, effective, and risk-free. But what if they are wrong? A truly successful cyber attack – one that does more than simply annoy defenders – is harder than it looks. Penetrating systems without getting caught requires technical expertise that is in short supply. Preoperational reconnaissance and intelligence gathering of the kind required to create politically interesting effects such as against national critical infrastructure, or to target military defence systems takes a long time and may not produce practical results. In 2015, it is also possible that neither Russian nor Ukrainian systems are sufficiently wired to allow for easy access and manipulation. Human-in-the-loop safeguards, for example, may prevent truly serious damage from occurring except on rare occasions. Both crit-

> *A truly successful cyber attack – that does more than simply annoy defenders – is harder than it looks.*

---

10 'The Russians and Ukrainians have some of the best computer people in the world, because of the Soviet legacy military industrial complex,' says Taras Kuzio, a Ukraine expert at the School of Advanced International Studies at Johns Hopkins University. 'These [Ukrainian] guys are fantastic. So if the Russians tried something like a cyberattack, they would get it right back. There would be some patriotic hackers in Ukraine saying, 'Just who are the Russians to do this to us?' from Mark Clayton. 'Where are the cyberattacks? Russia's curious forbearance in Ukraine,' *Christian Science Monitor*, 3 March 2014, http://www.csmonitor.com/World/Security-Watch/2014/0303/Where-are-the-cyberattacks-Russia-s-curious-forbearance-in-Ukraine.-video.

ical infrastructure and combat systems are designed to operate under a great deal of stress and unexpected events. Some states may already have calculated that the effects of cyber war are limited, temporary, and hard to repeat. Attackers also fear that digital weapons may work only once before defenders can plug the necessary holes. In this light, is developing a cyber war arsenal really worth it?

4   Conclusion

In 1972, when Chinese Premier Zhou Enlai was asked about the significance of the French Revolution of 1789, he famously said, 'It is too soon to say'.[11] With that logic in mind, it must be noted that the Internet is still a baby, and that cyber attacks are still in a nascent stage. Despite the prevailing 25 May 2015 ceasefire, the Russo-Ukrainian conflict is not over. Currently, it could be that neither side wants to escalate this somewhat localised conflict into the realm of interstate war, and this may inhibit operations otherwise warranted in less opaque circumstances. Both parties to the conflict are still exploring their best options, and both are surely upgrading their traditional and digital military arsenals. Finally, it is hard to say what current cyber operations may come to light in the future. However, in mid-2015, the preponderance of evidence suggests that the easy assumption that cyber attacks would unquestionably be used in modern warfare has come up wanting.

---

11   Alas, one of the greatest quotes in international relations of the 20th century may have been misunderstood, as Chou was actually referring to French protests of 1968. However, a diplomat present at the time said Chou's comment was 'too delicious to invite correction.' Dean Nicholas 'Zhou Enlai's Famous Saying Debunked,' *History Today*, 15 June 2011, http://www.history-today.com/blog/news-blog/dean-nicholas/zhou-enlais-famous-saying-debunked.

CHAPTER 6

REVOLUTION HACKING

NIKOLAY KOVAL

CyS Centrum LLC

1   INTRODUCTION: CYBER CONFLICT IN UKRAINE

During Ukraine's revolution in 2014, I served our country as the chief of its Computer Emergency Response Team (CERT-UA).[1] During my tenure, we responded to a wide variety of network security incidents. I can say with great confidence that the number and severity of cyber attacks against Ukraine rose in parallel with ongoing political events.

Before the revolution, Ukraine experienced a fairly typical array of incidents, the most frequent of which were botnet-driven[2] Distributed Denial of Service (DDoS) attacks. Often, these came in retaliation for unpopular government initiatives, such as when the

> *The number and severity of cyber attacks against Ukraine rose in parallel with ongoing political events.*

authorities tried to shut down the file-sharing website www.ex.ua. By the end of 2012, some of the public's frustration was channelled into politically motivated website 'defacements' (i.e. digital graffiti) within the government's Internet Protocol (IP) space.

In 2013, we began to discover a much more serious class of malware. Network vandalism had given way to a surge in cyber espionage, for which commercial cyber security companies developed a list of colourful names: RedOctober, MiniDuke, NetTraveler, and many more.

---

[1]   CERT-UA lies within the State Service for Special Communications and Information Protection of Ukraine.
[2]   In other words, the botnets were large enough that no other amplification was needed.

Once the revolution began in February 2014, even ordinary Ukrainians became familiar with the combination of hacking and political activism, or 'hacktivism', in which the attackers seek to wage psychological war via the internet. Although many people were exhausted by the momentous political events that had shaken our country, it was hard to ignore the publication of allegedly leaked Ukrainian government documents detailing a secret, fascist government agenda. The most prominent hacktivist group was CyberBerkut,[3] and it is their most famous attack which is detailed below.

In the course of so many incident responses we learned that, with sufficient evidence, it is usually possible to understand the general nature of an attack, including who the attackers might be and what they were seeking. Timing, context, victim identity, and malware sophistication are good indicators. Cutting-edge spyware is likely to be found on the computers of senior government officials or on important network nodes within national critical infrastructure. For example, in one case, we wondered why a private sector executive had been hit, and then discovered that he had previously been a high-ranking government official.

In my opinion, CERT-UA – in collaboration with network security firms such as Kaspersky Lab, Symantec, ESET, and others – was usually able to detect, isolate, and eliminate serious threats to network security in Ukraine.

However, in the course of our work, we also discovered another problem that any enterprise today should seek to address: a fundamental lack of user understanding of cyber security. At every institution, therefore, we tried to carry out a malware 'literacy campaign' to teach employees how infections begin and how attackers can subsequently control their computers to steal documents, all via a tiny, unauthorised program that can be maddeningly difficult to find.

2   Case Study: Hacking a Presidential Election

The most sensational hacktivist attack took place during Ukraine's presidential elections. On 21 May 2014, CyberBerkut compromised the Central Election Commission (CEC), disabling core CEC network nodes and numerous components of the election system. For nearly 20 hours, the software, which was designed to display real-time updates in the vote count, did not work properly. On 25 May – election day – 12 minutes before the polls closed (19:48 EET), the attackers posted on the CEC website a picture of Ukrainian Right Sector leader Dmitry Yarosh, incorrectly claiming that he had won the election. This image was immediately shown on Russian TV channels.

It is important to note here that this attack could in no way have determined the outcome of the election. In Ukraine, every citizen inks his or her vote on a real paper

---

3   For background on this hacker group, see Wikipedia entry 'CyberBerkut', https://en.wikipedia.org/wiki/CyberBerkut.

ballot, and all votes are manually verified. Each polling station in every corner of the country physically delivers its ballots to CEC headquarters in Kyiv for aggregation, reconciliation, and determination of the final tally. CEC's information technology (IT) infrastructure is a complex, geographically distributed system designed for fault tolerance and transparency. Polling stations have an 'anti-fraud' design that allows monitors to detect anomalies such as dramatically swinging vote counts and report them to the appropriate authorities. Any serious disruption during an election would generate immediate suspicion about its legitimacy, and spark a desire for a new election.

That said, I believe that we should not underestimate the ability of hackers – especially those that enjoy state sponsorship – to disrupt the political process of a nation. If CEC's network had not been restored by 25 May, the country would simply have been unable to follow the vote count in real-time. However, to what extent would that have caused citizens to question the integrity of the entire process? It is hard to know.

CEC was not the only election-related site compromised. There were many others, including some that were only tangentially related to Ukrainian politics when, for example, the word 'election' had unfortunately appeared somewhere on the site. But even when attacks against low-level sites were unsophisticated, and the sites basically continued to function, the attackers still got the press attention they sought.

The technical aspects of this hack also tell us something very important: the hackers were professionals. Beyond disabling the site and successfully displaying incorrect election results, CERT-UA discovered advanced cyber espionage malware on the CEC network (Sofacy/ APT28/Sednit). These two aspects of the

The technical aspects of this hack also tell us something very important: the hackers were professionals.

attack – disruption and espionage – may seem contradictory, but in fact they are quite complementary. Hackers must first conduct in-depth reconnaissance of a target prior to any serious attack.

To bolster its technical credentials as an elite hacker group, CyberBerkut claimed to have discovered and exploited a 'zero-day' vulnerability in CEC's Cisco ASA software. In my opinion, it is highly unlikely that a non-state hacker group would possess such a high level of technical expertise. If CyberBerkut really did exploit a zero-day, the group is likely supported by a nation-state.

During my tenure as chief of CERT-UA, the CEC compromise was probably the most technically advanced cyber attack we investigated. It was well planned, highly targeted, and had some (albeit limited) real-world impact. Preparation for such an attack does not happen overnight; based on our analysis of Internet Protocol (IP) activity, the attackers began their reconnaissance in mid-March 2014 – more than two months prior to the election. Neither does the level of required expertise suggest that this was the work of amateurs; at a minimum, the hackers had gained administrator-level access to CEC's network.

3   Conclusion: What Is to Be Done?

Ukraine today faces cyber security challenges on at least two fronts. First, there are technical attacks against a wide range of network infrastructure, including individual websites and whole Internet Service Providers (ISPs). These encompass everything from preoperational reconnaissance to social engineering against the target's employees. Second, there is an ongoing, content-driven information war within the online media space designed to influence and deceive the public.

More serious threats lie over the horizon. In recent incident response activities we have discovered samples of the most advanced forms of malware, including BlackEnergy2/SandWorm, Potao, Turla/Urobros, and more.

In the face of these threats, Ukraine is currently unprepared. At the strategic level, our senior officials are preoccupied with more pressing concerns. At the tactical level, our law enforcement agencies still fail to grasp the basic connection between email attachments, remote administrative software, and cyber espionage. Today, there is no unified mechanism to monitor Ukraine's network space, which hinders our ability to detect cases of unauthorised access in a timely fashion.

It is time for the government of Ukraine to pay attention to cyber security.

It is time for the government of Ukraine to pay greater attention to cyber security. Given our current national security crisis, this will not be easy. However, in spite of the challenging environment, many positive developments are taking place in Ukraine, such as the recent transformation of Kyiv's metropolitan police force.[4] A similar breakthrough can take place in our cyber security domain, but it must begin with the allocation of funds to hire and retain the right personnel through competitive salaries and more attractive working conditions.

---

4   Laura Mills. 'In Ukraine's Capital, a New Show of Force,' *The Wall Street Journal*, 6 August 2015, http://www.wsj.com/articles/in-ukraines-capital-a-new-show-of-force-1438903782.

CHAPTER 7

CYBER OPERATIONS AT MAIDAN: A FIRST-HAND ACCOUNT

GLIB PAKHARENKO

ISACA Kyiv

1   INTRODUCTION: CYBER CONFLICT IN UKRAINE

I would like to tell the story of what I experienced in Ukraine from the autumn of 2013 until the end of 2014. In this chapter, I will describe the nature and impact of numerous cyber attacks that took place during our revolution and the subsequent conflict between Ukraine and Russia.

As background, it is important to understand the strategic value of Ukraine to Russia. Ukraine is the largest country in Europe, with over 42 million citizens and 27 administrative divisions. In the past, its rich farmland and industrial base have been coveted by Russia, Turkey, Poland, and even by Nazi Germany. Ukraine has also made significant contributions in politics; the Ukrainian Cossacks created the first constitution in contemporary European history. Following the horrors of World War II, the country continued to suffer under Soviet rule until it regained its independence in 1991. Despite that, Russia has never really let go of Ukraine.

Ukraine has had internet connectivity since 1990. As everywhere else in the world, it has also had its share of cyber attacks. The majority of these have come in the form of Distributed Denial-of-Service (DDoS) incidents against politically or economically targeted websites. During election seasons, for example, hackers have frequently gone after the websites of political parties. In terms of cyber crime, Ukraine has long been home to carding, mobile operator fraud, spam factories, cyberlockers, pirated software, unauthorized bank transfers, and various attacks on rival businesses.

Responsibility for the enforcement of internet security in Ukraine belongs to the Ministry of Internal Affairs (MVS) and the Security Service of Ukraine (SBU).[1] Cyber security regulations are overseen by the State Service of Special Communication and Information Protection (SSSCIP),[2] but the ultimate responsibility for cyber crimes has never made explicit, and in this regard there has been competition between the MVS and SBU. Ukraine's Computer Emergency Response Team was created in 2007.

National cyber security legislation is still in its nascent stages. Many of our current laws date from the Soviet era, and need to be updated for the information age. The national critical infrastructure domain is still largely unregulated. Definitions related to 'cyber security' and 'information security' are unclear, as is the distinction between them.

Historically, the Ukrainian police have investigated straightforward cases related to illegal content, online gambling, and pornography. Their number of qualified personnel trained in cyber security was low, with little competency in computer or network forensics. Therefore, their most common tactic was simply to confiscate all IT equipment.

Given these circumstances, Ukraine is currently ill-prepared to combat advanced, nation-state level cyber attacks. In the future, its specialists would like to see the arrival of more non-governmental organisation (NGO) support from the European Union and United States, with a view to implementing modern best practices and internationally recognised standards.

2   THE IMPACT OF EUROMAIDAN

The 'Revolution of Dignity' in Ukraine began in late 2013 when citizens took to the streets to vent their fury at the decision of then-President Viktor Yanukovych not to sign an agreement of political association with the European Union (EU). This political movement became known as 'Euromaidan' – the Ukrainian word *Maidan* means 'square' in English, and refers to the main square in the capital city, Kyiv.

On November 30, mobile phone communications were systematically shut down through mobile operators, and armed police units physically attacked the protesters. However, the population was undeterred, and by December 2, more than 500,000 people crowded into *Maidan*. The sitting government made several more attempts to clear the city, using gas grenades and plastic bullets, and the author personally suffered a long-term injury from exposure to tear gas. The crackdown eventually led to the use of lethal force,[3] likely killing well over 100 protestors.[4]

---

1   The SBU is a former constituent part to the Soviet KGB, and is still coming to terms with its legacy ideology and post-Soviet corruption.
2   The SSSCIP was a former constituent part of SBU and has since had a conflicting relationship with its former parent over its role in the information security arena.
3   The author believes that Russian Security Services took part in these killings.
4   'List of people killed during Euromaidan', Wikipedia, https://en.wikipedia.org/wiki/List_of_people_killed_during_Euro-maidan.

The cyber attacks began on 2 December 2013 when it was clear that protesters were not going to leave *Maidan*. Opposition websites were targeted by DDoS attacks, the majority of which came from commercial botnets employing Black-Energy and Dirt Jumper malware.

Police confiscated mobile phones to acquire the protestors' web, email, social media, and financial activities. In one case, pornographic images were uploaded to a protestor's social media account, and were later used to prosecute him. Police seized comput-

> *The cyber attacks began on 2 December 2013 when it was clear that protesters were not going to leave Maidan.*

ers from the opposition party's premises, and according to one city official, the lighting in city hall (which had been a base of opposition activity) was switched off remotely, via the internet.

Opposition activists also conducted cyber attacks against the Ukrainian Government, using tools such as the Low Orbit Ion Cannon (LOIC) to launch DDoS attacks on the President's website. When one group of protestors entered the Ministry of Energy, the organisation sounded a 'red alert' at Ukrainian nuclear facilities, due to the fact that the national electricity grid is remotely controlled via the internet from headquarters.

During this period of intense cyber attacks in Ukraine, cyber criminal organisations proactively reduced their use of the Ukrainian Internet Protocol (IP) space, rerouting their malware communications through Internet Service Providers (ISP) in Belarus and Cyprus, which meant that, for the first time in years, Ukraine was not listed among the leading national purveyors of cyber crime.[5]

The largest and most sophisticated attacks coincided with the lethal shooting of protestors in *Maidan* (February 18-20, 2014). The mobile phones of opposition parliament members were flooded with SMS messaging and telephone calls in an effort to prevent them from communicating and coordinating defences. One precision attack (which targeted the protesters on only one street in Kyiv) entailed spamming the IMSI catcher device on mobile phones with fake SMS messages, threatening the recipient with prosecution for participation in the protest.[6]

In western Ukraine, the Government turned off the main opposition TV channel, and when protesters decided to enter police departments, those facilities were disconnected from the Public Switched Telephone Network (PSTN) and internet.

Despite all of these police actions, the now-radicalised protesters were unbowed, and continued their revolutionary campaign. Therefore, on February 22, 2014, Ukrainian President Yanukovich fled to Russia, and a new and reformist government was established in Kyiv.

---

5   HostExploit analysis, http://hostexploit.com/.
6   This tactic has also been used by Russian military units in eastern Ukraine.

3 CRIMEA AND DONBASS

By the end of April 2014, the Russian Government had responded to these events by occupying and annexing the Ukrainian peninsula of Crimea, as well as military intervention in eastern Ukraine, where hostilities continue to this day.

From the start of its Crimean operation, the Russian army moved to gain control of the peninsula's telecommunications infrastructure, severing cables and routing calls through Russian mobile operators. Ukrainian media companies lost their physical assets in Crimea, and local television programming shifted from Ukrainian to Russian channels. With physical access to its control infrastructure, Russia also commandeered the Ukrainian national satellite platform *Lybid*.

> *From the start of its Crimean operation, the Russian army moved to gain control of telecommunications infrastructure.*

In Kyiv, as soon as the Russian military occupied Crimea, the internal security staff of one of Ukraine's largest mobile operators immediately demanded the severing of communications links between Ukraine and the occupied territory. However, its pro-Russian management refused, and maintained unrestricted connectivity as long as possible, likely so that Russian security services could retain access to its internal systems, for intelligence gathering and other information operations.

Ukrainian mobile operators saw an increase in the volume of cyber crime emanating from Crimea, and it is likely that Russian security services acquired intelligence from information collected in this way.

Pro-Russia media, discussion forums, and social network groups were active in propaganda dissemination. The Crimea campaign was even buttressed by mass changes in *Wikipedia*, where Russian propaganda teams altered articles related to the events taking place there.

Today in Crimea, Russian authorities have implemented content filtering for internet access, including the censorship of Ukrainian news sites. In November 2014, Russia announced it would create a cyber warfare-specific military unit in Crimea.

Pro-Ukrainian hackers have attacked Crimean websites during the occupation, such as that of the Crimean Parliament[7] and a site linking to public web cameras.[8] They have also released allegedly official Russian documents related to the conflict which were claimed to be stolen from Russian government servers.[9]

As the conflict shifted to Donbass, cyberspace played an increasingly important role in military operations. Physical attacks destroyed cabling, broadcast infra-

---

7   'Vulnerabilities in www.rada.crimea.ua',12 March 2014, *Websecurity* http://websecurity.com.ua/7041/.
8   'Ukrainian Cyber Army: video intelligence', *Websecurity* April 23, 2015, http://websecurity.com.ua/7717/.
9   Aric Toler. 'Russian Official Account of Attack on Ukraine Border Guards', *bellingcat*, 30 May 2015 https://www.bellingcat.com/news/uk-and-europe/2015/05/30/russian-official-account-of-attack-on-ukraine-border-guards/.

structure, and ATM networks, and this served to isolate the region from Ukrainian media, communications, and financial services.[10] Military operations were coordinated with propaganda disseminated on Russian TV channels and internet-based media. Finally, the occupation army performs regular forensics checks on computers and mobile devices owned by the population in eastern Ukraine.

Russian signals intelligence (SIGINT), including cyber espionage, has allowed for very effective combat operations planning against the Ukrainian army. Artillery fire can be adjusted based on location data gleaned from mobile phones and Wi-Fi networks.[11] GPS signals can also be used to jam aerial drones. Ukrainian mobile traffic can be rerouted through Russian GSM infrastructure via a GSM signalling level (SS7) attack;[12] in one case, this was accomplished through malicious VLR/HLR updates that were not properly filtered. Russian Security Services also use the internet to recruit mercenaries.

> *Russian signals intelligence (SIGINT) has allowed for effective combat operations against the Ukrainian army.*

Generally speaking, the computer systems and mobile communications of Ukrainian government, military, and critical infrastructure are under permanent attack, and their communications are routinely intercepted and analysed for information of intelligence value. There are also many attacks on Ukrainian businesses: examples include the Ukrainian Railway Company, Kievstar mobile operator,[13] a SMART-TV retail shop,[14] and a city billboard.[15]

4   Cyber Tactics

Cyberspace is a complex domain. In the Ukraine conflict, we have seen many different types of actors, tools, and tactics. Hacktivists have used the Low Orbit Ion Cannon; criminals have used malware like Blackenergy and DirtJumper. But with cyber attacks, attribution and motive are not always clear, and the level of deception is high. The pro-Russia hacker groups Cyberberkut and Cyber-riot Novorissia have conducted DDoS attacks and released stolen email and office documents from Ukrainian officials. Russian media, parliament members, and pro-Russian

---

10 Some attacks against telecom infrastructure took place in Kyiv as well.
11 'In the area of ATO proposes to ban military use mobile phones', Голос України, 12 May 2015 http://golosukraine.com/publication/zakonoproekti/parent/41516-u-zoni-ato-proponuyut-zaboroniti-vijskovim-koristu/#.VYbMdnWlyko.
12 'How the Russians attacked Ukrainian mobile operators', *Delo.ua*, 26 May 2014, http://delo.ua/tech/kak-rossijane-atakova-li-ukrainskih-mobilnyh-operatorov-237121/.
13 Kyivstar is owned and controlled by Russian business, so this attack may be from a non-Russian actor.
14 The TV's firmware was compromised, after which the TV began to display channels from of pro-Russian, separatist eastern Ukraine.
15 The billboard then displayed pro-Russian messages.

Ukrainian politicians often mention these groups by name, but true attribution is difficult. For example, spam is used to deliver news about their operations.[16]

For DDoS, various types of network flooding have been used against web and DNS servers from spoofed source IPs.[17] Sometimes, the attacks overwhelmed internet channel bandwidth; at other times, they affected the capability of an internet router to process packets. The offending bots were located all over the world, but when Ukrainian ISPs began to filter traffic based on national IP ranges, the point of attack simply shifted to Ukrainian bots, which served to defeat this protection measure. During the revolution in Ukraine, DDoS attacks lasted up to weeks at a time, which had never been seen before. Cloud DDoS protection services provided some relief, but the attackers could usually find some worthwhile computer to shut down, such as when they blocked updates to an online media portal.

> *DDoS attacks lasted up to weeks at a time, which had never been seen before.*

Over time, computer security companies have improved their ability to place malware into 'families' and attacks into 'campaigns'. To some degree, this helps to provide attribution, especially when some sophisticated, persistent campaigns can only be the work of nation-state actors – for reasons of mission focus, cost, and the overall level of operational effort required.

Researchers believe, for example, that the Ouroboros/Snake malware family, which avoided detection for 8 years and actively targeted the Ukrainian Government, has Russian origins.[18] With enough data, it is possible to see large cyber espionage campaigns that encompass many different types of targets; it is also possible to see that they generally work within a particular time zone, such as Moscow.[19] One possible Russia-based campaign against Ukraine (and other nations), called Sandworm, exploits advanced 'zero-day' vulnerabilities and targets national critical infrastructure.[20] Finally, in 'Operation Armageddon', researchers believe that they tied malware activity to ongoing Russian military operations in Ukraine.[21]

---

16 Even the pro-Russian NGO 'Mothers of Soldiers,' which fights the mobilization efforts of the Ukrainian army, uses spam to distribute information.

17 The breadth of the attacks included IPv6->IPv4 to bypass DDoS filters, NTP amplification, slow HTTP POST packets against vulnerable Apache servers, DAVOSET, and SSL renegotiation against misconfigured web servers. The maximum volume I am aware of was <30 Gbt/s.

18 David E. Sanger and Steven Erlangermarch, 'Suspicion Falls on Russia as 'Snake' Cyberattacks Target Ukraine's Government', *New York Times*, 8 March 2014, http://www.nytimes.com/2014/03/09/world/europe/suspicion-falls-on-russia-as-snake-cyber-attacks-target-ukraines-government.html?_r=0.

19 'APT28: A Window into Russia's Cyber Espionage Operations?' *FireEye*, 27 October 2014, https://www.fireeye.com/blog/threat-research/2014/10/apt28-a-window-into-russias-cyber-espionage-operations.html.

20 Stephen Ward. 'iSIGHT discovers zero-day vulnerability CVE-2014-4114 used in Russian cyber-espionage campaign', *iSIGHT Partners*, 14 October, 2014, http://www.isightpartners.com/2014/10/cve-2014-4114/.

21 Robert Hackett. 'Russian cyberwar advances military interests in Ukraine, report says' *Fortune*, 29 April 2015, http://fortune.com/2015/04/29/russian-cyberwar-ukraine/.

5   Conclusion and Recommendations

Ukraine is vulnerable to Russia, both in traditional geopolitical space and in cyber-space. In 2015, Ukrainians are still dependent on Russian web resources, including social media (*Vkontakte*), email (Mail.ru), search engines (*Yandex*), antivirus software (Kaspersky), and much more. Our IT supply chain acquires hardware that is either produced in Russia or travels through Russia – this creates vulnerabilities out of the box, and facilitates future attacks.

Whereas Russia is a world leader in cyber espionage and attack, Ukraine's security services are new and inexperienced. In the current conflict with Russia, the only option available to Ukraine is simply a self-inflicted denial-of-service: block access to pro-Russian sites, remove access to Russian TV channels, limit the use of Russian hardware and software, ban mobile phone and social network usage for Ukrainian soldiers, and sever network access with occupied eastern Ukraine.

In the future, Ukraine must modernise its cyber security legislation. One critical aspect of that process will be transparency: it must publish proposed and new laws on government websites so that they are easy to read and understand. In the past, even the few websites available were often knocked offline by hackers.

There have been many lessons learned. Here are some of the author's personal recommendations to the Ukrainian Government:

- Clear Ukrainian IP space of botnets and misconfigured servers (NTP, DNS, etc.) that facilitate cyber attacks;
- Remove illegal and pirated software from critical infrastructure and public agencies;
- Reduce Ukraine's IT dependency in the context of crisis scenarios;
- Implement continuity standards for media and telecoms in conflict zones;
- Create mechanisms to reliably deliver messages from the government to its citizens in occupied territories;
- Incorporate anti-DDoS solutions into Internet-facing services;
- Ensure multiple, independent routes for internet traffic between Ukraine and the rest of the world;
- Implement effective filtering mechanisms on national traffic exchange points;
- Develop a culture of continuous cyber attack monitoring, investigation, information sharing, and research;
- Develop strong cyber security and cryptography capabilities across Ukraine;
- Implement effective civil society controls over unauthorised interception and collection of data;
- Improve emergency data erasure and disaster recovery capabilities;

- Provide resources to military and security services to effectively conduct large-scale cyber operations and computer forensics during their missions; and
- Ensure supply chain security for IT services coming from Russia.

Finally, the world should not underestimate Russia, which is seeking to re-establish its former empire, to include Ukraine and other parts of the defunct Soviet Union and Warsaw Pact. In the context of its wide-ranging political and military campaigns, Russia has developed a cyber attack capability that can target national critical infrastructures, via the internet, anywhere in the world.

CHAPTER 8

BEYOND 'CYBER WAR': RUSSIA'S USE OF STRATEGIC CYBER ESPIONAGE AND INFORMATION OPERATIONS IN UKRAINE

JEN WEEDON

FireEye

1   INTRODUCTION

'Cyber attacks' and 'cyber war' are all too often characterised as independent phenomena limited to the cyber domain, somehow distinct from the broader dynamics that define a conflict. An analysis of cyber conflict thus far suggests that such a perceived dichotomy is both inaccurate and unwise. Targeted internet-based assaults cannot be divorced from their underlying geopolitical contexts, and there is small likelihood that a 'cyber war' will ever take place that is limited only to the cyber domain. On the contrary, governments have been shown to use cyber tools and tactics as a broad instrument of statecraft, a tool for coercion, and a complement to kinetic forces in conflict scenarios.

Moscow's strategy in Ukraine has included a substantial investment in espionage and information operations, relying on the success of integrated cyber operations and computer network exploitation in particular. Russian cyber activities have included cyber espio-

> *Moscow's strategy in Ukraine has included a substantial investment in information operations.*

nage, 'prepping the battlefield', selective telegraphing of capabilities, and some hints at destructive activity. Together, these operations have no doubt inexorably contributed to Moscow's advantages over Kyiv, both on the ground and in shaping the conflict's narrative in the public arena. This orchestration should come as no surprise to Russian security analysts, as such an integrated approach is consistent with published Russian military doctrine. Russian strategic thinkers do not consider 'cyber war' (or even the prefix 'cyber') as a distinct concept. Rather, computer network operations are tools to be integrated into broader efforts to maintain political and military dominance in a given theatre and, more broadly, in the domestic and global courts of public opinion.

This chapter will ground strategic thinking on cyber conflict against the systematic cyber espionage that we believe Russia is leveraging in its conflict with Ukraine. Rather than a 'cyber war' waged in a distinct networked domain, Russia's strategy has been to masterfully exploit the information gleaned from its worldwide computer network exploitation campaigns to inform its conduct, purposely distort public opinion, and maintain its dominant position in Ukraine.

The author will examine three types of interrelated Russian cyber operations from a technical and targeting perspective:

1. Computer network exploitation (CNE) to gain a decisive information advantage;
2. 'Prepping the battlefield' via denial and deception; and
3. Limited incidents of cyber disruption and destruction.

2   THE ARCHITECTURE AND ARTISTRY OF RUSSIA'S STRATEGIC INFORMATION THEFT

Since the start of the Ukraine conflict, security companies have been increasingly tracking, cataloguing, and exposing sustained Russian CNE campaigns. Overall these Russian cyber threat groups have consistently focused on clandestinely stealing intelligence, most likely to give the Russian Government a strategic advantage. The targets of these operations have repeatedly included Ukrainian, European, and U.S. government targets, militaries, international and regional defence and political organisations, think tanks, media outlets, and dissidents. While it is difficult to assess with certainty whether these cyber threat groups are directly tasked or supported by Moscow, there is a growing body of evidence indicating these cyber actors are Russia-based, and that their activities highly likely benefit Moscow.

The security community's ability to detect, track, and ultimately expose Russian cyber operations seems to have improved since the Ukraine conflict began, even relative to overall trends in the industry on exposing threat activity. While determining a direct causation between the conflict in Ukraine and a seemingly marked uptick in observable Russian cyber activity is challenging, the timing is certainly notable. It is exceedingly unlikely that Russian actors only just started conducting aggressive CNE on a global scale, so why has our ability to track and expose their activity appear to have improved? One reason may be that Russia's current national security crisis has increased its government's collections requirements to state-supported hackers, which has in turn accelerated the groups' operational tempo. As a result, it may be more difficult for these actors to modify their tactics, techniques, and procedures (TTPs) on a timely basis, which often results in them tipping their hand.

To shed light on how this sustained information theft is being carried out, the following sections discuss some of the cyber tactics and compromised computer infrastructure that FireEye has associated with two prominent hacker groups that we believe operate from Russia, as well as a summary list of CNE-related activity that is likely being used to give Moscow a geopolitical and military advantage.

3 APT29 ('Advanced Persistent Threat'[1] Group 29)

APT29 is a sophisticated and highly capable Russian cyber espionage group with a diverse, constantly evolving toolset, and talented operators. The group maintains a globally dispersed and intricate attack infrastructure that doubtless requires substantial resources to maintain.

> *APT29 is a highly capable Russian cyber espionage group with a constantly evolving toolset.*

APT29's tools often leverage legitimate web services for malware command and control mechanisms, which can make them more difficult to detect because they appear to be benign communications at first glance.

3.1 APT29's Targets: Consistent with Russian State Interests
APT29 typically targets entities to steal information that is closely linked to Russian geopolitical interests and priorities. The group's recent operations suggest it is particularly focused on targets of intelligence value that are related to the Russia-Ukraine crisis and related policy responses. This includes: western governments (particularly foreign policy and defence-related targets); international security and legal institutions; think tanks; and educational institutions.

APT29 usually compromises its victims via socially engineered spear phishing emails– either with malicious email attachments, or through a link to download a malicious file from a compromised website. The group's decoy documents ('lures') often topically align with their targets' interests and work subject matter; this social engineering technique is common and can be very effective. APT29 has also been known to re-purpose and weaponise legitimate documents or information stolen from its previously compromised networks. Example lure topics from legitimate sources include content related to European Union sanctions on Russia, a voicemail

---

1   We refer to groups that we assess have a nexus to state sponsorship as 'Advanced Persistent Threat,' or 'APT' groups.

attachment sent from a reporter to a think tank scholar who writes on Russia-Ukraine issues,[2] a PDF report on terrorism, and discussions related to Caucasus regional development and democratisation.[3] APT29 has also used less tailored and pop culture-themed approaches, such as a faked e-fax, and videos of 'Office Monkeys'.[45]

3.2 APT29's Tools and Infrastructure: the Work of Professionals

The complex nature of APT29's malware and infrastructure (requiring significant financial resources and expertise for upkeep), combined with its operational security practices and target sets strongly suggests some level of Russian state sponsorship. Its typical work hours (as defined by active operations in networks the group has compromised) fall within the UTC+3 time zone, which aligns to the time zones of Moscow and St. Petersburg. Furthermore, APT29 has been known to temporarily halt its operations on Russian holidays.[6]

APT29 has been highly active throughout 2015, employing new data theft tools as well as pursuing new targets for stealing information. To maintain operational security, APT29 often configures its malware to activate only at predetermined times, and is adept at using misdirection and obfuscation TTPs[7] that hinder reverse engineering and other means of analysis. One complicated APT29 backdoor, HAMMERTOSS, is highly capable of evading detection, particularly by its ability to mimic the behaviour of legitimate users.[8] HAMMERTOSS accomplishes this stealthiness by leveraging commonly visited websites and web services to relay commands and steal data from victims. The tool works by:

- Checking in and retrieving commands via legitimate web services, such as Twitter and GitHub;
- Using compromised web servers for command and control (C2);
- Visiting different Twitter handles daily and automatically;
- Using timed starts, such as communicating only after a specific date or only during the victim's workweek;
- Obtaining commands via images containing hidden and encrypted data (steganography); and
- Extracting information from a compromised network by uploading files to commonly used cloud storage services.[9]

2   'The Connections Between MiniDuke, CosmicDuke and OnionDuke.' January 7, 2015. *F-Secure*. https://www.f-secure.com/weblog/archives/00002780.html.
3   Graham Cluley. 'MiniDionis: Where a Voicemail Can Lead to a Malware Attack.' July 16, 2015. http://www.tripwire.com/state-of-security/security-data-protection/cyber-security/minidionis-voicemail-malware/.
4   *Ibid.*
5   Sergey Lozhkin. 'Minidionis – one more APT with a usage of cloud drives.' *Kaspersky Lab*. July 16, 2015. https://securelist.com/blog/research/71443/minidionis-one-more-apt-with-a-usage-of-cloud-drives/.
6   FireEye Threat Intelligence, HAMMERTOSS: Stealthy Tactics Define a Russian Cyber Threat Group,' July 29, 2015. https://www.fireeye.com/blog/threat-research/2015/07/hammertoss_stealthy.html.
7   Kurt Baumgartner and Costin Raiu. 'The CozyDuke APT.' *Securelist*. April 21, 2015. https://securelist.com/blog/research/69731/the-cozyduke-apt/.
8   *Ibid.*
9   *Ibid.*

APT29 appears to deploy this advanced malware only against high-value networks where it needs not only to steal information but also to maintain persistent access to the victim's environment. In addition, APT29 possesses other advanced, stealthy

> *Malware needs not only to steal information but to maintain persistent access to the victim's environment.*

tools in its toolbox (which include the 'Dukes' malware[10]), and the group is constantly evolving its 'weaponry'.

4   APT28 (ALSO KNOWN AS TSAR TEAM/SOFACY/PAWN STORM)

APT28 is another Russian cyber espionage group that frequently targets European security organisations, Eastern European governments and militaries, international media outlets, think tanks, defence companies, domestic dissident populations, and entities in the Caucasus. This list is not exhaustive.[11] The following table summarises some of what currently know about APT28.[12]

Like APT29, APT28 works in a highly professional manner worthy of its 'advanced persistent threat' moniker. Security researchers believe its malware is written in a Russian language development environment, and that it has been systematically updating its tools, some of which are also able to target mobile devices[13] since 2007.

One way to appreciate the sophisticated nature of APT28 is through its exploitation of 'zero-day' vulnerabilities; that is, previously undiscovered and unpatched vulnerabilities. For example, in early 2015, APT28 likely exploited two zero-day vulnerabilities in Adobe Flash and Microsoft Windows in an attack against a government contractor.[14] In a separate incident in July 2015, APT28 rapidly integrated into its operations multiple zero-day vulnerabilities exposed in the highly public breach of the Italian exploit dealer Hacking Team.[15]

10   'Duke APT group's latest tools: cloud services and Linux support.' July 22, 2015. *F-Secure.* https://www.f-secure.com/we-blog/archives/00002822.html; Kurt Baumgartner, Costin Raiu. 'The CozyDuke APT.' *Kaspersky Lab.* April 21, 2015. https://securelist.com/blog/69731/the-cozyduke-apt/; Brandon Levene, Robert Falcone and Richard Wartell. 'Tracking MiniDionis: CozyCar's New Ride Is Related to Seaduke.' *Palo Alto Networks.* July 14, 2015.
11   'APT28: A Window into Russia's Cyber Espionage Operations?' FireEye Blog.October 27, 2014. https://www.fireeye.com/blog/threat-research/2014/10/apt28-a-window-into-russias-cyber-espionage-operations.html.
12   *Ibid.*
13   Dune Lawrence and Michael Riley. 'Hackers Target Hong Kong Protesters via iPhones.' *Bloomberg Business.* October 1, 2014. http://www.bloomberg.com/bw/articles/2014-10-01/hackers-target-hong-kong-protesters-via-iphones.
14   FireEye Labs. 'Operation RussianDoll: Adobe & Windows Zero-Day Exploits Likely Leveraged by Russia's APT28 in Highly-Targeted Attack.' April 18, 2015. https://www.fireeye.com/blog/threat-research/2015/04/probable_apt28_useo.html.
15   Jonathan Leathery. 'Microsoft Office Zero-Day CVE-2015-2424 Leveraged By Tsar Team.' *iSight Partners.* July 15, 2015. http://www.isightpartners.com/2015/07/microsoft-office-zero-day-cve-2015-2424-leveraged-by-tsar-team/.

Malware	Targeting	Russian Attributes
Evolves and Maintains Tools for Continued, Long-Term Use • Uses malware with flexible and lasting platforms • Constantly evolves malware samples for continued use • Malware is tailored to specific victims' environments, and is designed to hamper reverse engineering efforts • Developed in a formal code development environment **Various Data Theft Techniques** • Backdoors using HTTP protocol • Backdoors using victim mail server • Local copying to defeat closed/air gapped networks	**Georgia & the Caucasus** • Ministry of Internal Affairs • Ministry of Defence • Journalist writing on Caucasus issues • Kavkaz Center **Eastern European Governments & Militaries** • Polish Government • Hungarian Government • Ministry of Foreign Affairs in Eastern Europe • Baltic Host exercises **Security-related organisations** • NATO • OSCE • Defense attaches • Defense events and exhibitions	**Russian Language Indicators** • Consistent use of Russian malware over a period of six years • Lure to journalist writing on Caucasus issues suggests APT28 understands both Russian and English **Malware Compile Times Correspond to Work Day in Moscow's Time Zone** • Consistent among APT28 samples with compile times from 2007 to 2014 • The compile times align with the standards workday in the UTC +4 time zone, which includes major Russian cities such as Moscow and St. Petersburg

Figure 1-1 – APT28 Activities

5 A Crowded Playing Field: Additional Examples of Russian CNE

Numerous cyber security companies have characterised a range of suspected Russian state-sponsored cyber activity and malware. Overall, there are recurring themes in their findings, which suggests that Russian CNE campaigns are based on consistent taskings. Multiple cyber espionage campaigns ongoing across the globe since at least 2007 (and no doubt much earlier) has probably given these actors a considerable information advantage. A few examples are as follows.

Russian CNE campaigns are based on consistent taskings.

In September 2015, Kaspersky Labs published research exposing multiple Russian APT groups 'using and abusing' satellite-based internet links (particularly IP addresses in Middle Eastern and African countries) to hide their operational command and control. This infrastructure likely enables a high degree of operational security. One of the groups using this tactic is the same group behind the Snake/Uroburos/Turla malware, thought to be related to the infamous Agent. BTZ, which was used to penetrate U.S. military networks as early as 2008. Kaspersky's report outlined a specific campaign targeting government, embassies, military entities, universities, research organisations, and pharmaceutical companies worldwide.[16]

In August 2015, a group of security researchers described the enterprise-like effort behind the Gameover ZeuS malware and its prolific and FBI-sought author Evgeniy Mikhailovich Bogachev (a.k.a. 'Slavik'). The malware was used to facilitate both cyber crime and espionage. Further, the researchers discovered commands in the malware indicating that the actors sought to gather classified information from victims in Ukraine, Georgia, and Turkey,[17] suggesting a link between Russia's cyber crime syndicates and government espionage actors.

In late 2014, researchers exposed a long-active Russian group called 'Sandworm', whose victims included NATO, the Ukrainian Government, EU governments, energy and telecommunications firms, and an American academic organisation. The group used zero-day exploits and infected victims through a variety of means including malicious PowerPoint attachments and the BlackEnergy toolkit.[18]

Between 2013 and 2014, actors using the Snake/Uroburos/Turla malware targeted Ukrainian computer systems in dozens of cyber operations launched by 'committed and well-funded professionals'.[19] This malware is highly complex, reistant to countermeasures, and thought to have been created in 2005.[20]

Since 2013, 'Operation Armageddon' – a Russian cyber espionage campaign allegedly targeting Ukrainian government, law enforcement, and military officials – has likely helped provide a military advantage to Russia vis-à-vis Ukraine from secrets systematically gathered from cyber espionage.[21]

In 2012, suspected Russian actors reportedly used the Wipbot and Snake backdoors for long-term cyber espionage. The actors leveraged legitimate (but compromised) websites to systematically deliver malware, particularly to victims in Eastern Europe.[22]

6   Prepping the Battlefield

The cyber espionage activity previously described entails the penetration and exploitation of networks in order to steal sensitive information. However it is important to note that the network access required for CNE can, depending on

---

16 Stefan Stanase. 'Satellite Turla: APT Command and Control in the Sky'. *Securelist Blog*. September 9, 2015. https://securelist.com/blog/research/72081/satellite-turla-apt-command-and-control-in-the-sky/.

17 Michael Sandee. 'GameOver Zeus. Backgrounds on the Badguys and the Backends'.*FoxIT Whitepaper*. https://www.fox-it.com/en/files/2015/08/FoxIT-Whitepaper_Blackhat-web.pdf.

18 'iSIGHT discovers zero-day vulnerability CVE-2014-4114 used in Russian cyber-espionage campaign'. *iSight Partners*, October 14, 2014. http://www.isightpartners.com/2014/10/cve-2014-4114/.

19 'The Snake Campaign'. *BAE Systems*. 2014.www.baesystems.com/ai/snakemalware.

20 'Ukraine attacked by cyberspies as tensions escalated in recent months'. *Associated Press*. March 9, 2014. http://www.theguardian.com/world/2014/mar/09/ukraine-attacked-cyberspies-tensions-computer.

21 Lookingglass. 'Operation Armageddon: Cyber Espionage as a Strategic Component of Russian Modern Warfare – CTIG Report'. April 28, 2015. https://lgscout.com/operation-armageddon-cyber-espionage-as-a-strategic-component-of-russian-modern-warfare-ctig-report/.

22 Symantec Security Response. 'Turla: Spying tool targets governments and diplomats'. August 7, 2014. http://www.symantec.com/connect/blogs/turla-spying-tool-targets-governments-and-diplomats.

the intent of the attacker, also be used for disruptive or destructive CNA, including what military professionals call 'preparation of the battlefield' for potential conflict scenarios. [23,24] The cyber backdoors used to access environments illicitly or lay low and maintain persistence could also be used to enable future attacks.

Extensive preparation of the battlefield is consistent with Russian strategic thinking. During the Cold War, the Soviet Union developed highly detailed maps of U.S. and European cities – all the way down to individual buildings, terrain, and weather. This information would be invaluable in the event of invasion or occupation, as in Crimea.[25] Russian 'mapping' of an adversary's cyber infrastructure is in principle the same concept. Computer networks, however, are harder to map: like living organisms, they constantly evolve. Therefore, today's map might not be good tomorrow, which is why Russian malware implants like HAMMERTOSS are designed to sustain clandestine access.

> *Extensive preparation of the battlefield is consistent with Russian strategic thinking.*

6.1 Preparing for Attack?

Is Russia preparing for future cyber attacks on Western critical infrastructure? This is difficult to prove, but the Sandworm group has reportedly targeted supervisory control and data acquisition (SCADA) equipment, which is used in industrial and critical infrastructure settings, with the BlackEnergy toolkit.[26] The victims were production systems, not vendor-owned prototypes or systems that contained financial information, intellectual property, or political intelligence. Given the targets seemed to be production systems, there would likely be no benefit from an espionage perspective to infect these systems. Rather, the actors using the malware may have been looking for weaknesses to exploit in a future disruptive scenario. In addition, the use of a crimeware toolkit offers a degree of anonymity or plausible deniability for actors with more destructive purposes.

---

23 Jen Weedon and Jacqueline Stokes. 'Security in an Era of Coercive Attacks.' *FireEye Executive Perspectives Blog*. May 14, 2015. https://www.fireeye.com/blog/executive-perspective/2015/05/security_in_an_erao.html.

24 In the U.S., CNE and CNA may be carried out by different government agencies operating under different authorities, but not all countries will have this same dichotomy.

25 Nick Ballon. 'Inside the Secret World of Russia's Cold War Maps.' *Wired*. http://www.wired.com/2015/07/secret-cold-war-maps/

26 Kyle Wilhoit and Jim Gogolinski. 'Sandworm to Blacken: The SCADA Connection.' October 16, 2014. http://blog.trendmicro.com/trendlabs-security-intelligence/sandworm-to-blacken-the-scada-connection/.

7 DECEPTION AND TELEGRAPHING INTENT: APT28 AND TV5MONDE

Russia has a long history of using information operations and deception to create confusion or sow panic to ultimately create favourable conditions for their activity.[27] This tactic has simply evolved for the internet era to include online misinformation campaigns and propaganda, and extensive internet trolling. One of the more remarkable incidents this year included APT28's possible use of false flag operation against a French TV station.

In April 2015, hackers claiming to be the Islamic State-affiliated 'Cyber Caliphate' hacked France's *TV5 Monde* channel, shutting off transmissions for eighteen hours, and posting Islamic State propaganda on the *TV5 Monde's* Facebook and Twitter accounts. The attack also apparently resulted in significant damage to the channel's broadcasting infrastructure.[28]

This incident generated enormous publicity and speculation over Cyber Caliphate's apparently growing capabilities and intent. However, technical analysis of the attackers' network infrastructure (such as the IP block hosting the Cyber Caliphate's website, its server, and registrar)[29] as well as some other sensitive source reporting related to the malware used suggests that Russia's APT28 was in fact the more likely perpetrator of this attack. French Police concurred with this conclusion, stating 'Russian hackers linked to the Kremlin' may have been responsible'.[30] In a similar vein, *The New York Times* reported that a Russian organisation known as the 'Internet Research Agency' had conducted systematic online trolling and hoaxes in the U.S., including a spoofed Islamic State attack against a Louisiana chemical plant on the anniversary of 9/11.[31]

If APT28 (or another Russian hacker group) conducted these attacks, what were their motivations? There are a number of plausible scenarios, including:

- Russian actors may have been displeased at *TV5 Monde* coverage of the Ukraine conflict, and this was an act of retribution;
- Russian actors wanted to distract attention from the Kremlin's actions in Ukraine by shifting the focus of Western national security planners to the Islamic State;

---

27 Roland Heickerö. 'Emergin Cyber Threats and Russian Views on Information Warfare and Information Operations.' FOI, Swedish Defence Research Agency. March 2010. http://www.foi.se/ReportFiles/foir_2970.pdf.

28 Cale Guthrie Weissman. 'France: Russian hackers posed as ISIS to hack a French TV broadcaster.' *Business Insider*. June 11, 2015. http://www.businessinsider.com/new-discovery-indicates-that-russian-hackers-apt28-are-behind-the-tv5-monde-hack-2015-6.

29 Sheera Frankel. 'Experts Say Russians May Have Posed As ISIS To Hack French TV Channel.' Buzzfeed. June 9, 2015. http://www.buzzfeed.com/sheerafrenkel/experts-say-russians-may-have-posed-as-isis-to-hack-french-t#.wg4BeJ6xDP ; Eamon Javers. 'These cyberhackers may not be backed by ISIS.' *CNBC*. July 14, 2015. http://www.cnbc.com/2015/07/14/these-cyber-hackers-not-backed-by-isis.html.

30 Joseph Menn and Leigh Thomas. 'France probes Russian lead in TV5Monde hacking: sources.' *Reuters*. June 10, 2015. http://www.reuters.com/article/2015/06/10/us-france-russia-cybercrime-idUSKBN0OQ2GG20150610.

31 Adrian Chen. 'The Agency.' *New York Times*. June 2, 2015. http://www.nytimes.com/2015/06/07/magazine/the-agency.html?_r=0.

- Russian actors actively sought exposure as the perpetrators, and by doing so, telegraph that they were both willing and capable of pulling off such a scheme, while refining their ability to disrupt and destroy digital media broadcasting capabilities.

8 'Cyber War' in Ukraine – Not Much to See Here

There have been significant cyber espionage operations directed against victims related to Russia's strategic interests, particularly in regards to the situation in Ukraine. However we have not seen high profile, coercive and damaging attacks similar to those waged on Estonia in 2007 or Georgia in 2008.

We have not seen coercive and damaging attacks similar to Estonia or Georgia.

The publicly reported examples of CNA in Ukraine mostly include Denial of Service (DoS) and Distributed Denial of Service (DDoS) attacks designed to undermine Ukraine's telecommunications infrastructure. For the attackers, these were likely a low-risk way to disrupt the flow of information within the Ukrainian national security space, as well as a way to selectively and temporarily silence specific voices online. Some of the known incidents are listed below:

- November 2013: Russian hackers reportedly defaced and DDoS'ed the websites of several Ukrainian TV stations, news outlets, and politicians.[32]
- February 2014: Russian troops allegedly tampered with Ukraine's fibre optic cables and raided *Ukrtelecom*, which stated that it had 'lost the technical capacity to provide connection between the peninsula and the rest of Ukraine and probably across the peninsula, too'.[33] In Crimea, mobile, landline, and internet access were all affected.
- March 2014: As Russian troops entered Crimea, the main Ukrainian Government website was shut down for nearly 72 hours,[34] many other official government and media websites were targeted in DDoS attacks,[35] and the cell phones of many Ukrainian parliamentarians were 'hacked'.[36]

---

32 'Hromadske.tv under DDoS-attack.' *Institute of Mass Information.* November 26, 2013. http://imi.org.ua/en/news/42266-hro-madsketv-under-ddos-attack.html.

33 'Ukrtelecom's Crimean sub-branches officially report that unknown people have seized several telecommunications nodes in the Crimea.' February 28, 2014. http://en.ukrtelecom.ua/about/news?id=120467.

34 'Ukraine says communications hit, MPs phones blocked.' *Reuters.* March 4, 2014. http://www.reuters.com/article/2014/03/04/ukraine-crisis-cybersecurity-idUSL6N0M12CF20140304.

35 Cornelius Rahn, Ilya Khrennikov and Aaron Eglitis. 'Russia-Ukraine Standoff Going Online as Hackers Attack.' *Bloomberg.* March 6, 2014. http://www.bloomberg.com/news/articles/2014-03-05/russia-ukraine-standoff-going-online-as-hackers-at-tack.

36 Peter Bergen and Tim Maurer. 'Cyberwar hits Ukraine.' *CNN.* March 7, 2014. http://www.cnn.com/2014/03/07/opinion/bergen-ukraine-cyber-attacks/.

- May 2014: the pro-Russian hacktivist group *CyberBerkut* claimed responsibility for a breach of the systems of Ukraine's Central Election Commission with malware that would have deleted the results of the presidential election. However, Ukraine's Security Service (SBU) removed the malware and replaced the election software prior to the vote.[37]

Outside of these limited publicly reported incidents, it appears that the Kremlin has either not needed or not chosen to engage in extensive overt CNA during this conflict. One reason for this could be that Moscow wants to avoid the international criticism that followed its alleged cyber operations in the 2008 war in Georgia, and in Estonia in 2007. Instead, Moscow seems to be using more narrowly focused, limited operations in support of strategic state objectives, primarily via sustained cyber espionage rather than widespread attacks.

9   Information War, Not Cyber War

In the Russia-Ukraine conflict, computer network operations have not been limited to trite notions of 'cyber war.' Rather, an examination of the sustained tensions suggests that this has been a war waged with and by the strategic theft and manipulation of information, and not extensive application of destructive cyber attacks. Russia's unrelenting cyber espionage campaigns over time, and against so many targets, have no doubt given it a considerable advantage in understanding, anticipating, and in some instances outmanoeuvring its enemies. This approach may have rendered DDoS and other destructive attacks less necessary or preferable.

> *This has been a war waged with and by the strategic theft and manipulation of information.*

While we do not always have definitive attribution, the malicious cyber tools and attacker infrastructure used by these suspected Russian government-backed actors in many ways mimic what we would expect from Russian intelligence operatives, defined by stealth, artistry in tradecraft, and a high regard for operational security. Yet, as mirrored in Russia's real-life politics, some of the actors also appeared flippant and even brazen at times, characteristics that could reflect an absence of fear of getting caught or any sense of effective deterrence. In this sense, such behaviour will no doubt continue, and it remains of the utmost important to anticipate and defend against this activity, both for short-term network security and for long-term international stability.

---

37   "'Cyber-attack' cripples Ukraine's electronic election system ahead of presidential vote." *RT.* May 24, 2014. http://rt.com/news/161332-ukraine-president-election-virus/.

CHAPTER 9

CYBER PROXIES AND THE CRISIS IN UKRAINE

TIM MAURER

New America

1 INTRODUCTION

In July 2015, I travelled to Kyiv to investigate the role of cyber proxy actors as part of a long-term, global research project on the issue. The Ukrainian crisis seemed like the perfect case study to explore how states use non-state actors and their capabilities. The findings confirmed some of my assumptions but also revealed some surprises. This article outlines what I learned during the trip based on interviews with 11 individuals including current and former government officials, private sector representatives, security researchers, and Eugene Dokukin, the 'commander' of the Ukrainian Cyber Forces, in addition to a review of existing literature.[1]

To start, the crisis in Ukraine has several ingredients that appear to make the use of proxies by a state likely, namely (1) an ongoing hot conflict, fuelling (2) incentives for the state to use proxy capabilities and (3) significant capabilities residing outside of but available to the state. With regard to the second, this includes the general political incentive to be able to claim plausible deniability as well as incentives for the state to augment its own capabilities by adding those provided by non-state actors.

It is also helpful to distinguish between two dimensions when analysing proxy actors to ensure greater analytical clarity. First, analysing proxy actors is part of the broader academic inquiry into the governance of violence best described by the title

---

1 'Cyber warrior steps up effort to help in war with Russia,' *KyivPost*, February 10, 2015, http://www.kyivpost.com/content/kyiv-post-plus/cyber-warrior-steps-up-effort-to-help-in-war-with-russia-380184.html?flavour=mobile.

of Deborah Avant's seminal book *The Market for Force – The Consequences of Privatizing Security*. In that book, Avant investigates the market for force and the role of public and private actors including proxies.[2] The second, narrower dimension focuses on proxy actors used 'to commit internationally wrongful acts using ICTs.'[3] This is the language used in the most recent report of the Group of Governmental Experts (GGE) that is leading the international community's global cybersecurity norms effort under the auspices of the United Nations. Unlike the first dimension which examines proxy actors more broadly including those that are used by states for defensive purposes, this second lens is about proxy actors used to cause harm to another party.

This short chapter will look at both private actors involved in the general provision of security for the benefit of the state, and private actors using force against a third party to the benefit of the state, but will focus on the latter. The first section outlines in greater detail the conditions present in the region assumed to contribute to the existence of proxy actors. The second part describes the proxy actors that are publicly known to have been active during the crisis.

2   THE MAKING OF A HOT CONFLICT

The hot conflict between Ukraine and Russia was the result of simmering political tension that escalated in November 2013, when former Ukrainian president Viktor Yanukovych abandoned plans to sign a trade agreement with the EU. Yanukovych's decision incited mass protests that were met with a violent government crackdown. In November, long before Yanukovych's flight in February and the build-up of Russian troops on the Crimean border, reports emerged that Russian hacker groups were executing Distributed Denial of Service

> *Long before Yanukovych's flight, Russian hacker groups were executing DDoS attacks and defacing websites.*

(DDoS) attacks and defacing websites critical to the Yanukovych government's relationship with Russia. This period was characterised by low-level hacking targeting highly visible websites, either rendering them unavailable or changing their content.

On February 28, shortly after Yanukovych left the country, unmarked soldiers, that Russia's President Putin later acknowledged[4] to be Russian troops, seized a military airfield in Sevastopol and Simferopol international airport. Concurrently, armed sol-

---

2   'The Market for Force The Consequences of Privatizing Security,' Cambridge University Press, 2005, http://www.cambridge.org/US/academic/subjects/politics-international-relations/comparative-politics/market-force-consequences-privatizing-security.

3   United Nations, General Assembly, *Report of the Group of Governmental Experts on Developments in the Field of Information and Telecommunications in the Context of International Security,* United Nations, July 22, 2015, http://www.un.org/ga/search/view_doc.asp?symbol=A/70/174.

4   'Vladimir Putin admits for first time Russian troops took over Crimea, refuses to rule out intervention in Donetsk,' *National Post*, April 17, 2014, http://news.nationalpost.com/news/world/vladimir-putin-admits-for-first-time-russian-troops-took-over-crimea-refuses-to-rule-out-intervention-in-donetsk.

diers tampered with fibre optic cables, raiding the facilities of Ukrainian telecom firm *Ukrtelecom*, which stated afterward that it had 'lost the technical capacity to provide connection between the peninsula and the rest of Ukraine and probably across the peninsula, too'.[5] In addition, cell phones of Ukrainian parliamentarians were hacked and the main Ukrainian government website was shut down for 72 hours after Russian troops entered Crimea on March 2. Patriotic Ukrainian hacker groups such as 'Cyber Hundred' and 'Null Sector' retaliated with DDoS attacks of their own against websites of the Kremlin and the Central Bank of Russia.[6] The day before the presidential election, Ukraine's Security Service (SBU) discovered malware in the systems of the Central Election Commission designed to compromise data collected on the results of the election, revealing how close Russian hackers had come to sabotaging the results.[7] The hacker group 'Cyber Berkut' claimed responsibility.[8]

3   INCENTIVES FOR THE STATE TO USE CAPABILITIES IN PRIVATE HANDS

A general political incentive for states to use proxies is summed up by the concept of 'plausible deniability'. Developed in the context of maritime privateering, it was:

> *Political incentive for states to use proxies is summed up by the concept of 'plausible deniability'.*

> 'invented [by state rulers] at the turn of the seventeenth century. If a 'private' undertaking that a ruler authorised met with success, s/he could claim a share in the profits. If the enterprise caused conflict with another state, the ruler could claim it was a private operation for which s/he could not be held responsible'.[9]

While some of the specific elements of maritime privateering are no longer relevant today, the general concept and logic for this type of behaviour still apply and exist today. For example, the Russian Government denied any involvement in the Ukrainian crisis for many months, in spite of eyewitness accounts and news reports plainly stating otherwise. One particularly horrible example of plausible deniability was the mass murder of the passengers on Malaysia Airlines flight 17.

The benefits of plausible deniability also apply to the Ukrainian Government. The Ukrainian Cyber Forces, led by Eugene Dokukin, is a volunteer group that

---

5   'Feb. 28 Updates on the Crisis in Ukraine,' *The New York Times News Blog*, February 28, 2014, http://thelede.blogs.nytimes.com/2014/02/28/latest-updates-tensions-in-ukraine/?_r=0.

6   'Kremlin website hit by 'powerful' cyber attack,' *Reuters*, March 14, 2014, http://www.reuters.com/article/2014/03/14/us-russia-kremlin-cybercrime-idUSBREA2D16T20140314.

7   'Cyber-attack' cripples Ukraine's electronic election system ahead of presidential vote,' RT, 24 May, 2014, http://www.rt.com/news/161332-ukraine-president-election-virus/.

8   'Ukraine election narrowly avoided 'wanton destruction' from hackers (+video),' *The Christian Science Monitor*, June 17, 2015, http://www.csmonitor.com/World/Passcode/2014/0617/Ukraine-election-narrowly-avoided-wanton-destruction-from-hackers-video.

9   Janice Thomson. *Mercenaries, Pirates, and Sovereigns* (Princeton, NJ: Princeton University Press, 1994), 21.

occasionally publishes data from the Russian Ministry of the Interior, and at one point threatened to shut down the internet in the Crimea and other cities in eastern Ukraine.[10] There is no evidence suggesting that the Ukrainian Government coordinates or directly supports any of the Ukrainian Cyber Forces' activities, and my own research supports this conclusion. At the same time, the Government benefits from its activities with or without its involvement. For the Ukrainian Government, another set of incentives is arguably more important than the political ones: its own limited capabilities, and the possibility to rely on proxy actors to augment these capabilities in the face of a much more powerful opponent.

The Russian Government is considered to be among the most sophisticated actors with significant in-house cyber capabilities,[11] and the government in Ukraine faced a dire situation at the beginning of the conflict. Its military had essentially been falling apart since the end of the Soviet Union and Kyiv was ill-prepared for a conflict with Russia. As Dmitry Gorenburg points out:

> 'At the time of its creation, the Ukrainian military was considered the fourth most powerful conventional military force in the world, behind only the United States, Russia, and China. However, these forces were allowed to atrophy throughout the post-Soviet period, with virtually no funding provided for the maintenance of equipment or troop training. Reforms were not carried out and there were no attempts at rearmament to replace aging Soviet equipment'.[12]

The responses from several interviewees confirmed this assessment.

4   CAPABILITIES OUTSIDE THE STATE

In order for a state to be able to pursue the incentives of using proxy actors, private actor capabilities must exist in the first place. With regard to cyberspace, such capabilities include those present within a state's territory and beyond. Regarding the former, significant capabilities have been present in Ukraine and Eastern Europe since the 1980s. Misha Glenny, the award-winning journalist, recounts in his 2011 book *Dark Market – How Hackers Became the New Mafia* that:

> 'The hackers of Eastern Europe played a particularly important role in cracking security devices played on software…Bulgaria, Ukraine and Russia set the pace, with the Romanians not far behind.'[13]

---

10   'Ukraine's Lonely Cyberwarrior vs. Russia,' *The Daily Beast*, February 18, 2015, http://www.thedailybeast.com/articles/2015/02/18/ukraine-s-lonely-cyber-warrior.html.
11   'Russia Tops China as Principal Cyber Threat to US,' *The Diplomat*, March 3, 2015, http://thediplomat.com/2015/03/russia-tops-china-as-principal-cyber-threat-to-us/.
12   Dmitry Gorenburg. 'Russia and Ukraine: Not the Military Balance You Think,' *War on the Rocks*, November 10, 2015, http://warontherocks.com/2014/11/russia-and-ukraine-not-the-military-balance-you-think/.
13   Misha Glenny. *McMafia: A Journey Through the Global Criminal Underworld* (New York, Vintage Books: 2009), 59; see also Nadiya Kostyuk's chapter in this book.

Ukraine was the cradle of CarderPlanet, which was 'changing the nature of cyber-crime around the world'.[14] One explanation why technically skilled people in the region decided to pursue cybercrime to make a living was the lack of other opportunities. For example, a job in the Ukrainian Government for somebody in his 20s pays roughly $3,000 – a year, not a month. And while Samsung has one of its largest R&D centres in Kyiv, the private IT industry is neither large nor attractive enough to absorb all of the skilled labour, unlike in Israel, for example.[15] Interestingly, 'CarderPlanet was penetrated and compromised by the Russian Secret Police almost as soon as it was set up' but:

> 'why would the KGB waste resources on investigating networks that are ripping off American and European credit cards? A complete waste of time. So for the moment, Moscow was content to observe and store information. They knew exactly who was who in the Odessa carding community'.[16]

Yet, it was not only the FSB that knew what was happening in Eastern European countries. In 2009, Brian Krebs, an expert on cybercrime in the region and widely read not only by law enforcement officials in the U.S. but also Ukraine, wondered:

> 'whether authorities in those countries would be any more willing to pursue cyber crooks in their own countries if they were forced to confront just how deeply those groups have penetrated key government and private computer networks in those regions?'

An example is Dmitry Ivanovich Golubov, once considered a top cybercrime boss by U.S. law enforcement, but now a leader of the Ukrainian Internet Party participating in parliamentary elections. Russian agencies reportedly provide little assistance with shutting down networks such as the Russian Business Network. Last but not least, cyber criminals also do their best to avoid attracting local law enforcement attention. As Krebs notes:

> 'Some of the most prolific and recognizable malware disbursed by Russian and East European cyber crime groups purposefully avoids infecting computers if the program detects the potential victim is a native resident.'[17]

In sum, there is no shortage in the region of labour skilled in information technology and hacking, while a mature industry is missing, and government salaries of a few thousand dollars a year pale in comparison to reports of thousands or millions of dollars made in the latest cyber heist.

---

14   Misha Glenny. *McMafia: A Journey Through the Global Criminal Underworld*, 48.
15   'Nearshoring: Top 20 largest In-House R&D offices in Ukraine,'GoalEurope, October 4, 2013, http://goaleurope. com/2013/10/04/nearshore-outsourcing-top-20-largest-rd-offices-in-ukraine/.
16   Misha Glenny. *McMafia: A Journey Through the Global Criminal Underworld*, 52-53.
17   'Story-Driven Résumé: My Best Work 2005-2009', *KrebsonSecurity*, December 9, 2010, http://krebsonsecurity.com/2009/12/ story-driven-resume-my-best-work-2005-2009-3/.

There are several important findings regarding proxies and the conflict in Ukraine. The first is that proxy actors are active as part of the conflict in Ukraine. The second is that the amount of cyber proxy activity has remained relatively low. There are two likely explanations for this: there has been a relatively low number of significant cyber incidents associated with the conflict other than during its initial phase as described above; and while there was clearly a significant wave of patriotism and willingness by Ukrainian citizens to volunteer and support the government, several interviewees suggested that the government in Kyiv did not have the ability to absorb and coordinate these extra capacities. In other words, to draw from the political science literature on power, while significant cyber power resources in the hands of private actors existed, the Ukrainian Government was not able to effectively mobilise these resources to actually project power. Kyiv's cyber power was inhibited by a lack of what Alexander Klimburg calls 'integrated national capability'.[18]

Thirdly, the conflict does not appear to have mobilised the most sophisticated non-state actors with cyber capabilities in the region – the cybercriminals – to change their profit-driven behaviour to more politically-driven action. While the conflict apparently politicised and led to a split of the criminal underground community in the autumn of 2014, the effect was ephemeral and once the cybercriminals realised that their spat started to affect their business, 'money trumped politics', according to Konstatin Korsun, head of council at the NGO Ukrainian Information Security Group and director at the private cybersecurity company Berezha Security.[19]

> *Once cybercriminals realised that their spat started to affect business, 'money trumped politics'.*

A closer look reveals a range of proxy actors has been active. In the context of a broader analysis of the market for force, it is notable that the crisis in Ukraine demonstrated that cybersecurity is a domain where private actors possess significant capabilities and are used by states for both defensive and offensive purposes. For example, the limited capabilities of the Ukrainian Government have been augmented through NATO assistance, namely its Cyber Defence Trust Fund, to train and improve Ukraine's cyber defences. Interestingly, the lead NATO member providing that assistance, Romania, has itself not been providing this assistance directly through its government, but is relying on a proxy actor, a state-owned company called Rasirom, to provide the service.[20]

---

18   Joseph S. Nye, Jr. *The Future of Power* (New York: Public Affairs, 2011).
      Alexander Klimburg, 'Mobilising Cyber Power,' *Survival* 53.1 (2011), 56.
19   'Kostiantyn Korsun,' LinkedIn, accessed August 25, 2015, https://ua.linkedin.com/pub/kostiantyn-korsun/1b/12b/580.
20   'Romania Turns Hacking Crisis Into Advantage, Helping Ukraine,' *The New York Times*, May 13, 2015, http://www.nytimes.com/aponline/2015/05/13/world/europe/ap-eu-romania-ukraine-cyber-warfare.html; 'NATO-Ukraine Trust Fund on Cyber Defence,' Romania's Permanent Representation to NATO, accessed August 25, 2015, http://nato.mae.ro/en/local-news/804.

While criminal groups have not been active players in the Ukraine conflict, the most prominent proxy actors have been hacktivist groups. These groups include pro-Kyiv OpRussia, Russian CyberCommand (which considers itself to be part of Anonymous),[21] Cyber Ukrainian Army, Cyber Hundred, Null Sector,[22] and the pro-Moscow CyberBerkut and Anonymous Ukraine.[23] Their activities have been limited to DDoS attacks, web defacements, and the occasional leaking of government files. The most serious incident involved the aforementioned targeting of the Ukrainian voting system during the Ukrainian Presidential election. While Ukrainian government officials and many news reports blame the Russian Government for indirectly orchestrating these operations, as well as for the crude 'hack attacks' on Ukrainian state websites, the Russian Government has vehemently denied accusations that it has any influence over these groups. Evidence for a relationship between pro-Russian separatists or hacker groups such as Cyber Berkut and the Russian Government remains lacking.

The Ukrainian Cyber Force has been among the most prominent Ukrainian hacktivist groups. It is led by Eugene Dokukin and a group of volunteers he recruited through social media, whose number has fluctuated from several dozens to a few hundred, and primarily includes ordinary citizens without a technical background.[24] The Ukrainian Cyber Force combines a series of different activities, ranging from the unauthorised monitoring of CCTV cameras in eastern Ukraine and Russia, to reporting troop and separatist activities to web companies in an effort to shut down their accounts, launching DDoS attacks against websites, and leaking sensitive documents from the Russian Government. While Dokukin has given a series of interviews and shares information about his actions with the media and the government, there is no evidence that the government coordinates or supports him financially or otherwise. Instead, the government has been turning a blind eye.

Related to the conflict in Ukraine are the findings of several industry reports. The U.S.-based security company FireEye published a report titled '*APT28: A Window into Russia's Cyber Espionage Operations?*', detailing the activities of a group conducting political espionage against East European countries and security organisations. FireEye:

> 'conclude[s] that we are tracking a focused, long-standing espionage effort. Given the available data, we assess that APT28's work is sponsored by the Russian Government'.[25]

---

21 Jeffrey Carr. 'Rival hackers fighting proxy war over Crimea,' *CNN*, March 25, 2014, http://www.cnn.com/2014/03/25/opinion/crimea-cyber-war/.

22 'Cyber Wars: The Invisible Front,' *Ukraine Investigation*, April 24, 2014, http://ukraineinvestigation.com/cyber-wars-invisible-front/.

23 'Cyber Berkut Graduates From DDoS Stunts to Purveyor of Cyber Attack Tools,' *Recorded Future*, June 8, 2015, https://www.recordedfuture.com/cyber-berkut-analysis/.

24 'Cyber warrior steps up effort to help in war with Russia,' *KyivPost*, February 10, 2015, http://www.kyivpost.com/content/kyiv-post-plus/cyber-warrior-steps-up-effort-to-help-in-war-with-russia-380184.html.

25 'APT28 – A Window Into Russia's Cyber Espionage Operations?' *FireEye*, October 27, 2014, https://www2.fireeye.com/apt28.html.

Perhaps the most interesting report is the one published by the Finnish firm F-Secure titled '*BlackEnergy & Quedagh – The convergence of crimeware and APT attacks*'. The authors highlight that in 2014, malware named BlackEnergy, originally developed and used for criminal profit-driven purposes, was deployed against government organisations in Ukraine by a group the report calls 'Quedagh'. The report concludes by stating that:

> '*the use of BlackEnergy for a politically-oriented attack is an intriguing convergence of criminal activity and espionage. As the kit is being used by multiple groups, it provides a greater measure of plausible deniability than is afforded by a custom-made piece of code.*'[26]

6   CONCLUSION

The conflict in Ukraine includes a range of proxy actors and proxy activity. This should be expected given the existence of a hot conflict, the presence of significant cyber capabilities in private hands, and incentives for the nations involved to use these private capabilities. However, the amount of cyber proxy activity has remained relatively low, much like the overall level of computer network operations compared to what some experts predicted. It is notable that the conflict does not appear to have politicised and mobilised the most sophisticated non-state actors with cyber capabilities – the cybercriminals – to change their profit-driven behaviour to more politically-driven action. Moreover, the Ukrainian Government has not had the capacity and strategy in place to be able to absorb the additional capabilities provided by volunteers. Kyiv has therefore not been able to mobilise and project the full potential of Ukraine's power due to the limited use of its true power resources. While the Ukrainian Government regularly accuses the Russian Government of using proxies, there seems to be less vehemence from the Russian side criticising, for example, the activities of the Ukrainian Cyber Forces. According to one interviewee, one explanation is that the Russian Government has more to gain from being able to point to the existence of Ukrainian proxies in order to thereby indirectly legitimise the existence of Russian proxies.

While this chapter hopefully shed some light on the role of proxy actors in the Ukraine conflict, it is necessary to point to some important limitations and issues that were beyond the scope of this short piece. First, the term 'proxies' lacks a clear definition. While it is used in the GGE report, it is not defined, even though the report distinguishes 'proxies' as a separate type of actor from state and non-state actors. Developing a more systematic and nuanced analytical framework for proxies is therefore the focus of my current research. This will hopefully be useful for future empirical research on proxy actors around the world, as well as for ongoing policy discussions through the GGE and elsewhere.

---

26   'The convergence of crimeware and APT attacks,' *F-Secure*, 2014, https://www.f-secure.com/documents/996508/1030745/blackenergy_whitepaper.pdf.

CHAPTER 10

RUSSIAN INFORMATION WARFARE: LESSONS FROM UKRAINE

MARGARITA LEVIN JAITNER

Swedish Defense University

1 INTRODUCTION

'Information is now a species of weapon',[1] write Russians Maj. Gen. (R) Ivan Vorobyev and Col. (R) Valery Kiselyov. Closer to the truth is that Russia has a long history of using information as a weapon – both in the context of mobilising its own population[2] and in demonising foreign powers.[3]

Therefore, it is only natural that Russia has employed Information Warfare (IW) in Ukraine: from the onset of the 'Euromaidan' demonstrations, to the annexation of Crimea, and as a dimension of ongoing military operations in eastern Ukraine. And it is equally unsurprising that, in the internet era, Moscow has developed effective tactics for waging IW in cyberspace.

This chapter discusses contemporary Russian IW theory and analyses Russian IW activities on the ground in Crimea and in eastern Ukraine. While the dynamic and diffuse nature of IW makes it difficult to gauge its precise impact, this chapter argues that Russian IW in Crimea and in eastern Ukraine has been highly successful, and that the West is currently playing catch up vis-à-vis Russia in this arena.

---

1   Vorobyov, I. and Kiseljov, V. 'Russian Military Theory: Past and Present.' *Military Thought* 2013 (3).
2   Peter Kenez. *The birth of the propaganda state: Soviet methods of mass mobilization, 1917-1929* (Cambridge University Press, 1995).
3   David M. Glantz. *Surprise and Maskirovka in Contemporary War.* Soviet Army Studies Office, Army Combined Arms Center, Fort Leavenworth KS, 1988). http://www.dtic.mil/get-tr-doc/pdf?Location=U2&doc=GetTRDoc.pdf&AD=ADA216491.

2 Information Security and Cyber Security in Russian Military Theory

In Russian government and academic circles, information is understood to be a form and source of great power. This was true well before the advent of the internet and cyberspace – which have not changed Russian IW strategy, but only its tactics.

In the West, cyber security and information security are considered to be two different things. In Russia, however, cyber is subordinate to information security, which allows national security planners to oversee both technical data (e.g. the integrity of password files) and cognitive data (e.g. political information on websites). Thus, any information found on the World Wide Web could be a 'missile' fired at Russia that is more dangerous than a typical cyber attack as currently understood in the West.

The logical consequence of this Russian perspective is to define and to protect the borders of the Russia's 'information space' (*информационное пространство*), and this philosophy is to be found easily in Russian doctrines, strategies, and activities both at home and abroad – including in Ukraine.

For example, Russia's *National Security Strategy 2020* states that 'nationalist, separatist, radical religion' is a danger to nation-states, and that a 'global information struggle' is now intensifying. The document proposes to counter this threat by disseminating 'truthful' information to Russian citizens, including via the promotion of native internet platforms encompassing social media.[4]

As for the importance of cyberspace, numerous official documents describe computer network operations as an integral part of Russian information security, including: *Information Security Doctrine of the Russian Federation*,[5] *Conceptual Views Regarding the Activities of the Armed Forces of the Russian Federation in the Information Space*,[6] and *Basic Principles for State Policy of the Russian Federation in the Field of International Information Security*.[7]

> *Information superiority in cyberspace is an essential goal.*

Academic discourse within the Russian military is similar. From a historical perspective, progress in computer science has wrought a new generation of warfare in which the achievement of information superiority in cyberspace is an essential goal. Within any desired zone of influence, this includes attacks against and defence of

---

4   Security Council of the Russian Federation. *Стратегия национальной безопасности Российской Федерации до 2020 года.* (National Security Strategy to 2020) (Moscow, 2009).

5   Security Council of the Russian Federation. 2000. *Доктрина информационной безопасности Российской Федерации.* (Information Security Doctrine of the Russian Federation.) (Moscow, 2000).

6   Ministry of Defence of the Russian Federation. *Концептуальные взгляды на деятельность Вооруженных Сил Российской Федерации в информационном пространстве.* (Conceptual Views Regarding the Activities of the Armed Forces of the Russian Federation in the Information Space) (Moscow, 2011).

7   Security Council of the Russian Federation. *Основы государственной политики Российской Федерации в области международной информационной безопасности на период до 2020 года.* (Basic Principles for State Policy of the Russian Federation in the Field of International Information Security to 2020.) (Moscow, 2013).

both technical data and cognitive information, as well as and psychological operations, or PSYOPS.

Maj. Gen. (R) Ivan Vorobyev and Col. (R) Valery Kiselyov have written that information is 'not just an addition to firepower, attack, manoeuvre, but transforms and unites all of these'.[8] Col. (R) Sergei Chekinov and Lt. Gen. (R) Sergei Bogdanov go even further: 'Today the means of information influence reached such perfection that they can tackle strategic tasks'.[9]

> *Information can disorganise governance, delude adversaries and reduce an opponent's will to resist.*

Checkinov and Bogdanov point out – in the aftermath of the annexation of Crimea and the current destabilisation of Ukraine – that information can be used to disorganise governance, organise anti-government protests, delude adversaries, influence public opinion, and reduce an opponent's will to resist. Furthermore, it is critical that such activities begin prior to the onset of traditional military operations.[10]

At least since Soviet times, Russia considers itself to be a victim of IW, engaged in a battle between the 'historical Russian world' (of which Ukraine is a part) and the West where the US is its principal antagonist.[11] Professor Igor Panarin has described a 'first information war' during the Cold War that resulted in the demise of the Soviet Union. Today, he sees an 'Operation ANTI-PUTIN' modelled on an earlier 'Operation ANTI-STALIN'. He contends that Western IW was behind both the Arab Spring[12] and Euromaidan, and that WikiLeaks' Julian Assange is an agent of the British MI6.[13] Panarin believes there is a 'second information war' taking place against countries such as Russia and Syria which began at least by the time of the Russo-Georgian war in 2008.[14] Russian President Vladimir Putin has characterised the rift between Russia and the West as an incompatibility of values («духовные ценности»).[15]

Panarin is far from being the only contemporary Russian military thinker arguing this line. A group of five authors recently wrote in Russia's *Military Thought* that 'The NATO countries led by the US … have set up a powerful information operations (IO) system and are going on expanding and improving it'.[16]

---

8   Vorobyov and Kiseljov 'Russian Military Theory: Past and Present.' *Military Thought*, 2013 (3).
9   Sergei G. Checkinov and Sergei A. Bogdanov. 'Asymmetrical Actions to Maintain Russia's Military Security.' *Military Thought*, 2010 (1).
10 Sergei G. Checkinov and Sergei A. Bogdanov. 'The Art of War in the Early 21st Century: Issues and Opinions.' *Military Thought*, 2015 (24).
11 Igor Panarin. *Информационная война и коммуникации.* (Information warfare and communications.). Moskva, Russia: Goryachaya Liniya – Telekom, 2014a.
12 *Ibid.*
13 Igor Panarin. Posting on Facebook , 29 June, 2014b. http://www.facebook.com/permalink.php?story_fbid=487886764691548&id=100004106865632&fref=ts. Accessed 19 December, 2014.
14 Igor Panarin. 2014a.
15 Vladimir Putin. '*Путин защитит традиционные семейные ценности.* (Putin to defend traditional family values)'. Vesti, 12 December, 2013a. http://www.vesti.ru/doc.html?id=1166423; Vladimir Putin. '*Наши духовные ценности делают нас единым народом*' (Our values unite us as peoples. Speech in Kyiv 27.07.2013.). YouTube, 2013b. https://www.youtube.com/watch?v=YW1WYh_gvJg Accessed 20 December 2014.
16 Dylevski, I.N., Elyas, V.P., Komov, S.A., Petrunin, A.N. & Zapivakhin V.O. 'Political and Military Aspects of the Russian Federation's State Policy on International Information Security.' *Military Thought*, 2015 (24).

Even Russia, however, is not a monolith.[17] Some military scholars have criticised the prevailing view and have suggested that a distinction should be drawn between attacks on technical and cognitive data, detailing a 'technospheric war' largely corresponding to the Western perception of 'cyber war'.[18] Similarly, a publicly available draft of the next *Cyber Security Strategy of the Russian Federation* problematises the difference between the Russian and the Western views on the matter, suggesting that cyber security and information security be treated as distinct challenges. However, to date these remain unimplemented proposals.

3   RUSSIAN IW IN CRIMEA AND NOVOROSSIYA[19]

Russian IW in Ukraine began well before the current conflict. The Security Services of Ukraine (SBU) warned that its government officials had been targeted by Russian espionage malware (variously called 'Snake', 'Uroboros' or 'Turla') since 2010.[20,21,22] Successful cyber espionage can have a strategic impact. In a military context, it can be directly linked to a desire to gain information superiority on the battlefield,[23] and can sometimes be easy to associate with ongoing military operations.[24]

In Crimea, just as soon as insignia-less armed fighters appeared on the scene (the same dynamic later occurred in eastern Ukraine), Russian media referred to them as 'friendly people' who were 'good to civilians',[25] while the Ukrainian side called them the 'little green men' from Russia. For weeks, Vladimir Putin[26] and Russian

> *The course of events was enveloped in a sophisticated effort to control the flow of information.*

---

17   Balybin, C., Donskov, Yu. and Boyko A. 'Electronic Warfare Terminology in the Context of Information Operations.' *Military Thought,* 2014 (23) 3.

18   Yurii Starodubtsev, Vladimir Bukharin and Sergei Semenov (2012). Техносферная война (War in the technosphere). *Военная Мысль (Military Thought) 2012(7).*

19   Novorossiya – historically a region north of the Black Sea, annexed by the Russian Empire following the Russo-Turkish wars. The term was revived to denote a confederation of the self-proclaimed Donetsk People's Republic and Lugansk People's Republic in eastern Ukraine.

20   Security Service of Ukraine, SBU. Служба безпеки України попереджає про 'фейкові' електронні розсилки від імені державних органів. (Security Service of Ukraine warns of 'fake' e-mails on behalf of public authorities). 26 September, 2014. http://www.sbu.gov.ua/sbu/control/uk/publish/article?art_id=132039&cat_id=39574.

21   'Snake Cyber-espionage Campaign Targetting Ukraine is Linked to Russia.' *InfoSecurity Magazine,* 11 March 2014. http://www.infosecurity-magazine.com/news/snake-cyber-espionage-campaign-targetting-ukraine/.

22   'Turla: Spying tool targets governments and diplomats.' *Symantec,* 7 August 2014. http://www.symantec.com/connect/blogs/turla-spying-tool-targets-governments-and-diplomats.

23   James J. Coyle. 'Russia Has Complete Information Dominance in Ukraine.' *Atlantic Council,* 12 May 2015. http://www.atlanticcouncil.org/blogs/new-atlanticist/russia-has-complete-informational-dominance-in-ukraine.

24   'Operation Armageddon: Cyber Espionage as a Strategic Component of Russian Modern Warfare.' *Lookingglass,* 28 April 2015. https://lgscout.com/wp-content/uploads/2015/04/Operation_Armageddon_FINAL.pdf.

25   Aleksandr Leonov. 'Солдаты будущего: чем вооружены «вежливые люди» в Крыму. (Future soldiers: The friendly men's equipment in Crimea.).' *Forbes,* 7 March 2014. http://m.forbes.ru/article.php?id=251676.

26   Vladimir Putin. Путин: 'В Крыму нет российских солдат. Это самооборона Крыма. (Putin: There are no Russian soldiers. This is Crimea's popular defense.).' *YouTube,* 2014b. https://www.youtube.com/watch?v=qzKm7uxK8ws. Accessed 20 December 2014.

Defence Minister Sergei Shoigu[27] denied the participation of Russian troops in the Crimea takeover – even though Ukrainian troops on the peninsula were forced into a quick, large-scale surrender.[28][29]

In warfare, there has always been a tight relationship between IW and traditional military operations. In Crimea, the entire course of events – from the takeover of the Simferopol parliament to the disputed referendum and the Russian annexation of Crimea – was enveloped in a sophisticated effort to control the flow of information. Russian IW extended across the entire spectrum of communication in both the cyber and non-cyber domains, targeting its physical, logical, and social layers.

In early March, *Ukrtelecom* reported kinetically damaged fiber-optic trunk cables, as well as the temporary seizure of its company's offices. Further disclosures detailed the jamming of Ukrainian naval communications.[30] SBU Chief Valentyn Nalyvaichenko declared that Ukrainian government officials' mobile communications were subjected to an 'IP-telephonic attack'.[31] And on the World Wide Web, government sites and news portals suffered Distributed Denial of Service (DDoS) attacks and defacements – all of which contributed to a significant information blackout.[32][33]

The 'hacktivist' group *Cyberberkut*[34] has repeatedly claimed to have gained access to telephone recordings and e-mail correspondence between Ukrainian, European Union (EU) and US officials – and released some content to prove it. *Cyberberkut* also allegedly attacked the Ukrainian electronic voting system and defaced several NATO websites.[35]

The importance of gaining information superiority in warfare can be seen in how much time and resources have been spent in creating official, semi-official, and unofficial sources of war-related information, including dedicated channels on YouTube.[36]

The success of IW is hard to gauge, but these attacks likely made it more difficult for Kyiv to gain a clear picture of what was happening in Crimea – which in turn presumably hampered its decision-making process. Even unsophisticated cyber attacks tend to generate significant media attention, and as a bonus can sow general distrust in systems and their security architecture.[37]

---

27 Sergey Shoigu. 2014. 'Шойгу о российской технике в Крыму: 'чушь и провокация'. (Shoigu on Russian military in Crimea: 'nonsense and provocation').' *BBC Russkaya Sluzhba*, 5 March 2014. http://www.bbc.co.uk/russian/russia/2014/03/140305_crimea_troops_shoigu.

28 Yuzhniy Kurier. 'Все. Украинские солдаты в Крыму сдаются. (The End. Ukrainian soldiers in Crimea surrender.).' *Yuzhniy Kurier*, March 19, 2014. http://courier.crimea.ua/news/courier/vlast/1146781.html.

29 'CNN.' 'Украинские войска в Крыму сдаются силам самообороны. (Ukrainian troops surrender to Crimean self-defence forces.).' edited by RT, 19 March 2014. http://russian.rt.com/inotv/2014-03-19/CNN-Ukrainskie-vojska-v-Krimu.

30 Tim Maurer and Scott Janz. 'The Russia-Ukraine Conflict: Cyber and Information Warfare in a Regional Context.' *The International Relations and Security Network*, 17 October 2014. http://www.isn.ethz.ch/Digital-Library/Articles/Detail/?id=184345.

31 Pierluigi Paganini. 'Crimea – The Russian Cyber Strategy to Hit Ukraine.' *InfoSec Institute*, 11 March 2014. http://resources.infosecinstitute.com/crimea-russian-cyber-strategy-hit-ukraine/.

32 Tim Maurer and Scott Janz. 'The Russia-Ukraine Conflict: Cyber and Information Warfare in a Regional Context.'

33 Piret Pernik. 'Is All Quiet on the Cyber Front in the Ukrainian crisis?' *RKK ICDS International Centre for Defence and Security*, 7 March 2014. http://www.icds.ee/et/blogi/artikkel/is-all-quiet-on-the-cyber-front-in-the-ukrainian-crisis/.

34 'Киберберкут' http://cyber-berkut.org/en.

35 Pierluigi Paganini. 'Crimea – The Russian Cyber Strategy to Hit Ukraine.'

36 'YouTube.' 2014. Database query: 'Новости Новороссии'. Accessed 13 December 2014.

37 Tim Maurer and Scott Janz. 'The Russia-Ukraine Conflict: Cyber and Information Warfare in a Regional Context.'

Ukrainian military commentator Dmitry Tymchuk, speaking on behalf of the 'Information Resistance' group,[38] accused the interim government in Kyiv of lacking clarity and moving too slowly,[39] and Ukrainian parliament (Verhovna Rada) member Gennady Moskal complained that Ukrainian troops had not received permission to use their weapons in time.[40]

Today, the war in eastern Ukraine can also be described as a hall of IW smoke and mirrors. On 17 April, 2014, Vladimir Putin referred to the south-eastern part of Ukraine as *Novorossiya*, and a similarly named 'confederation' was formally created on May 24, 2014.[41] However, an analysis of web data shows that cyber preparations were made prior to this announcement: *Novorossiya* websites such as novorus.info and novorossia.su were registered with who.is in March 2014, and the official websites of the People's Republics of Donetsk and Lugansk were registered before the entities came into being.[42] Finally, Moscow has consistently denied that its military personnel are engaged in Ukraine, but web-based studies have found evidence of their deployments to Ukraine[43] as well as their involvement in the crash of the Malaysian Airlines flight 17,[44] via social media and imagery analysis.[45]

4 THE UNIQUE CHARACTERISTICS OF RUSSIAN IW

The Russian political narrative – aimed at both domestic and foreign audiences – describes a 'Russian World' (*Русский Мир*), 'Russian values', and even a 'Russian soul'. The narrative's articulation begins at the very top, in the person of Vladimir Putin, and flows downward in a pyramidal fashion through traditional media and cyberspace all the down to the grassroots level. It targets not just Russian citizens but the entire Russian-speaking population of planet Earth. Beyond that, it is expected that the narrative's influence will organically spread outside the diaspora.

The basic storyline is easy to comprehend and to convey, and is intended to be become a foundation for the interpretation of current and future world events. In this narrative, Russia is a misunderstood and misjudged superpower, and a necessary counterweight to Western liberal values. By contrast, the West has experienced

---

38 'Information Resistance' is, according to its own description on http://sprotyv.info/en/about-us, a non-governmental project that aims to counteract external threats to the informational space of Ukraine'. The group provides operational data and analytics. As one of the project's front figures, Dmitry Tymchuk has provided analysis to, amongst others, Kyiv Post and Huffington Post.
39 Dimitro Tymchuk. 'О предательстве (On betrayal).' *Gazeta.ua*, March 2014. http://gazeta.ua/ru/blog/42707/o-predatelstve.
40 Yuzhniy Kurier. 'Все. Украинские солдаты в Крыму сдаются. (The End. Ukrainian soldiers in Crimea surrender.).' *Yuzhniy Kurier*, 19 March 2014. http://courier.crimea.ua/news/courier/vlast/1146781.html.
41 Vladimir Putin. 'Прямая линия с Владимиром Путиным.' Phone-in with Vladimir Putin. (Transcript). 17 April 2014. http://kremlin.ru/news/20796.
42 See who.is listings for novorus.info (http://who.is/whois/novorus.info), novorossia.su (http://who.is/whois/novorossia.su)
43 'Selfie Soldiers: Russia Checks in to Ukraine.' *Vice News*, 16 June, 2015.
44 'Bellingcat.com' By and for citizen investigative journalists: Russia. http://www.bellingcat.com/tag /russia/.
45 NATO ACO – Allied Command Operations. 'New Satellite Imagery Exposes Russian Combat Troops Inside Ukraine'. *NATO Allied Command Operations: News*, 28 August 2014. http://aco.nato.int/new-satellite-imagery-exposes-russian-combat-troops-inside-ukraine.aspx.

a decay of 'traditional values' and acts hypocritically in the international arena. As a result, the West's philosophy, systems, and actions should not be trusted.

At the bottom of the pyramid, the Russian political narrative is absorbed into individual group ideologies in different ways. For example, nationalists focus on Russia's historic power, while communist groups decry capitalism. Each group self-selects and customises the narrative in unique ways that correspond to their own natural biases. And this stovepiping dynamic also tends to bypass critical peer review from the wider public.

This group dynamic capitalises on the pre-established interpersonal trust characteristic of online social media – a by-product of information overload in the internet era. There are many groups which are naturally sceptical of mainstream information channels, such as the population of the Former Soviet Union, where citizens have long had little trust in official media. In Moscow, the word of friends and colleagues is immeasurably more important than that of mass media.[46]

One of the latest developments in this arena has been the rise of professional 'trolls' and other (sometimes anonymous) 'opinion agents'. Such operations (in Russian military terminology 'maskirovka' (маскировка), or denial and deception) can be countered through the effective analysis of open source information, but usually not in a timely manner. Therefore, analysts and scholars must exercise caution, because online persona, images, messages, and campaigns can be wholly fabricated.

5   Conclusion

The global internet offers military and intelligence agencies the opportunity to expand and enhance IW, and it simultaneously presents their targets and victims with novel challenges. Russian IW – both in traditional media and in cyberspace – tangibly contributed to the successful annexation of Crimea, and is playing an important role in the ongoing crisis in eastern Ukraine. On balance, this author believes that Russia, and not the West, currently has the lead in contemporary IW.

Unlike propaganda in Soviet times, which was largely a unidirectional, top-down phenomenon, today's IW encompasses a worldwide audience that is both narrative-bearing and narrative-developing. Domestic, diaspora, and foreign audiences interact with current events in real time as they travel through online platforms such as social media. This dynamic makes it more challenging for propagandists to predict how and where the narrative will evolve, but to some degree it is possible to presume how certain political groups will interpret the narrative and how they will describe it to their followers.

In sum, the traditional 'fog of war' has changed in the internet era. The ubiquity and anonymity of internet communications offer all nations including Russia

---

46   Markku Lonkila. 'Russian Protest On-and Offline: The role of social media in the Moscow opposition demonstrations in December 2011.' *UPI FIIA Briefing Papers* 98, 2012.

> *In sum, the traditional 'fog of war' has changed in the internet era.*

new IW opportunities, even as defenders also have more tools and tactics at their disposal to counter hostile actions. In Ukraine, 'conventional' cyber attacks by Russia were negligible,[47] but social media-based, narrative-focused attacks including disinformation have been common. And while it is possible to counter adversary operations with accurate open source analysis (for journalists,[48] scholars, and activists[49]), this is unfortunately difficult to do in a timely manner.

47   However, even unsophisticated cyber attacks such as DDoS and website defacements tend to garner widespread media exposure, and can sow distrust in the security of systems. This occurred during the invasion of Crimea, when Russia sought to capitalise on events that unfolded far too quickly for methodical information analysis to take place.

48   Jessikka Aro. 'Yle Kioski Investigated: This is How Pro-Russia Trolls Manipulate Finns Online – Check the List of Forums Favored by Propagandists'. *YLE Kioski*, 24 June 2015. http://kioski.yle.fi/omat/troll-piece-2-english.

49   Sites such as www.stopfake.org were launched inviting people to join the 'struggle against fake information about events in Ukraine' by verifying online allegations. 'Stopfake.org.' 2015. Accessed: 14 June 2015. http://www.stopfake.org; 'Bellingcat kontert Kritik mit neuen Satellitenbildern'. *Zeit Online*. 12 June 2015. www.zeit.de/politik/ausland/2015-06/bellingcat-russland-mh17-satellitenfotos-manipulation; Dmitry Volchek and Claire Bigg. 'Ukrainian bloggers use social media to track Russian soldiers fighting in east'. *The Guardian*, 3 June 2015. http://www.theguardian.com/world/2015/jun/03/bloggers-social-media-russian-soldiers-fighting-in-ukraine.

CHAPTER 11

MISSING IN ACTION: RHETORIC ON CYBER WARFARE

LIISA PAST

NATO CCD COE

1   INTRODUCTION

In the Russo-Ukrainian conflict, there has been much talk of 'hybrid warfare', encompassing every aspect of war including cyber operations. Much of cyber operations is classified and hidden from public view, but there are numerous ways in which information becomes known, including via intelligence leaks and open source analysis. This chapter focuses on leadership communications and what they can tell us about conflict in cyberspace.

In geopolitics, heads of state are the ultimate decision-makers, especially during a national security crisis. Leaders are expected to show rhetorical as well as executive leadership. The media takes it from there, but the public still struggles to find a consistent evaluation, primarily relying on experts and opinion leaders.[1] As the head of state seeks his or her 'rally around the president' moment,[2] domestic and international observers analyse their explanations and emotions – as well as their proffered initiatives and guidance.[3] From a national podium, heads of state have an inherent advantage, as their arguments are 'more likely to resonate with the public than the opinions of leaders voicing a more local outlook.'[4]

Communication and discourse analysis in international affairs rests on the idea that language cannot be taken at face value. Words carry definitional meaning, but dif-

---

1   Timothy E Cook. *Governing with the News* (Chicago and London: University of Chicago Press, 1998).
2   Birgitte Lebens Nacos. *Terrorism and the Media: From the Iran Hostage Crisis to the Oklahoma City Bombing* (New York: Columbia University Press, 1996).
3   Jeffrey E Cohen. *Presidential Responsiveness and Public Policy-Making, The Public and the Policies That Presidents Choose* (Ann Arbor: The University of Michigan Press, 1997).
4   *Ibid*, 32.

ferent audiences will perceive them differently. Critical analysis can yield insight into the true beliefs and motivations of any speaker, including policy-makers. Meaning is 'mediated through language'[5] and all words have 'social values'[6] that vary with context.

This chapter analyses Russian and Ukrainian leadership statements, speeches, press releases and other rhetoric from 2014 and 2015, especially the English-language elements, written for a global audience and printed in international media. The author also searched major international news outlets for the keywords 'Ukraine', 'Russia', 'cyber', and 'information warfare'. In all cases, focus remained on the rhetoric attributable to a head of state or other high-level political player,[7] with an eye toward uncovering their underlying motivations, beliefs, and ideologies.

2   ANALYTICAL FOCUS

This analysis is designed to yield insight into numerous areas of international concern. Above all, the world would like to understand more about the emerging threat of cyber warfare. New developments in research and technology, as well as in the means and methods of war, are usually far ahead of their codification in doctrine.

Computer network operations fit nicely within the concept of hybrid warfare that has been so characteristic of the Russo-Ukrainian conflict. Cyber attacks are similar to covert operations, information operations, denial and deception, false flag and no-flag attacks: they give national command and control structures some degree of plausible deniability. These aspects of war tend to be highly classified; therefore, an analysis of political rhetoric may yield significant insight into what politicians, soldiers and spies simply cannot discuss in public forums, namely, one of the most vexing challenges of cyber attacks: attribution.

> *An analysis of political rhetoric may yield significant insight into what politicians cannot discuss in public forums.*

Political leaders must appeal to the hearts and minds of their domestic and international audiences, with the help of emotional and sometimes long-winded speeches. National security establishments must provide legal support for their actions through the release of press statements and promulgation of doctrine. With these in hand, analysts may be able to understand much more about the otherwise covert nature of cyber attacks. In 2015, Russia has a fairly well-developed military doctrine on cyber and information warfare, while that of Ukraine is still in its infancy. This analysis offers a deeper understanding of each nation's non-explicit political objectives related to cyber warfare.

---

5   Henrik Larsen. *Foreign Policy and Discourse Analysis: France, Britain and Europe* (London: Routledge advances in International Relations and Politics, 1997), 11.
6   *Ibid*, 14.
7   Unfortunately, on the current 'President of Ukraine' website, documents and speeches by former Ukrainian President Viktor Yanukovych cannot be found.

3   RUSSIA

Since the turn of the century, Russia has been publicly admiring European values while simultaneously emphasising sovereignty and a strong national defence.[8] Moscow insists that 'each nation in the region should be given a right to experiment with its own democratic model that fits its national and international conditions'.[9] This tension may only grow stronger with time, and we may see further Russian moves away from shared values in the future as Moscow confronts not only Ukraine but also the West more generally, including in Syria.

Regarding Ukraine, Russia insists it is a bystander and even a victim. Putin said, 'There are still many threats and challenges in the world today. As you may know, in Europe, militant nationalism is raising its head here and there – the one that once led to the appearance of the Nazi ideology. I will not dwell on each of the hotspots separately – we all know where the danger is. Incidentally, the situation in our neighbouring brotherly Ukraine is an example of the disaster and loss such an irresponsible policy can bring about.'[10] In explaining Gazprom's tough stance vis-à-vis Ukraine, for example, Putin has argued that there was no other choice but to take a hard line against Kyiv,[11] again placing Russia as a bystander, not an active party.

Putin has consistently delegitimised Poroshenko's government:

> 'There can only be one assessment: this was an anti-constitutional takeover, an armed seizure of power [that] significantly destabilised the east and southeast of Ukraine [...] we see the rampage of reactionary forces, nationalist and anti-Semitic forces going on in certain parts of Ukraine, including Kyiv [...] Are the current authorities legitimate? The Parliament is partially, but all the others are not. The current Acting President is definitely not legitimate [...] one set of thieves [is] being replaced by another. [...] We will not fight with the Ukrainian people [but] I do not have a partner at the top level there'.[12]

Throughout the Ukraine crisis which began in 2014, Vladimir Putin has not once used the word 'cyber'. This does not signify a lack of interest in the subject, or that Russia has not engaged in computer network operations, but it does demonstrate a preference not to discuss the issue, which in turn likely means that cyber warfare as a distinct form of attack, from

Throughout the Ukraine crisis, Vladimir Putin has not once used the word 'cyber'.

---

8   Andrei P. Tsygankov. *Russia's Foreign Policy: Change and Continuity in National Identity* (Rowman & Littlefield Publishers, 2013), 181.
9   *Ibid.*
10   'Meeting with Presidents of Armenia, Belarus, Kyrgyzstan and Tajikistan' Website of the President of Russia, 8 May 2014), http://en.kremlin.ru/events/president/news/20980.
11   'Message to the leaders of European countries regarding the supply and transit of Russian gas across the territory of Ukraine' Website of the President of Russia, 15 May 2014, http://en.kremlin.ru/events/president/news/page/82.
12   'Vladimir Putin answered journalists' questions on the situation in Ukraine' Website of the President of Russia 3 April 2014), http://en.kremlin.ru/events/president/news/20366.

Russia's perspective, has not played a major role in the Ukraine conflict. There have been some commercial reports alleging specific Russian cyber attacks, such as that by the security firm FireEye,[13] but these are typically dismissed as Western propaganda. According to Kremlin spokesman Dmitry Peskov, 'We know that blaming Russia for everything has turned into a sport'.[14]

Putin did refer to the stories about phone hacking and surveillance of top politicians, which were prominent in the news in 2014:

> *'As for the facts of cyber espionage that you mentioned, it not only amounts to overt hypocrisy in relationships between allies and partners, but also a direct violation of the state's sovereignty, an infringement on human rights and an invasion of privacy. We are looking forward to jointly developing an international information security system'.*[15]

This quote may indicate an underlying assumption of Russian doctrine: today, everyone is spying on everyone, there are currently no acceptable international laws to govern such activities in cyberspace, and Russia must be a part of any credible effort to develop such norms.

Although Russia claims not to be directly involved in the Ukraine conflict, Moscow still wants to direct its peace-making efforts. Putin has championed a consideration of Ukraine's eastern regions[16] has produced a diplomatic solution called the Putin Plan[17] and 'gave the instruction to hold consultations with foreign partners, including the IMF and the G8 countries, on organising financial assistance for Ukraine'.[18]

4   UKRAINE

Many of these quotes came from the President of Russia's website, and are directly attributable to Vladimir Putin. However, most of the conflict-related quotes in this section – from the President of Ukraine's website – are from news articles and press releases that quote Ukrainian President Petro Poroshenko. Unlike on the Russian site, full-length Ukrainian speeches are a smaller proportion of the presidential communications. That said, Ukraine has been much clearer than Russia in identify-

---

13   'APT28 – A Window Into Russia's Cyber Espionage Operations?' *FireEye*, https://www2.fireeye.com/apt28.html.

14   Owen Matthews. 'Russia leading the way in the cyber arms race,' *Irish Examiner*, 13 June 2015, http://www.irishexaminer.com/lifestyle/features/big-read-russia-leading-the-way-in-the-cyber-arms-race-336675.html.

15   'Interview to Prensa Latina and ITAR-TASS' Website of the President of Russia, 11 July 2014, http://en.kremlin.ru/events/president/news/46190.

16   'On the start of contacts with Ukraine's Choice public movement in Donetsk and Lugansk' Website of the President of Russia, 22 June 2014, http://en.kremlin.ru/events/president/news.

17   'The 'Putin Plan' for settling the conflict in Ukraine' Website of the President of Russia, 3 September 2014, http://en.kremlin.ru/events/president/news/46554.

18   'Instructions regarding the situation in Ukraine' Website of the President of Russia, 27 February 2014, http://en.kremlin.ru/events/president/news/20347.

ing cyberspace as a separate and active domain of conflict. Various terms have been used, such as 'cyber security',[19] 'informational cyber-security system of Ukraine',[20] and 'cyber and information security'.[21] These terms may refer

Ukraine has been much clearer than Russia in identifying cyberspace as a separate and active domain of conflict.

to slightly different things at different times, but in general, there was more cyber warfare-related content to analyse.

From the beginning of the conflict, Ukraine has suffered a variety of network attacks. In February 2014, the Ukrainian telecommunications firm Ukrtelecom reported that 'unknown people'[22] had damaged a fibre backbone cable that resulted in the loss of communication between Crimea and the rest of Ukraine. Not long after, Ukrainian security chief Valentyn Nalivaichenko announced, 'I confirm that an ... attack is under way on mobile phones of members of the Ukrainian parliament for the second day in a row'.[23] The most sophisticated attack came against the Ukrainian Central Election Commission (CEC) during Ukraine's Presidential elections.[24] However, there was no official attribution for any of these attacks provided by the government in Kyiv.

There were at least two cases of cyber attack attribution, both to Russia. The Security Service of Ukraine linked the disruption of mobile communications and the defacement of websites to pro-Russian hackers and to pro-Russian forces in Crimea. There was no direct link made to Moscow, perhaps in part because the 'IP-telephonic' attack was aimed at top Ukrainian politicians irrespective of their political allegiance.[25] On another occasion, when the hacktivist group CyberBerkut claimed responsibility for an attack on German government websites, Ukrainian Prime Minister Arseny Yatseniuk placed the blame on Russian intelligence: 'I strongly recommend that the Russian secret services stop spending taxpayer money for cyberattacks against the Bundestag and Chancellor Merkel's office'.[26]

In the case of downed Malaysian airliner MH17, which Poroshenko called terrorism,[27] the President stated that 'The State Security Service of Ukraine has inter-

19 'President met with U.S. Congress delegation,' Office of the President of Ukraine, 6 August 2014 http://www.president.gov.ua/en/news/prezident-zustrivsya-z-delegaciyeyu-kongresu-ssha-35766.

20 'NSDC decision: Ukraine asks the UN, NATO, EU, OSCE and strategic partners for help,' Office of the President of Ukraine, 28 August 2014, http://www.president.gov.ua/en/news/ukrayina-zvertayetsya-za-dopomogoyu-do-oon-nato-yes-obsye-de-33573.

21 'Presidents of Ukraine and Lithuania have held the Seventh session of the Council of Presidents' Office of the President of Ukraine, 24 November 2014. http://www.president.gov.ua/en/news/prezidenti-ukrayini-i-litvi-proveli-some-zasidannya-radi-pre-34105.

22 Ukrtelecom. 'Ukrtelecom's Crimean sub-branches officially report that unknown people have seized several telecommunications nodes in the Crimea,' 28 February 2014, http://en.ukrtelecom.ua/about/news?id=120467.

23 Dave Lee. 'Russia and Ukraine in cyber 'stand-off', *BBC News*, 5 March 2014 http://www.bbc.com/news/technology-26447200.

24 SRK/NN/SS, 'Hackers attack Ukraine election website,' *PressTV*, 25 October 2014, http://www.presstv.com/detail/2014/10/25/383623/ukraines-election-website-hacked.

25 Max Smolaks. 'Security Service Of Ukraine Claims Politicians' Phones Are Under Attack,' *TechWeek Europe*, 4 March 2014, http://www.techweekeurope.co.uk/workspace/security-service-ukraine-claims-politicians-phones-attack-140643.

26 Erik Kirscbaum. 'Ukraine says Russia behind cyber attack on German government,' *Reuters*, 8 January 2015, http://www.reuters.com/article/2015/01/08/us-germany-cyberattack-idUSKBN0KH0IY20150108.

27 'Address of the President on the occasion of the crash of Malaysia Airlines aircraft,' Office of the President of Ukraine, 18 July 2014, http://www.president.gov.ua/en/news/zvernennya-prezidenta-z-privodu-tragediyi-z-litakom-aviakomp-33262.

cepted a conversation in which one of the leaders of the mercenaries boasted about bringing down the plane in his reporting to his Russian supervisor, a colonel of the General Intelligence Unit of Russia's Armed Forces'[28] and 'terrorists have already declared their desire to hide the evidence and transport the aircraft's black boxes to Moscow'.[29]

In eastern Ukraine, Poroshenko contends that the separatist movement is 'fully controlled' by Russian leadership[30] and even in government-controlled territory, he announced that '[t]he Security Service of Ukraine unmasked and neutralised the terrorist group coordinated by special forces of the Russian Federation'.[31]

To international audiences, Poroshenko has focused primarily on the broader topic of hybrid warfare, taking care to fit within the narratives and terminology of the West. At the 2015 Munich Security Conference, he said that '[f]or over a year Ukraine has been facing dramatic consequences of an undeclared hybrid warfare. It is very important that the states in the region devote more attention to hybrid threats. […] Today, a former strategic partner is waging a hybrid war against a sovereign state, a co-founder of the United Nations. Mounds of lies and propaganda have been heaped into a wall of hatred, erected between two once friendly nations'.[32] While analysts have yet to agree on a common definition of hybrid warfare, it certainly encompasses Internet-based propaganda, information operations, and computer hacking.

> *To international audiences, Poroshenko has focused primarily on the broader topic of hybrid warfare.*

Looking toward the future, Poroshenko has positioned himself as a 'President of Peace'[33] 'on the forefront of the global fight for democracy'.[34] Russia is the clear antagonist: 'all military threats and challenges are related to Russia,'[35] and Moscow's war 'has brought Ukraine to the brink of its survival'.[36] Poroshenko argues that not just Ukraine, but the whole world needs a resolution to this conflict,[37] and that 'democracies must support each other'.[38] Ultimately, Ukraine's national security goal

---

28 *Ibid.*
29 *Ibid.*
30 'President's statement on ceasefire from February 15,' Office of the President of Ukraine, 15 February 2015, http://www.president.gov.ua/en/news/zayava-prezidenta-pro-pripinennya-vognyu-z-0000-15-lyutogo-34723.
31 'Head of the Security Service of Ukraine reports to the President: Terrorist group coordinated by Russian special forces was neutralized,' Office of the President of Ukraine, 16 August 2014, http://www.president.gov.ua/en/news/zneshkodzheno-teror-istichnu-grupu-yaku-koordinuvali-specsluz-33478.
32 'Speech by President of Ukraine Petro Poroshenko at the Munich Security conference,' Office of the President of Ukraine, 7 February 2015, http://www.president.gov.ua/en/news/vistup-prezidenta-ukrayini-petra-poroshenka-na-myunhenskij-k-34663.
33 Petro Poroshenko. Speech by President of Ukraine Petro Poroshenko at the Munich Security Conference 2015.
34 Petro Poroshenko. 'Address by the President of Ukraine Petro Poroshenko to the Joint Session of the United States Congress,' 18 September 2014, http://www.president.gov.ua/en/news/vistup-prezidenta-ukrayini-petra-poroshenka-na-spilnij-sesiy-33718.
35 'President: New Military Doctrine is based on the duration of threat from Russia and demands full compatibility of the Armed Forces with NATO standards,' Office of the President of Ukraine, 2 September 2015, http://www.president.gov.ua/en/news/nova-voyenna-doktrina-vihodit-z-trivalosti-zagrozi-z-boku-ro-35907.
36 *Ibid.*
37 Petro Poroshenko. President's statement on ceasefire from February 15 2015.
38 Petro Poroshenko. Address by the President of Ukraine Petro Poroshenko to the Joint Session of the United States Congress 2014.

is 'full NATO membership'.[39] The President asserted that 'Ukraine is not a NATO member now. Unfortunately, we are not allies de jure. Yet, de facto we are more than just partners … Ukraine is the eastern outpost of Euro-Atlantic civilisation, which is now defending not only sovereignty, territorial integrity and independence of our country.'[40]

5   THE ROLE OF NON-STATE ACTORS

In the cyber domain, non-state, sometimes anonymous actors can play a significant role in any conflict. During the Ukraine crisis, numerous groups such as Cyber-Berkut have positioned themselves as independent, Internet-based guerrillas, and to some degree they have influenced the course of events. In general, there is too little public information available for analysts to determine if any of these non-state actors has a direct or indirect government connection.

In Ukraine, one of the most prominent non-state cyber leaders is Eugene Dokunin, who describes himself as a 'lone wolf waging a furious battle against the thousands of paid hackers and trolls in Russia'.[41] Whereas governments may not boast about their achievements, rogue actors do. Dokunin's group claims to have blocked more than 170 PayPal and other online accounts belonging to separatists, and frozen almost $3 million of their cash. In one attack, they compromised networked printers in separatist regions, forcing them to spew out documents glorifying Ukraine, as well as the popular chant 'Putin is a dick', which is sung in football stadiums across Ukraine'.[42] Dokunin reserves some of his ire for the sitting government in Kyiv: 'The Ukrainian Government hasn't invested a cent in cyber warfare, even though this is also an information war'.

6   CONCLUSION

Communication analysis reveals that both Putin and Poroshenko have adopted similar rhetorical strategies – 'good vs. evil' and 'us vs. them' – in an effort to rally citizens around the flag. They emphasise the righteous nature of their cause, their leadership in working toward a solution, and other countries' approval of their political stances. This is an exercise in national identity building, while portraying the adversary as illegitimate, dangerous, and even terrorist in nature. To resolve the

---

39   'Speech by President of Ukraine Petro Poroshenko at the session of the National Security and Defense Council of Ukraine with participation of NATO Secretary General Jens Stoltenberg,' Office of the President of Ukraine, 22 September 2015, http://www.president.gov.ua/en/news/vistup-prezidenta-ukrayini-poporoshenka-na-zasidanni-radi-na-36007.

40   Petro Poroshenko. Speech by President of Ukraine Petro Poroshenko at the session of the National Security and Defense Council of Ukraine with participation of NATO Secretary General Jens Stoltenberg, 2015.

41   Vijai Maheshwari. 'Ukraine's Lonely Cyberwarrior vs. Russia,' *The Daily Beast*, 18 February 2015, http://www.thedailybeast.com/articles/2015/02/18/ukraine-s-lonely-cyber-warrior.html.

42   *Ibid.*

> *Russia has focussed on national interests, while Ukraine has appealed to the international community.*

situation, Russia has offered its services as an indispensable negotiator. By contrast, Ukraine has oriented its national strategy to the West and to NATO. Russia has focussed on national interests, while Ukraine has appealed to the international community for understanding and support.

Even while Russia and Ukraine have been engaged in a modern, 'hot' military conflict, its leaders have shed very little light on cyber warfare. Russia has referred to it only in high-level, diplomatic terms. Ukraine, despite the fact that it has suffered numerous cyber attacks, primarily frames the issue within the larger concept of hybrid warfare. Neither country denies that cyberspace is now a theatre of warfare, or that it is part of the Ukrainian conflict, but neither has argued that cyberspace is an integral aspect of it. And for the most part, this echoes the sentiments of other authors and chapters in this volume.

CHAPTER 12

STRATEGIC COMMUNICATIONS AND SOCIAL MEDIA IN THE RUSSIA UKRAINE CONFLICT

ELINA LANGE-IONATAMISHVILI

SANDA SVETOKA

NATO Strategic Communications Centre of Excellence

1 INTRODUCTION

The new information environment has changed the nature of warfare. The events in south-east Ukraine have demonstrated that a conflict can be won without firing a single shot and some of the key battles can take place in the cyber and communications domains rather than on the land, air and sea. As Thomas Elkjer Nissen said in his recent book, the internet, cyberspace, and social media can be used to collect intelligence or even to target people and organisations. Such tactics may be employed in isolation, but they are much more likely to be an integral part of a larger strategy.[1]

> *Key battles can take place in the cyber and communications domains rather than on the land, air and sea.*

The operation for the take-over of Crimea was a particularly bold example of an influence operation where the traditional role of conventional forces was mini-

---

1   Thomas Elkjer Nissen. *#TheWeaponizationOfSocialMedia. @Characteristics_of_ Contemporary_Conflicts*. Copenhagen: Royal Danish Defence College, 2015.

mised. As the conflict continues to develop in the east of Ukraine, Russia continues to exploit the opportunities offered by new technologies and the new information environment. It does so with the purpose of influencing the hearts and minds of its audiences: if Russia succeeds in mobilising its supporters, demonising its enemy, demoralising its enemy's government and armed forces, and legitimising its own actions, then really there is no need for conventional fighting in order to subdue Ukraine.

In the modern-day operations cyberspace plays an increasingly important role. A targeted attack by an adversary in the cyber environment is often understood as an attack on the computerised systems which help us run our daily lives and businesses, sustain critical infrastructure and conduct financial transactions amongst other things. As the former White House advisor Richard Clarke writes, a cyber-attack can mean that these vital systems go down and we see exploding oil refineries, derailing trains, runaway satellites, food shortages, and much more.[2] But what we do not often realise is that we can be attacked in the cyber environment by an adversary presenting manipulative information to us with the intent to affect our perception of the situation and our decision-making, and provoke some resulting action. The real-life consequences of this 'soft' cyber-attack can be as severe as an attack on a critical infrastructure.

2 STRATEGIC COMMUNICATIONS AND CYBERSPACE

Strategic Communications (StratCom) is a mind-set which implies placing communications at the heart of a strategy. It means that our activity is narrative-driven and we communicate it to different audiences through coordinated words, images and deeds. Cyberspace plays an increasingly important role in StratCom as our dependency on modern technologies, computer networks and the internet grows day by day. We use it for receiving and conveying information, for coordinating our actions and also for analysing the environment around us in order to detect and evaluate potential threats.

Cyberspace is often used in a conflict in order to take out the communications systems of an adversary. However, the conflict in Ukraine has demonstrated that cyberspace can also play a role in conducting a narrative-driven operation where the main targets are not the machines or networks but the minds of the people.

The internet and social media, due to their ability to multiply information at high speed and at little cost, are increasingly used for propaganda, information warfare, and influence operations, all of which can tangibly change both the perception and behaviour of the target audience. It is a highly dynamic, user-driven, constantly changing environment where it is easy to get a message to 'go viral', and also difficult

---

2   Richard A. Clarke and Robert Knake. *Cyber War: The Next Threat to National Security and What to Do About It.* New York: HarperCollins, 2011.

to track the initial source of information, verify its authenticity, and separate fact from fiction.

With the increasing popularity of social media platforms, the concept of social cyber attack is gaining traction.[3] It allows for a low-cost, speedy way of manipulating society's perceptions in order to cause disruptive behaviour in real life. The social cyber attacks observed during the crisis in Ukraine led to an assumption that at least part of them were implemented in an organised way, as part of a larger influence strategy.

3   Psychological Operations (PSYOPS) and Social Media

Psychological Operations (PSYOPS) is a military activity which is aimed at influencing the perceptions, attitudes and behaviours of target populations. The perception is usually affected by either emotional appeals or rational arguments, corresponding to the master narrative, and in social media, where one has to compete with a flood of information and large amounts of information noise, elements like surprise, cognitive dissonance, easily recognisable symbols or some eye-catching techniques are used in order to draw the audience into the PSYOPS product.

In PSYOPS the influence over a target group is often achieved by spreading rumours. Those can be:

- Hate rumours: exploit ingrained dislikes and prejudices of a target population.
- Fear rumours: exploit a human tendency to believe the worst.
- Hope rumours: exploit wishes for a favourable turn of events.

Modern technology allows particularly easy exploitation of digital material in order to produce falsified or ambiguous content which can be used for deception and manipulation. Textual messages (posts, status updates, comments) can also be crafted according to the same principles.

Social media provides fruitful soil for PSYOPS as it is largely a trust-based network since it is formed on a networks of friends or like-minded group members. Hence the information coming from an individual or group can be more trusted than that coming from an official mass-media outlet or government communicators. This trust can be manipulated to achieve particular effects. It allows targeting of groups of people connected by certain social ties which increases the chance of the desired effect on perception and behaviour.

It is also very easy to hide the real identity or original source of information on social media as well as manipulate digital data such as imagery. Hence the concept

3   Rebecca Goolsby. *On Cybersecurity, Crowdsourcing and Social Cyber-Attack*. Washington: Wilson Center. U.S. Office of Naval Research, 2013.

of social cyber attack becomes increasingly important as it is based on manipulated information being spread under false identities to networks of users.

4   UNDERSTANDING SOCIAL CYBER ATTACKS

A social cyber attack, as defined by Dr Rebecca Goolsby, involves acting under false pretences or anonymously, by either releasing a manipulated signal into the social media or by manipulating an existing signal in order to achieve the desired effects: chaos, panic, mass disorders. This type of cyber attack offers a different view to the traditional views on attacks in the cyber environment, as the effects of these attacks are purely psychological.

Spreading rumours is one of the most effective tactics of the social cyber attack, as those can create fear, hate or unfounded hope in the target audience which will most likely result in real-life action:

> *Spreading rumours is one of the most effective tactics of social cyber attack.*

for example, mass protests, withdrawing money from banks, or organised attacks on certain groups or individuals whose image has been portrayed as the enemy.[4]

Social cyber attack can also involve traditional hacking if the information to be manipulated and released needs to be obtained or published this way. Since the concept of the social cyber attack is very new, it is often difficult to determine what activity should be classified as one. One might argue that the key component to social cyber attack is the narrative which drives it. The actions by the pro-Russian 'Cyber Berkut' (*КиберБеркут*) and its nemesis, the pro-Ukrainian 'Cyber Hundred' (*Киберсотня*) can serve as examples.

Cyber Berkut is frequently in the news, propagating the Russian political narrative as well as hacking both the Ukrainian Government and other countries. The group successfully attacked and defaced the websites of the North Atlantic Treaty Organisation (NATO) and the NATO Cooperative Cyber Defence Centre of Excellence (NATO CCD COE), claiming that its activities were in retaliation for NATO support for Ukraine.[5] However, the key to Cyber Berkut's activities is the narrative which it uses to justify and promote its activities. Cyber Berkut claimed credit on its social networking site VKontakte page for hacking electronic advertising billboards in the centre of Kyiv prior to a Ukrainian parliamentary election on 24 October 2014, displaying videos of numerous prominent Ukrainian politicians and labelling them war criminals:[2]

> *[English translation] 'We Cyber Berkut intend to use every opportunity to defend the interests of Ukrainian citizens from the arbitrariness of nationalist*

---

4   *Ibid.*
5   The post and video can be found here: http://vk.com/wall-67432779_14678

fringe and the oligarchic elite …Today, we have used a few dozen billboards in Kyiv, Ukraine to remind people about the futility of farcical elections …We reiterate once again that no one will change our lives for us. If the people will continue to hope that the authorities in the offices there are people concerned about the problems of ordinary citizens, Ukraine will be more immersed in the chaos of civil war. The United States and the West first brought into the government people who are ready to sell our country to please their owners, and now want to put the same traitors in Parliament. Today, everyone has to realise that his decision depends the future of our country, and the sooner we crack down on neo-Nazi government and deputies, who are just cashing in on this war, the sooner the country's peace and order.'

This narrative was also spread on social media networks. Analysing this statement, one can identify clear attempts to construe enemy images of the Ukrainian Government and induce fear in the population by calling it neo-Nazi and threatening chaos and civil war. The hacking of the billboards had no other meaning than to conduct a social cyber attack by propagating this narrative and spreading rumours through manipulated information.

5   Social Media in the Russian-Ukrainian Conflict

During the war in Ukraine, social media has become home to intense conflict-related information updates, impassioned arguments, and debate.[6] The social media space has been abused, and pro-Russian forces have given the world a masterclass.

At the beginning of the conflict, we saw strategic communications in action. Over Twitter and YouTube, unknown attackers released an intercepted phone conversation between the U.S. Assistant Secretary of State Victoria Nuland and Geoffrey Pyatt, the U.S. Ambassador to Ukraine.[7] In one stroke, the perpetrators sought to discredit Western policy and to announce their access to Western lines of government communication. Thus we saw both a technical exploit on an information system and a psychological attack on the West via social media.

During the course of the conflict, Russia's narrative has been tightly scripted and disseminated, both on traditional media (in 'breaking' and 'eyewitness' accounts on television) and in cyberspace via social media. These venues are mutually reinforcing, encompassing older and younger readers with varying degrees of access to technology. For example, one can no longer watch Ukrainian television in eastern Ukraine; similarly, Russian television channels are no longer available in western Ukraine.

---

6   See, for example, Irina Anilovskaja. *Война: переписка одноклассников*, Alfra Reklama, 2014.
7   Anne Gearan. 'In recording of U.S. diplomat, blunt talk on Ukraine' *Washington Post*, 6 February 2014, https://www.washingtonpost.com/world/national-security/in-purported-recording-of-us-diplomat-blunt-talk-on-ukraine/2014/02/06/518240a4-8f4b-11e3-84e1-27626c5ef5fb_story.html.

On social media, pro-Russian voices have systemically cultivated fear, anxiety, and hate among the ethnically Russian (and other non-Ukrainian populations) of Ukraine. They have manipulated and distributed images of purported atrocities by the Ukrainian army, including: mass graves of tortured people, civilians used for organ trafficking, burning crops to create a famine, recruiting child soldiers, the use of heavy weapons against civilians, and acts of cannibalism.[8]

Via social media, such information – whether offered with some evidence or merely in the form of rumours – often criss-crosses the globe in minutes, and a well-organised social media campaign can easily influence a target population's perceptions and behaviours.

The Latvian media company LETA conducted an analysis of Twitter posts during the first six months of 2014, and identified an increasing polarisation between pro-Russian and pro-Ukrainian social media users as the conflict escalated, especially following the violence in Odessa.[9] The researchers wrote that 12.2% of all tweets related to the conflict in eastern Ukraine were 'aggressive', dominated by pro-Russian stances, most intense relative to human casualties, and included epithets such as 'fascist' and 'ruscist'.[10]

Numerous social media postings appear to be disseminated in order to manipulate people in eastern Ukraine.

The conflict in Ukraine has seen numerous social media postings that appear to be deliberately disseminated in order to manipulate people in eastern Ukraine and beyond. During the May 2014 violence in Odessa, someone posted the following to Facebook:

[English translation] 'Hello. My name is Igor Rosovskiy. I am 39 years old. I live in the city of Odessa. I have worked as an emergency physician for 15 years. Yesterday, as you know, there was a terrible tragedy in our city, some people killed other people. They killed them in a brutal way by burning them alive, not in a drunken stupor, not to get their grandmother's inheritance, but because they share the political views of nationalists. First they brutally beat their victims, then burned them alive. As a doctor, I rushed to help those whom I could save, but the fighters stopped me. They didn't let me go to the wounded. One rudely pushed me, promising that I and other Jews would suffer a similar fate. I saw a young man I could have saved if I could have taken him to the hospital, but my attempts at persuasion were met with a blow to the face and lost glasses. In fifteen years I have seen much, but yesterday I wanted to cry, not from the blows and humiliation,

8   More information about the false information related to Russian – Ukrainian can be found at *StopFake.org*, 21 August 2014, http://www.stopfake.org/en/russia-s-top-100-lies-about-ukraine/

9   G.C. 'Ukraine's murky inferno: Odessa's fire examined.' *The Economist Eastern Approaches blog.* 8 May 2014, http://www.economist.com/blogs/easternapproaches/2014/05/odessas-fire-examined.

10 '*Ruscist*' is an invented word with offensive meaning, a combination of the words 'Russian' and 'fascist'.

but from my helplessness in being unable to do anything. In my city, such things did not happen even during the worst times of Nazi occupation. I wonder why the world is silent.'

The Russian-language social networking website *Vkontakte* saw more than 5,000 shares of this post within 24 hours, and it was quickly translated into English, German, and Bulgarian. However, analysts subsequently discovered that Dr. Rozovskiy's profile picture was actually that of a dentist from the North Caucasus, and now believe this social media post to be a hoax.[11]

On 4 June 2014, Pavel Astakhov, the Children's Ombudsman under the President of the Russian Federation, announced on his Instagram account that 'more than 7,000' Ukrainian refugees had fled Ukraine and arrived in the Rostov Oblast in the previous 24 hours. The next day, that number had risen to 8,386. Russian mass media reported these numbers, but Rostov authorities apparently contradicted them, where the Governor's office reported that the number of refugees did not exceed 712.[12]

In July 2014, 3-year-old boy was allegedly tortured and crucified by the Ukrainian military in a public square in Slovyansk, Ukraine. The Russian state-run TV *Channel One* broadcast the 'eyewitness' testimony of Galina Pyshnyak, who stated that she and others were forcibly brought to the central square to witness the public execution. The interview took place at a refugee camp in Russia's Rostov region and was widely disseminated on social media.[13] However, Russian journalist Yevgeny Feldman of *Novaya Gazeta*, as well as journalists from Russia's independent channel *Dozhd*, challenged the report with contradictory testimonies from multiple interviews in Slovyank, in which numerous residents denied any knowledge of the incident.[14]

Throughout 2014, the list of rumours from eastern Ukraine grew to be quite long: the Kyiv government and European Union were building concentration camps; the forest was full of right-wing killers; the May 9 Victory Day holiday had been cancelled;[15] property would be confiscated; and use of the Russian language was prohibited. On one occasion, terrified locals called the Donbas Water Company after social media informed them that the region's water supply had been poisoned.[16]

These stories can be contrasted with the 'Polite People' campaign on *Vkontakte*, which supported the Russian invasion of Crimea with pictures of Russian troops posing alongside girls, mothers with children, the elderly, and pets.[17]

---

11   'Odesa Doctor Or Random Dentist? Claims Of Atrocities, Anti-Semitism Face Scrutiny,' *Radio Free Europe/Radio Liberty*, 27 June 2015, http://www.rferl.org/content/ukraine-unspun-odesa-doctor-dentist-false-claim/25372684.html.

12   'Rostov officials refuted information about thousands of Ukrainian refugees,' *StopFake.org*, 6 June 2014, http://www.stopfake.org/en/rostov-officials-refuted-information-about-thousands-of-ukrainian-refugees/.

13   'Беженка из Славянска вспоминает, как при ней казнили маленького сына и жену ополченца,' Первый канал, 12 July 2014, http://www.1tv.ru/news/world/262978.

14   Евгений Фельдман, Жители Славянска – о том, был ли распятый мальчик Первого канала на самом деле (w/eng subs), 13 July 2014, https://www.youtube.com/watch?v=UA1LE6iKMfk.

15   Lily Hyde, 'Rumors and disinformation push Donetsk residents into wartime siege mentality,' *Kyiv Post*, 3 May 2014, http://www.kyivpost.com/content/ukraine-abroad/rumors-and-disinformation-push-donetsk-residents-into-wartime-siege-mentality-346131.html.

16   *Ibid.*

17   NATO Strategic Communications Centre of Excellence. *Analysis of Russia's Information Campaign against Ukraine*, 2014.

6   Troll Farming

Who tweets in support of politics? Who posts Facebook updates in support of military operations? Of course, there are millions of true believers in the world, adherents to every cause under the sun. However, it is also possible to fabricate support for anything, especially in cyberspace. The social media offers great opportunities for state and non-state actors to use fake identities or automatically generated accounts to disseminate their narrative to audiences as widely as possible.

On 24 May 2014, hacked and leaked email correspondence (revealed on b0ltai.org) allegedly from a company called the 'Internet Research Agency' in St. Petersburg, Russia, offered evidence of the existence of a professional 'troll farm', including the firm's relationship to the Russian Government. Media reports suggested that recruitment of employees had occurred prior to the onset of military operations, and that workers were tasked with writing 100 internet posts per day.[18]

For strategic communications, these developments are critical to understanding modern information operations including disinformation and PSYOPS, as a well-orchestrated social media campaign could significantly affect the prevailing political narrative.

It is possible to analyse the social media domain in an effort to separate fact from fiction, to investigate when accounts were created, whether they have credible content or a real networks of real friends, but to do this accurately and in a timely manner is an extraordinary challenge for anyone, including law enforcement and counterintelligence organisations.[19]

7   Conclusion

The suspicious and seemingly targeted use of social media in the Russian-Ukrainian conflict offers considerable evidence that social media is being extensively used to support military actions on the ground. To some degree, the information operations have generated fear, uncertainty, and doubt about the economic, cultural, and national security of Ukraine, especially in the eastern provinces where there are strong historical ties to Russia.

Social media is extensively used to support military actions on the ground.

The goal of these social media operations may be to convince Ukrainians that the *Euromaidan* movement has led only to political chaos in the country, and has not been in Ukraine's best long-term interests. This message can be contrasted with

---

18   Александра Гармажапова, 'Где живут тролли. И кто их кормит', *Novaya Gazeta*, September 9, 2013, http://www.novayag-azeta.ru/politics/59889.html.

19   Kenneth Geers and Roelof Temmingh. 'Virtual Plots, Real Revolution,' *The Virtual Battlefield: Perspectives on Cyber Warfare*, ed. Kenneth Geers and Christian Czosseck, 294-302 (Tallinn: NATO CCD COE, 2009).

some examples of social media commentary from Crimea: that its incorporation into Russia has led to safety and stability on the Crimean peninsula.

The use of cyberspace both to attack the infrastructure and to influence 'people's hearts and minds' is a new phenomenon that has been increasingly used in recent conflicts to support military operations on the ground. This kind of warfare will not disappear; on the contrary the combination of actions which are targeted at infrastructure and human psychology will be used in more sophisticated and unpredictable ways in the future. A three step approach could be recommended for security experts and national decision makers to prepare better to meet these kind of challenges:

> **Identify**. Governments and defence organisations should enhance their capabilities to identify the detrimental use of social media. Information campaigns which entail propaganda and automated or fake accounts to rapidly disseminate information should be closely monitored and analysed. This also includes additional efforts in order to understand how these campaigns are organised and what effects they can have on public perception.

> **Challenge**. Examples by citizen journalists have shown that revealing false facts to the public is an effective approach in mitigating the effects of disinformation. At the same time it is important not to engage in counter-propaganda as this fuels the information war and creates public distrust rather than diminishing the power of misinformation. Humour perhaps could be more helpful in countering aggressive propaganda as it hampers the ability to achieve its aim – subduing the society of the target country. The initiatives in Twitter like @DarthPutinKGB or @Sputnik_Intl are good examples of how to challenge Russia's disinformation campaign with irony and jokes.

> **Learn and prepare**. The development of the unifying strategic narrative – the story which entails the set of the values and beliefs of your country or organisation – is the best defence against propaganda which questions them. A long-term educational effort to enhance critical thinking and media (including social media) literacy would also contribute greatly to society's self-defence against manipulation.

CHAPTER 13

UKRAINE: A CYBER SAFE HAVEN?

NADIYA KOSTYUK

University of Michigan

1   INTRODUCTION

Since the end of the Cold War, there has been a proliferation in online criminal activity in Eastern Europe, and Ukraine is no exception. Famous for its hacker community, Ukraine ranks among the Top 10 countries in the world in cyber crime[1] and number 15 as a source of Distributed Denial of Service (DDoS) attacks.[2] In 2012, five Ukrainian nationals stole more than $72 million from U.S. bank accounts;[3] in 2013, Ukrainian hackers stole 40 million sets of debit and credit card details from the US retail chain Target;[4] in 2014, the RAND Corporation wrote that Russian and Ukrainian (the primary language of Ukraine) were the lingua franca of online hacker forums.[5] In this light, it is natural to wonder if Ukraine is today a safe haven for cyber criminals.

To be sure, there have been some law enforcement successes, such as when numerous European countries and Europol (with the aid of the Ukrainian government) arrested five hackers who stole at least €2 million from banks all around the world.[6] However, there are major countervailing factors at play in Ukraine, which include ongoing political, military, and economic crises and the absence of *zhyvoii*

1   Victor Zhora, e-mail to the author, July 30, 2015.
2   'Украина вошла в рейтинг стран с наибольшим количеством DDoS-атак.' Minfin, June 8, 2015.http://minfin.com.ua/2015/06/08/7407564/.
3   Taylor Armerding. 'Ukraine Seen as a Growing 'haven for Hackers' March 13, 2012. http://www.csoonline.com/article/2131155/network-security/ukraine-seen-as-a-growing--haven-for-hackers-.html.
4   Charles Riley and Jose Pagliery. 'Target Will Pay Hack Victims $10 Million.' CNNMoney. March 19, 2015. http://money.cnn.com/2015/03/19/technology/target-data-hack-settlement/.
5   Lillian Ablon, Martin C. Libicki, and Andrea A. Golay. Markets for Cybercrime Tools and Stolen Data: Hackers' Bazaar. Rand Corporation, 2014.
6   Supra, note 4.

potreby (urgent need),[7] which together provide little hope that Ukraine will be able to climb down from its perch atop the world's cyber crime ladder in the near future.

In many ways, Ukraine is a perfect case study to examine the vexing dynamics of cyber crime. Its government has few cyber security regulations, its society is home to talented computer programmers, and its economy is struggling. This chapter begins with a brief description of Ukraine's current cyber crisis, to include the primary reasons why cyber crime flourishes there. Next, it discusses the future of the region based on interviews with Ukrainian and Western cybersecurity experts from public and private sectors and academia. Finally, the chapter ends with recommendations based on best practices in cyber security – all of which can help Kyiv to improve its cyber security posture. Beyond Ukraine, these insights can be applied to numerous other countries in the region.

> *In many ways, Ukraine is a perfect case study to examine the vexing dynamics of cyber crime.*

2   Ukraine as a Cyber Safe Haven

Once the internet conquered post-Soviet daily life, many talented computer programmers who had already dabbled in illegal activities such as stealing music and movies realised that they could make a living as professional hackers. There were few cyber security regulations in Ukraine and so, as in so many other countries, cyber crime quickly evolved from a mischievous hobby to a lucrative occupation.[8]

Several factors contributed to making Ukraine a cyber safe haven. First, its Soviet school STEM (science, technology, engineering, and mathematics) education is among the best in the world. Second, its underwhelming economic performance since independence in 1991 has led these STEM specialists to explore alternative career paths, often online. Third, Ukraine's social and cultural norms dictate that stealing from the West is not always a bad thing. This factor is compounded by the relatively impersonal nature of cyberspace.[9]

At the policy level, 'cyber crimes' such as stealing intellectual property and copyright infringement were not even considered illegal in Ukraine until recently. For instance, the popular Russian social media website *vkontakte.ru* used to be a source of large-scale music and movie piracy.[10] Ukraine recently has begun to develop a common lexicon on cyber security (a pre-requisite for progress in this

---

7   Vlad Styran, Skype interview, July 6, 2015.
8   Supra, note 5.
9   The author can testify through personal experience.
10   Kathryn Dowling. 'VKontakte Case Puts Russian Music Piracy into Spotlight.' August 11, 2014. http://www.bbc.com/news/business-28739602.

new domain),[11] but the multiple cyber units within the Ukrainian government[12] still tend to operate independently, and rarely collaborate.[13] Moreover, as in other Eastern European countries, government employees are poorly paid and lack resources, which in turn motivates skilled specialists to leave for the private sector. Finally, due to the high level of corruption in Ukraine, even when a cyber criminal is caught, he or she can usually bribe an official to have the charges reduced or dropped.[14]

3   Ukraine as a Cyber Target

Even though Ukraine is not a rich country and is relatively new to online banking, its enterprises nonetheless lost ₴65 million[15] to cybercrime in 2014.[16] The origin of these attacks is unclear, but numerous interviewees agreed that the cyber criminals were not physically located in Ukraine. Most likely, they would follow the hacker's first 'zapovid' ('commandment'), the so-called 'gypsy' rule: 'tam de zhyvesh, tam ne kradesh' ('you do not steal in the place where you live').[17] When asked whether Russia could be a source of such attacks, Vlad Styran, an information security consultant at Berezha Security, answered affirmatively, but explained that some groups originally operating from Russia have moved to Ukraine, mostly to the self-proclaimed Donetsk National Republic (DNR) and the Luhansk National Republic (LNR).[18] However, these groups may not be attacking Ukraine directly, but Western countries farther afield, similar to online criminals in Romania, Turkey, and Belarus.[19] In Ukraine, the domestic climate, technical capabilities, and resources are better suited to criminals who engage in credit card fraud,[20] and as long as they steal money in small amounts, no one will touch them.[21] Cyber criminals physically based in Ukraine have also begun to look for more comfortable conditions in which to operate, as Ukrainian law enforcement agencies have begun to collaborate with Western agencies.[22] Thus the number of cyber criminals in Ukraine may finally be declining.[23]

The conflict in eastern Ukraine has given rise to numerous high-level cyber attacks. As part of its military operations, Russia has used cyber warfare tactics against Ukrainian websites, some of which are physically hosted in Ukraine, while some are

---

11 Oleksandr V. Potii, Oleksandr V. Korneyko, and Yurii I. Gorbenko. 'Cybersecurity in Ukraine: Problems and Perspectives.' *Information and Security: An International Journal* 32 (2015): 2.

12 More detailed description will be provided later

13 Kostiantyn Kosrun, Skype Interview, July 6, 2015.

14 Glib Pakharenko, Interview, June 29, 2015.

15 ₴ – Hryvnia – Ukrainian unit of currency.

16 As mentioned by Guzii who works at the MVD department that deals with card (credit and debit) fraud operations.

17 Supra, note 14; supra, note 7.

18 The interviewee referred to the fact that it became quite hard for hackers to operate in Russia without being under constant government control.

19 Supra, note 7.

20 Glib Pakharenko, e-mail to the author, July 5, 2015.

21 *Ibid.*

22 *Ibid.*

23 *Ibid.*

not.[24] National Security Agency (NSA) Director Vice Admiral Michael Rogers stated that Russia conducted cyber operations to support its Crimea conquest.[25] Independent researchers also discovered a cyber espionage operation called Armageddon that was designed to provide a 'military advantage to Russian leadership by targeting Ukrainian government and law enforcement agencies,'[26] and included DDoS attacks against Ukrainian and NATO media outlets, and targeted attacks against Ukrainian election commission websites.[27] In all, hackers hit Ukrainian government, business, online media, and e-commerce sites.[28] Finally, it should be noted in this context that Ukraine's information and telecommunication networks generally use Russian hardware and software, a situation that would significantly help Russia to spy on its southern neighbour.[29]

4 UKRAINE'S CYBER SECURITY AGENDA

While cyber crime has flourished in Ukraine, the same cannot be said for the development of Kyiv's cyber security policy, which is simply not currently a high priority. In Ukraine, only 41.8% of the population is now online, compared to 84.2% in the United States and 61.4% in Russia.[30] Furthermore, the majority of Ukrainian internet connectivity lies in the country's major cities and very few electronic devices are used for online financial transactions.

> *While cyber crime has flourished in Ukraine, the same cannot be said for the development of Kyiv's cyber security policy.*

Currently, there is little cyber security legislation in Ukraine. The more prominent laws include 'On Information,' 'On State Secrets,' 'On Data Protection in Information and Telecommunication Systems,' 'On the National Security of Ukraine,' and 'On State Service for Special Communication and Information Protection of Ukraine.' In 2012, Parliament began to propose amendments to these laws. Today, there is an increasing focus on cyber crime awareness, and the government is in the process of creating a new ministry devoted to information technology (IT).

---

24   Sam Jones. 'Ukraine PM's Office Hit by Cyber Attack Linked to Russia.' *Financial Times*, August 7, 2014. http://www.ft.com/intl/cms/s/0/2352681e-1e55-11e4-9513-00144feabdc0.html.

25   Bill Gertz. 'Inside the Ring: Cybercom's Michael Rogers Confirms Russia Conducted Cyberattacks against Ukraine.' *Washington Times*, March 12, 2014. http://www.washingtontimes.com/news/2014/mar/12/inside-the-ring-cybercoms-michael-rogers-confirms-/?page=all.

26   'LookingGlass Cyber Threat Intelligence Group Links Russia to Cyber Espionage Campaign Targeting Ukrainian Government and Military Officials.' *Looking Glass*, April 29, 2015.

27   Tony Martin-Vegue. 'Are We Witnessing a Cyber War between Russia and Ukraine? Don't Blink – You Might Miss It.' CSO Online, April 24, 2015. http://www.csoonline.com/article/2913743/cyber-attacks-espionage/are-we-witnessing-a-cyber-war-between-russia-and-ukraine-dont-blink-you-might-miss-it.html.

28   Primarily with DDoS attacks from supra, note 11.

29   For example, via Russia's Система Оперативно-Розыскных Мероприятий, or 'System for Operative Investigative Activities', a technical system run by the Russian security services to search and surveil telephone and Internet communications. Supra, note 11, page 2; Andrei Soldatov, Skype interview, July 15, 2015.

30   'Online Panel Ukraine and Online Data Collection Ukraine | DataDiggers Online Data Collection.' DataDiggers Online Data Collection. July 27, 2015. http://www.datadiggers.ro/?page_id=75217.

Victor Zhora, CEO and Co-Founder at Infosafe IT LLC, contends that a major problem with existing Ukrainian legislation is the lack of a clear definition for cyber crime. The only operational definition is in Article 361 of the Criminal Codex of Ukraine: 'Illegal interference with the operation of computers (PCs), automated systems, computer networks or telecommunications networks'.[31] However, it is not clear what 'illegal interference' actually means.

Recently, lawmakers have considered new legislation – the 'Cybersecurity Law of Ukraine' – which seeks to: update existing laws; create conditions for cooperation between the private and publics sectors; protect critical information infrastructure; develop a comprehensive legal framework; build a secure national security network; educate future specialists; fight cyber crime and cyber terrorism; strengthen the state's defence in cyberspace; prevent other states from interfering in Ukraine's internal affairs; neutralise attacks on Ukraine's information resources; and ensure Ukraine's full participation in European and regional cybersecurity organisations.[32] However, such a comprehensive agenda faces numerous acute challenges before it can be properly implemented.[33]

For example, 'the strategy of creating a secure national segment of cyberspace' lacks a working definition of critical national infrastructure (CNI), as well as a valid list of CNI. At this stage in Ukraine's economic development, there is little CNI with internet-based management, but that number is beginning to rise.[34] Another example is 'ensuring full participation of Ukraine in European and regional systems'. Although Ukrainian cyber security experts already share information and intelligence with Western colleagues, this collaboration is not nearly as effective as it could be, because the West does not yet 'respect [them] and do not share information with [them].'[35]

For the foreseeable future, Ukrainian CNI will rely on reasonably sound private sector approaches.

It is debatable, given the ongoing war in eastern Ukraine, how urgent this process is, especially given that all countries are currently struggling to protect CNI. Even if adopted, the draft Cybersecurity Law of Ukraine will take years to fully implement.[36] Therefore, for the foreseeable future, Ukrainian CNI such as telecoms,[37] banks,[38] and insurance companies[39] will rely on reasonably sound private sector approaches to their cyber security challenges.[40]

---

31 'Несанкціоноване втручання в роботу електронно-обчислювальних машин (комп'ютерів), автоматизованих систем, комп'ютерних мереж чи мереж електрозв'явку; supra, note 1.

32 Supra, note 11, figure 1-1.

33 Some of those challenges were mentioned earlier.

34 Ukraine's CNI objects are not controlled via the Internet, as mentioned in the skype interview with Vlad Styran on July 6, 2015 (Supra, note 7).

35 Supra, note 14.

36 Its implementation has three stages: 1) 2014-2016; 2) 2016-2017; and 3) 2017 – the following years.

37 Telecom operators are mostly protected as a huge portion of the population uses these services. They do no necessarily suffer from cyber attacks but they suffer from their clients' abuse of the system. From supra, note 7.

38 Banks are in second place in terms of protection and in first place in terms of damage.. It is quite a new trend in Ukraine as banks mostly operate using their clients' money. Last year, we witnessed the first cyber attacks on Ukrainian banks. From supra, note 7.

39 Insurance companies take the third place on the level of protection. They are active in protecting their companies from cyber attacks not because they are subjects to those attacks, but mostly because they are part of some international group, which requires them to follow the EU or U.S. requirements or because they need to create their image. Supra, note 7.

40 *Ibid.*

Figure 1-1 – Organisation of the cyber security system of Ukraine

5   CYBERSECURITY ORGANISATIONS

Figure 1-1 depicts Ukraine's governmental organisations that deal with cyber crime: the Security Service of Ukraine (SBU); the State Service of Special Communication and Information Protection of Ukraine (SSSCIP); the Ministry of International Affairs of Ukraine (MVS) with its Department on Combating Cybercrimes; the Ministry of Defence of Ukraine (MO) with its Electronic Warfare Troops; the Defence Intelligence Service; and the Foreign Intelligence Service.[41] These agencies, of course, have different domains and priorities, and they rarely collaborate on common problems.[42] For example, MVD cyber units have a difficult time working with the SBU, which does not focus on external affairs, a crucial element in locating international hackers.[43] Glib Pakharenko, the ISACA Kyiv Chapter membership director, said: 'When NATO meets with various cyber forces in Ukraine, they only observe how these forces fight with each other and blame each other for failures.'[44]

SSSCIP is the only organisation that works exclusively on cyber security issues. Its main activities include: 'interaction with the administration domain UA.; protection of state information resources; interaction with state authorities; international cooperation in the protection of information resources; unified antivirus protection system; and determining the level of protection of information and telecommunication authorities' systems.'[45] SSSCIP has numerous internal offices, including the Centre for Antivirus Information Protection (CAIP),[46] the Assessment of Protection of State Information Resources, the Cybernetic Protection System, and the Registry

---

41   Supra, note 11.
42   Supra, note 7.
43   *Ibid.*
44   Supra, note 7.
45   Supra, note 39.
46   Supra, note 11.

of Information and Telecommunication Authorities' Systems. Its Computer Emergency Response Team of Ukraine (CERT-UA) handles international cooperation.

Each agency faces its own unique challenges and suffers from its own, unique criticism. For example, one interviewee said of CERT-UA: '[its specialists] just visit Europe and tell [the Europeans] how amazing they are. They [only] do PR and make contacts in Ukraine and abroad.'[47] Others, however, disagreed, arguing that in 2013 CERT-UA processed 232 incident reports from foreign CERTs[48] and was 'quite effective' despite 'significantly limited powers', a lack of qualified specialists, insufficient resources, and a low level of outside trust.[49] Two interviewees, Kostiantyn Korsun of Berezha Security and Glib Pakharenko of ISACA Kyiv, added that CERT-UA's bigger problem is the country's almost exclusive current focus on fighting Russian aggression in eastern Ukraine.[50]

> *CERT-UA's bigger problem is the country's almost exclusive focus on fighting Russian aggression in eastern Ukraine.*

At the MVD, Vasyl Guzii, a specialist in *kartkove shakhraistvo* (credit card fraud operations)⋅ asserted that no '*sdelka iz pravosudiiem*' ('deal with law enforcement agencies' in Russian) exists in Ukraine.[51] However, Styran was not so sure, suggesting that '*verbyvannia*' ('recruitment') was common.[52] In effect, this means that instead of arresting hackers, law enforcement agencies simply offer *krysha* (protection)[53] in exchange for future favours.[54] The overall level of corruption in Ukraine is high, even at the SBU.[55]

Despite everything, there is progress to report. Beyond the new draft law on cyber security and the proposed new IT ministry[56] Ukraine is setting up an Interagency Board[57] to counter strategic cyber threats (see Figure 1-2). This initiative will of course take time to blossom, and there are already doubts about technical talent, bureaucratic implementation, and overall SBU power in this new initiative.[58] So, for the time being, it is likely that the Ukrainian government will continue to rely on an approach favoured in the United Kingdom: *pereklastu* or delegating many cyber crime-related tasks, including client protection, to the private sector.[59]

---

47 Supra, note 7.
48 Supra note, 11.
49 "незважаючи на суттєве обмеження повноважень в сфері розслідування комп'ютерних злочинів (це не належить до їхньої компетенції), відсутність достатньої кількості кваліфікованих фахівців, недостатні матеріальну базу та рівень фінансового забезпечення, низький рівень довіри з боку як бізнес-структур, так навіть і органів державної влади." Supra, note 1.
50 However, Korsun pointed out that nearly all countries – especially in Eastern Europe – face the same challenges of low salaries and poor skillsets. He added that the SBU, in this regard, is not so different to CERT-UA. Supra, note 13.
51 Vlad Styran. 'Securit13 Podcast : Эпизод 30: Let the Magic Begin.' March 20, 2015. http://securit13.libsyn.com/-30-let-the-magic-begin.
52 Supra, note 7.
53 'Roofing' means that the law enforcement agencies do not pay attention to criminal's misbehavior in exchange for favors.
54 Supra, note 14.
55 *Ibid.*
56 Ol'ha Karpenko. 'В Украине создадут министерство IT.' *AIN*, June 18, 2015. http://ain.ua/2015/06/18/586897.
57 Supra, note 11.
58 Филипповский, Игорь. ЛІГАБізнесІнформ, June 25, 2015. http://biz.liga.net/all/it/stati/3046442-deputaty-doshli-do-interneta-est-zakonoproekt-o-kibeprostranstve.htm.
59 Supra, note 7.

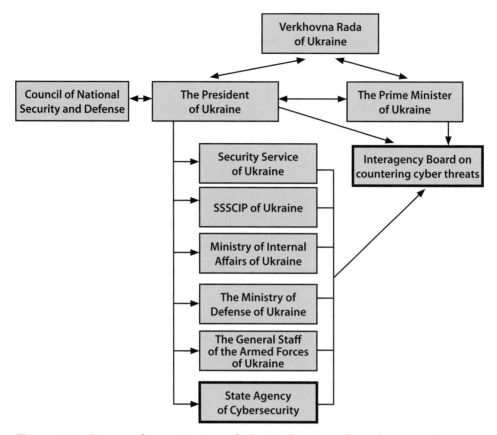

Figure 1-2 – Proposed organisation of Ukraine's system for cyber security

6 RECOMMENDATIONS

The following 'best practices' could significantly strengthen Ukraine's cyber security posture for the future.

6.1 National

- <u>Metrics</u>. Analysts believe that cyber crime is rife in Ukraine, but there are no accurate measurements or reliable studies that have documented this problem. Some Western[60] and Ukrainian companies[61] are now addressing this issue, but without better data and analysis, it is hard to separate fact from fiction.
- <u>Prevention</u>. Until Ukraine invests more in proactive cyber defence, it will remain in a reactive mode *vis-à-vis* cyber criminals, a serious problem in the age of light-speed communications.

---

60   Such as RAND.
61   Supra, note 14.

- Corruption. Ukraine must address bribes, protection,[62] and the unethical recruitment of hackers. In one infamous case, a fraudulent cyber crime 'call centre', which in fact was used to steal credit card information, actually operated from a Ukrainian prison.[63]
- Culture. Ukraine must promote cyber crime awareness and enforce existing law. Ukrainian citizens must recognise that stealing money from the West is against the law, and they must be willing to report such crimes to law enforcement.[64]
- Education. Kyiv must invest in the academic side of cyber security, to include software engineering, critical infrastructure protection, and more.[65] Some steps have already been taken, including the creation of *kiberpolitseiski* (cyber police) departments at the Kyiv and Kharkiv MVD Institutes;[66] further, the MVD has collaborated with various departments of the Kyiv Polytechnic Institute (KPI). The Science Park of the KPI promotes science-intensive products on domestic and foreign markets that provide better cybersecurity solutions. [67,68]
- Civil Society. The Ukrainian Government requires pressure from below to assist in the implementation of so many needed changes. Even from abroad, the Ukrainian diaspora can help.
- Oversight. Ukrainian lawmakers often receive foreign assistance to help the country adopt and implement reform, but currently there is no effective oversight body helping to manage this process.[69]
- Public sector labour force. The Ukrainian government must find a way to hire qualified cyber security professionals and retain them with quality training and attractive salaries. It must be said that this challenge is not unique to Ukraine.[70]

6.2 Regional and International
- Collaboration. Ukrainian cyber security institutions must develop a higher level of trust with their international counterparts, especially in the West. This begins with practical cooperation on current high-interest criminal cases, to include resource and information sharing. In the past, such collaboration has not always been effective, and sometimes never occurred at all.[71] Points of departure include Mutual Legal Assis-

---

62 *Ibid.*
63 Supra, note 7.
64 These two measures will be discussed later.
65 So far, eighteen universities carry out training specialists in information security on bachelor's and master's levels in Ukraine. From: Standards of higher education 1701 'Information Security', accessed on July 21, 2015, http://iszzi.kpi.ua/index.php/ua/biblioteka/normativno-pravova-baza/nmk-informatsijna-bezpeka.html .
66 Supra, note 50.
67 *Ibid.*
68 'Science Park 'Kyivska Polytechnika'.' Accessed September 1, 2015.
69 Supra, note 7.
70 Supra, note 14.
71 *Ibid.*

tance Treaties (MLAT) and the European Convention on Cybercrime which Ukraine ratified in 2005.

- Western Assistance. Most of the digital equipment in Ukraine was manufactured in Russia, so there is an urgent need for EU and NATO nations to assist Ukraine in replacing it. Some concrete steps have already been taken: NATO has allocated funds for Ukraine's 'cyber defences, command and control structures, and logistics capabilities';[72] Microsoft announced a partnership with the Ukrainian Government on cyber security;[73] U.S. Senators Mark Kirk and Mark Warner announced a 'bipartisan amendment creating a law enforcement partnership between the United States and Ukraine to combat cybercrime and improve cybersecurity';[74] and Romania launched an initiative to support the Ukraine Cyber Defence Trust Fund.[75]
- Cyber security strategy. Ukraine must harmonise its cyber security policies and legislation with those of the most technologically advanced members of the international community. The European Network and Information Security Agency (ENISA) has a strong record of providing guidance in cyber security policy development and best practices; Ukraine should take full advantage of this resource.

7 Conclusion

Ukraine, with its talented hackers and minimal cyber security regulations, is a perfect case study to examine the many challenges that Eastern European countries face as they seek to improve their cyber security posture. Ukraine has more than enough STEM expertise, but it must be refocused and repurposed toward a more transparent and accountable legal and cultural online environment. The development of Ukrainian civil society can accomplish all of these objectives, but the international community – including the Ukrainian diaspora – can help Kyiv to realise them much more quickly. Unfortunately, however, Ukraine's current political, economic, and military crises are likely to prevent it from climbing down the world's cyber crime ladder in the near term.

> *Ukraine has more than enough STEM expertise, but it must be refocused and repurposed.*

---

72 Andrew Rettman. 'Mr. Putin Isn't Done in East Ukraine.' *EUObserver*, June 26, 2015. https://euobserver.com/defence/129317.

73 'Ukrainian Government Partners with Microsoft on Cyber Security.' *Ukrainian Digital News*, April 7, 2015. http://uadn.net/2015/04/07/ukrainian-government-partners-with-microsoft-on-cyber-security/.

74 'Kirk, Warner to Introduce Cybersecurity Amendment to Ukrainian Aid Bill on Monday.' *Kirk Senate*. March 23, 2014. http://www.kirk.senate.gov/?p=press_release&id=1033.

75 'Romania Turns Hacking Crisis into Advantage, Helping Ukraine Fight Russian Cyber Espionage.' *Azerbaijan State News Agency*, May 18, 2015. http://azertag.az/en/xeber/Romania_turns_hacking_crisis_into_advantage_helping_Ukraine_fight_Russian_cyber_espionage-855844.

CHAPTER 14

A Legal Framework for Cyber Operations in Ukraine

Jan Stinissen
NATO CCD COE

1   Introduction

Do the cyber attacks that we have seen during the Ukraine conflict constitute cyberwar? This chapter considers this question from a legal perspective. The term 'cyberwar' has no precise legal meaning. Even the term 'war' is less important than it used to be. Contemporary international law distinguishes 'armed conflict', 'armed attack', and 'use of force', but the question is how to place cyber conflict into that framework. In Ukraine, are we seeing 'cyber armed conflict' or merely cyber crime?

Cyber operations have to be considered within the context of the whole conflict. Although cyber can be used as stand-alone operation, the more likely case – and this holds true in Ukraine – is that cyber is used as a facilitator for other, more traditional types of warfare. The law applicable to the conflict as a whole should be applied to the cyber activities that are part of it. In other words, the wider context determines the legal framework for cyber operations. Particularly relevant is whether the conflict in Ukraine is an 'armed conflict' that leads to the application of the Law of Armed Conflict (or international humanitarian law).

This chapter will first briefly outline the applicability of international law to cyberspace. Then it will describe the legal framework of the conflict, related to the subsequent phases of the conflict, from the protests at Maidan Square in November 2013 to the present day. After that, the associated cyber activities will be placed in this legal context.

2   International Law and Cyber Operations

The applicability of international law to cyberspace has long been debated. Most Western countries posit that existing international law applies. Some countries, such as China and Russia, have proposed a unique and separate set of norms.[1] Today, it is generally recognised that international law applies, which is illustrated by the 2013 report of the Governmental Group of Experts, established by the United Nations (UN) General Assembly. It states that 'International law, and in particular the Charter of the United Nations, is applicable and is essential to maintaining peace and stability and promoting an open, secure, peaceful and accessible ICT environment.'[2] However, the better question now concerns exactly *how* to apply international law in the cyber domain, and this is not a debate that will be resolved in the near future.[3] NATO 'recognises that international law, including international humanitarian law and the UN Charter, applies in cyberspace'.[4] It also considers cyber defence to be an intrinsic part of its collective defence task, and has declared that a cyber attack could have the impact as harmful as a conventional armed attack, which could lead to the invocation of Article 5 of the North Atlantic Treaty.[5]

In this chapter, the author takes as a premise that existing international law applies to cyberspace.

3   Legal Framework for the Conflict in Ukraine

Cyber activities conducted as part of a wider conflict are governed by that conflict's legal framework.

Cyber activities conducted as part of a wider conflict are governed by that conflict's legal framework. This section will describe the wider conflict in Ukraine. Section 1.4 will examine specific cyber incidents and how they fit into the larger legal puzzle.

---

1   United Nations, General Assembly, *Letter Dated 9 January 2015 from the Permanent Representatives of China, Kazakhstan, Kyrgyzstan, the Russian Federation, Tajikistan and Uzbekistan to the United Nations Addressed to the Secretary-General*, A/69/723, 2015. An earlier version was submitted in September 2011.

2   United Nations, General Assembly, *Report of the Group of Governmental Experts (GGE) on Developments in the Field of Information and Telecommunications in the Context of International Security*, A/68/98, 24 June 2013. The Group consisted of representatives of 15 nations, including the United States, Russia, and China. In their Report of July 2015, the GGE recommended a set of norms of behavior of states in cyberspace. For an analysis of this report, see Henry Rõigas and Tomáš Minárik. '2015 UN GGE Report: Major Players Recommending Norms of Behaviour, Highlighting Aspects of International Law', *INCYDER database*, NATO CCD COE, 31 August 2015, https://ccdcoe.org/2015-un-gge-report-major-players-recommending-norms-behaviour-highlighting-aspects-international-l-0.html.

3   One of the prominent publications in this field is the *Tallinn Manual*. It discusses applicability of international law to cyber warfare, in particular the legal framework for the use of force and the law of armed conflict. The *Tallinn Manual* is prepared by an international group of experts on the invitation by the NATO Cooperative Cyber Defence Centre of Excellence, Tallinn, Estonia: Michael N. Schmitt, gen. ed., *Tallinn Manual on International Law Applicable to Cyber Warfare* (Cambridge: Cambridge University Press, 2013). Currently the *Manual* is under revision, a project coined *Tallinn 2.0*, including an analysis of international law applicable to cyber operations below the threshold of armed attack.

4   Wales Summit Declaration, 5 September 2014, para 72.

5   NATO's fundamental principle which states that 'if a NATO Ally is the victim of an armed attack, each and every other member of the Alliance will consider this act of violence as an armed attack against all members and will take the actions it deems necessary to assist the Ally attacked,' 'What is Article 5?', NATO, last updated 18 February 2005, http://www.nato.int/terrorism/five.htm.

3.1 Euromaidan (November 2013 – February 2014)

A few weeks before the European Union (EU) Eastern Partnership Summit in Vilnius, Lithuania, on 27-28 November 2013, during which the Ukraine – EU Association Agreement was to be signed, tensions in Ukraine were rising between those in favour and those opposed to closer relations with the EU. On 21 November, President Viktor Yanukovych decided to abandon the Association Agreement. This was followed by massive pro-EU demonstrations in *Maidan Nezalezhnosti* (Independence Square) in Kyiv. The clashes with the authorities grew violent. By mid-February, the events had escalated significantly, and had taken over 100 lives.

Before the *Euromaidan* protests began, tensions in Ukraine had already triggered hostile activity in cyberspace. Politically motivated hacker groups launched Distributed Denial-of-Service (DDoS) and other cyber attacks against a wide range of targets. On 28 October, the hacker group 'Anonymous Ukraine' started 'Operation Independence' (#OpIndependence), favouring Ukraine's independence from any external influence, including the EU, NATO, and Russia.[6] Operation Independence included DDoS attacks and website defacements against both Western and Russian sites. During *Euromaidan* DDoS attacks and defacements against both sides continued. Information leaks were used for propaganda purposes. Operation Independence leaked emails from opposition leader Vitali Klitchko and his political party, the Ukrainian Democratic Alliance for Reforms. Unknown hackers leaked the U.S. officials' phone call which included the infamous statement, 'f*ck the EU.'[7]

3.1.1 Legal Analysis

The *Euromaidan* protests were the violent culmination of a conflict between government authorities and pro-Western, civilian groups. Although the controversy was about Ukraine's external relations, it was primarily an internal matter between a state and an opposition within that state. And while the conflict engendered considerable violence – one only has to look at the number of casualties – at that stage, it could not be seen as an 'armed conflict'. It was not a conflict with 'armed forces on either side engaged in hostilities [...] similar to an international war'.[8] The incidents had the character of internal disturbances, civilian uprising, and violent clashes between protesters and police.

3.2 Forming Interim Government and Annexation of Crimea (February – March 2014)

On 21 February, President Yanukovych fled to Russia, and an Interim Government was formed, uniting the opposition. Events unfolded rapidly in Crimea. Pro-Russian gunmen seized key government buildings. On 1 March, the upper house of the Russian Parliament approved the deployment of troops in Ukraine to protect the

---

6   Eduard Kovacs. 'Anonymous Ukraine Launches OpIndependence, Attacks European Investment Bank', *Softpedia*, 31 October 2013, http://news.softpedia.com/news/Anonymous-Ukraine-Launches-OpIndependence-Attacks-European-Investment-Bank-395790.shtml.

7   Listen to recording here: https://www.youtube.com/watch?v=CL_GShyGv3o.

8   ICRC Commentary to Common Article 3 of the 1949 Geneva Conventions.

Russian speaking minority. Russian military forces (coined 'little green men') were reportedly present in Crimea and blocked the positions of Ukrainian troops.[9] A referendum, initiated by the Crimean Parliament, was held in Crimea on 16 March, which declared that 97% of voters supported joining Russia. Two days later, President Vladimir Putin signed a bill declaring Crimea to be part of the Russian Federation.[10] These events were crucial in setting the stage for the ongoing conflict in eastern Ukraine, and led to a dramatic change in relations between Russia and the West.

In cyberspace, there was a simultaneous rise in malicious activity during the military operations in Crimea. Operations were conducted against Ukraine's mobile infrastructure, the mobile phones of members of the Ukrainian Parliament, and security communications. Some traditional methods were used, including the seizure of *Ukrtelecom* offices and the physical cutting of telephone and internet cables.[11] Digital attacks included DDoS targeting Ukrainian, Crimean, NATO, and Russian websites. The pro-Russian hacker group *CyberBerkut* was particularly active against NATO,[12] while groups like *OpRussia* and *Russian CyberCommand* directed their actions against Russian websites.[13] Polish, Ukrainian, and Russian websites were also defaced, including the site of *Russia Today*, sometimes with historical references to World War II.[14]

Information leaks continued. A sensitive conversation between the Estonian Minister of Foreign Affairs Urmas Paet and EU High Representative for Foreign Affairs and Security Policy Catherine Ashton was made public, revealing their discussion of information suggesting that both sides, the opposition *and* the government, were responsible for sniper killings during the Maidan protests.[15] Anti-Russian motivated information leaks included the disclosure of the names of members of *Berkut*, the anti-riot police,[16] as well as documents belonging to a Russian defence contractor.[17]

During this time, it also became clear that the spyware *Snake* (also known as *Ouruboros* or *Turla*) was used against several targets in Ukraine, including the government. *Snake* is sophisticated malware, known to be in use for at least eight years, whose origin is uncertain, but believed to be developed in Russia.[18]

---

9   Vitaly Shevchenko. '"Little green men" or "Russian invaders"?', *BBC News*, 11 March 2014, http://www.bbc.com/news/world-europe-26532154.

10 See for an overview of events: 'Ukraine crisis: timeline', *BBC News*, http://www.bbc.com/news/world-middle-east-26248275.

11 John Leyden. 'Battle apparently under way in Russia-Ukraine conflict', *The Register*, 4 March 2014, http://www.theregister.co.uk/2014/03/04/ukraine_cyber_conflict.

12 Adrian Croft and Peter Apps. 'NATO websites hit in cyber attack linked to Crimea tension', *Reuters*, 16 March 2014, http://www.reuters.com/article/2014/03/16/us-ukraine-nato-idUSBREA2E0T320140316.

13 Jeffrey Carr. 'Rival hackers fighting proxy war over Crimea', *Reuters*, 25 March 2014, http://edition.cnn.com/2014/03/25/opinion/crimea-cyber-war/. Contrary to what its name suggests, *Russian CyberCommand* is a hacker group acting *against* Russian authorities.

14 Darlene Storm. 'Political hackers attack Russia, Nazi defacement, threaten US CENTCOM with cyberattack', *Computerworld*, 3 March 2014, http://www.computerworld.com/article/2476002/cybercrime-hacking/political-hackers-attack-russia--nazi-defacement--threaten-us-centcom-with-cybera.html.

15 Ewen MacAskill. 'Ukraine crisis: bugged call reveals conspiracy theory about Kiev snipers', *The Guardian*, 5 March 2014, http://www.theguardian.com/world/2014/mar/05/ukraine-bugged-call-catherine-ashton-urmas-paet.

16 Jeremy Bender. 'EXPERT: The Ukraine-Russia Cyberwar Is 'More Serious And Damaging' Than The Annexation Of Crimea', *Business Insider*, 10 March 2014, http://www.businessinsider.com/ukraine-russia-cyberwar-extremely-serious-2014-3.

17 Bindiya Thomas. 'Rosoboronexport Denies Loss of Confidential Data in Cyber Attack', *Defense World.net*, 25 March 2014, http://www.defenseworld.net/news/10275/Rosoboronexport_Denies_Loss_of_Confidential_Data_in_Cyber_Attack#.VbzA8fmMCXQ.

18 Sam Jones. 'Cyber Snake plagues Ukraine networks', *Financial Times*, 7 March 2014, http://www.ft.com/cms/s/0/615c29ba-a614-11e3-8a2a-00144feab7de.html#axzz3gDUpc1wz.

3.2.1 Legal Analysis

Although the UN and EU expressed their grave concerns about Russia's annexation of Crimea, and NATO called it a violation of international law,[19] Russia defended its actions as the lawful protection of the Russian speaking minority in Crimea. States have the right to act when necessary to rescue their nationals abroad. However, in this case, there were no indications that native Russians were in danger. Even if that were the case, it could only have justified their evacuation, *not* the occupation of the entire peninsula.[20] A second possible justification for Russian intervention was an invitation by the Ukrainian authorities, i.e. President Yanukovych. But, after Yanukovych was replaced by the Interim Government, his actions could not be attributed to Ukraine anymore.[21] A third possible justification is the right to self-determination for the people of Crimea. However, while this right exists for 'peoples' within the existing borders of a state, it does not allow for a complete political separation.[22]

Russia's annexation of Crimea was a breach of international law by violating the territorial integrity of Ukraine. Russia also breached the 1994 Budapest Memorandum and the 1997 Treaty on Friendship, Cooperation, and Partnership.[23] The Black Sea Fleet Status of Forces Agreement allowed for a Russian military presence in Crimea, but not at the scale as

> *Russia's annexation of Crimea was a breach of international law.*

was the case in March 2014. But was this armed intervention also a use of force, a violation of Article 2(4) of the UN Charter?[24] Moving armed forces to the territory of another state, without the consent of that state, should definitely be considered a use of force.[25] That is exactly what happened: troops belonging to the Russian Black Sea Fleet in Crimea left their bases, and there were clear indications that other Rus-

---

19 '[A] spokesman for UN Secretary-General Ban Ki-moon delivered a statement saying that he was 'gravely concerned about the deterioration of the situation' in Ukraine and planned to speak shortly with Putin. It also called for 'full respect for and preservation of the independence, sovereignty and territorial integrity of Ukraine' and demanded 'immediate restoration of calm and direct dialogue between all concerned'. Representative of the Union for Foreign Affairs and Security Policy Catherine Ashton stated that the EU "deplores" what it called Russia's decision to use military action in Ukraine, describing it as an "unwarranted escalation of tensions". She called on "all sides to decrease the tensions immediately through dialogue, in full respect of Ukrainian and international law". She added that: 'The unity, sovereignty and territorial integrity of Ukraine must be respected at all times and by all sides. Any violation of these principles is unacceptable'. North Atlantic Council condemned what it called Russia's military escalation in Crimea and called it a breach of international law'. International reactions to the annexation of Crimea by the Russian Federation, Wikipedia, accessed 1 August 2015, https://en.wikipedia.org/wiki/International_reactions_to_the_annexation_of_Crimea_by_the_Russian_Federation.

20 See also: Marc Weller, in BBC News, 'Analysis: Why Russia's Crimea move fails legal test', *BBC News*, 7 March 2014, http://www.bbc.com/news/world-europe-26481423.

21 See also: Christian Marxsen, 'The Crimea Crisis – An International Law Perspective', *Zeitschrift für ausländisches öffentliches Recht und Völkerrecht (Heidelberg Journal of International Law)* 74/2 (2014): 367-391; Remy Jorritsma. 'Ukraine Insta-Symposium: Certain (Para-)Military Activities in the Crimea: Legal Consequences for the Application of International Humanitarian Law', *Opinio Juris*, 9 March 2014, http://opiniojuris.org/2014/03/09/ukraine-insta-symposium-certain-para-military-activities-crimea-legal-consequences-application-international-humanitarian-law/; Ashley Deeks. 'Here's What International Law Says About Russia's Intervention in Ukraine', *New Republic*, 2 March 2014, http://www.newrepublic.com/article/116819/international-law-russias-ukraine-intervention.

22 Marxsen. 'Crimea Crisis', 14; Jorritsma. 'Legal Consequences'.

23 The 1994 Budapest memorandum was intended to provide Ukraine security in exchange of accession to the Treaty on the Non-Proliferation of Nuclear Weapons. Russia, the United States, and the United Kingdom committed to 'respect the independence and sovereignty and the existing borders of Ukraine'. The 1997 Treaty on Friendship, Cooperation, and Partnership between Russia and Ukraine was to guarantee the inviolability of the borders between both states. See also: Marxsen, 'Crimea Crisis', 4-5.

24 Charter of the United Nations, San Francisco, 26 June 1945, Article 2(4).

25 See also: Deeks. 'What International Law Says'.

sian troops were sent to Crimea to secure strategic sites, block Ukrainian troops, and essentially force them to leave the peninsula.

States can take measures in response to violations of international law. In this case the European Union and the United States imposed sanctions on Russia.

Could Russia's actions be seen as an armed attack, in which case Ukraine would have had the right to use force in self-defence?[26] Like 'use of force', 'armed attack' is not defined in the UN Charter; in essence, a state determines on a case-by-case basis whether it considers an attack against it as an 'armed attack'. A violent attack with military forces resulting in damage and casualties would certainly be seen as an armed attack. In the case of Crimea, however, hardly a shot was fired. On the other hand, it is difficult to argue that Ukraine would *not* have the right to use force to drive Russian troops out of Crimea.[27]

Irrespective this analysis of the *legal basis* of the intervention in Crimea, what would be the *legal regime* for the operations conducted by the parties to the conflict, including the cyber operations? Did the situation qualify as an 'international armed conflict' where the Law of Armed Conflict applies? The criterion here is that it relates to hostilities between nation-states. In Crimea, however, the situation was unclear. Firstly, there was no fighting, although the threshold for 'armed' is low.[28] Secondly, Russia denied the troops present were theirs and referred to them as 'local self-defence groups'. However, reports indicated the active involvement of Russian troops[29] and, eventually, Putin admitted that Russian troops were present.[30] Even in the event that only local forces were active, a situation of international armed conflict could still prevail if they were acting under Russia's control.

> *The Law of Armed Conflict applies in a situation of total or partial occupation.*

The Law of Armed Conflict also applies in a situation of a total or partial occupation, even if the occupation did not meet armed resistance.[31] Occupation is a 'hostile substitution of territorial power and authority'.[32] This is precisely the case in Crimea, where Russia exercises territorial control without the consent of the Ukrainian Government.

---

26   Charter of the United Nations, Article 51.
27   Deeks. 'What International Law Says.'
28   'Any difference arising between two States and leading to the intervention of members of the armed forces is an armed conflict within the meaning of Article 2, even if one of the Parties denies the existence of a state of war. It makes no difference how long the conflict lasts, or how much slaughter takes place. The respect due to the human person as such is not measured by the number of victims', ICRC Commentary to the Geneva Conventions of 1949, 20-21.
29   For example: 'Ukrainian and Russian troops in standoff at Crimean military base – As it happened', *The Guardian*, 3 March 2014, http://www.theguardian.com/world/2014/mar/02/ukraine-warns-russia-crimea-war-live; and 'Russian troops storm Ukrainian bases in Crimea', *BBC News*, 22 March 2014, http://www.bbc.com/news/world-europe-26698754
30   'Putin Admits Russian Troop Role in Crimea Annexation', *Voice of America*, 17 November 2014, http://www.voanews.com/content/putin-admits-russian-troop-role-in-crimea-annexation/2523186.html; 'Putin admits Russian forces were deployed to Crimea', Reuters, 17 April 2014, http://uk.reuters.com/article/2014/04/17/russia-putin-crimea-idUKL6N0N921H20140417.
31   Geneva Conventions, 12 August 1949, Common Article 2.
32   Hague Regulations: Regulations concerning the Laws and Customs of War on Land, 18 October 1907, Article 42. See also: Jorritsma, 'Legal Consequences.'

3.3 Hostilities in Eastern Ukraine (April 2014 – Present)

Following the annexation of Crimea, the world's attention was quickly drawn to the onset of hostilities in eastern Ukraine. Protesters from the Russian speaking minority in the cities of Donetsk, Luhansk, and Kharkiv occupied government buildings and called for independence.[33] Pro-Russian 'separatist groups' emerged. The Ukrainian authorities responded by starting an 'anti-terrorist operation'. On 17 April, the first violent deaths occurred in eastern Ukraine; in the Black Sea city of Odessa, 42 people died in clashes. On 11 May, Donetsk and Luhansk declared themselves to be independent republics.

Petro Poroshenko was elected President of Ukraine on 25 May, but this poll could not be held in large parts of the conflict-ridden east. A cease-fire agreement,[34] signed in Minsk on 5 September 2014, collapsed when fighting started again in January 2015. A second agreement signed in the capital of Belarus on 11 February, *Minsk II*, provided for a ceasefire, the withdrawal of heavy weapons from the front line, a release of prisoners of war, and constitutional reform in Ukraine.[35] This second agreement has also been violated, although currently, in September 2015, the situation seems to have calmed down. NATO reported the active involvement of Russian troops in eastern Ukraine,[36] but Russia has consistently denied involvement.

Cyber operations have continued throughout the conflict. In May 2014, cyber means were used in an attempt to disrupt the presidential elections, including an effort to falsify the outcome. *CyberBerkut* may have taken part and some analysts believe that Russia was behind it.[37] In August 2014, hackers conducted a DDoS attack against Ukraine's election commission website, just prior to the parliamentary polls.[38]

There are numerous publicly-known examples of intelligence gathering through cyber means, all of which reportedly have a Russian connection. In the Summer of 2014, the *Blackenergy* spyware was used against Ukrainian government institutions.[39] In August, the *Snake* malware was employed against the Ukrainian Prime Minister's Office, as well as a number of foreign embassies.[40] In April 2015, *Lookinglass* reported on a Russian campaign to extract classified documents from Ukrainian military and law enforcement agencies in an effort to support pro-Russian military

---

33   'Ukraine crisis: Timeline', *BBC News*, accessed 1 August 2015, http://www.bbc.com/news/world-middle-east-26248275.

34   Protocol on the results of consultations of the Trilateral Contact Group, Minsk, 5 September 2014, http://mfa.gov.ua/en/news-feeds/foreign-offices-news/27596-protocolon-the-results-of-consultations-of-the-trilateral-contact-group-minsk-05092014.

35   'Ukraine ceasefire: New Minsk agreement key points', *BBC News*, 12 February 2015, http://www.bbc.com/news/world-europe-31436513.

36   See for example: 'NATO Commander: 'Conditions in Eastern Ukraine Have to Change'', OPB, 6 February 2015, http://www.opb.org/news/article/npr-nato-commander-conditions-in-eastern-ukraine-have-to-change/, and 'Nato urges Russia to stop fuelling Ukraine conflict', *The Irish Times*, 15 April 2015, http://www.irishtimes.com/news/world/europe/nato-urges-russia-to-stop-fuelling-ukraine-conflict-1.2176718.

37   Mark Clayton. 'Ukraine election narrowly avoided 'wanton destruction' from hackers (+video)', *The Christian Science Monitor*, 17 June 2014, http://www.csmonitor.com/World/Passcode/2014/0617/Ukraine-election-narrowly-avoided-wanton-destruction-from-hackers-video.

38   'Hackers attack Ukraine election website', *Presstv*, 25 October 2014, http://www.presstv.ir/detail/2014/10/25/383623/ukraines-election-website-hacked/. See also: Vitaly Shevchenko, 'Ukraine conflict: Hackers take sides in virtual war', BBC News, 20 December 2014, http://www.bbc.com/news/world-europe-30453069.

39   David Gilbert. 'BlackEnergy Cyber Attacks Against Ukrainian Government Linked to Russia', *International Business Times*, 26 September 2014, http://www.ibtimes.co.uk/blackenergy-cyber-attacks-against-ukrainian-governm)ent-linked-russia-1467401.

40   Sam Jones. 'Russia-linked cyber attack on Ukraine PM's office', *CNBC*, 8 August 2014, http://www.cnbc.com/id/101905588.

operations in Ukraine.[41] *ISight Partners* reported that Russian *Sandworm* hackers used a 'zero-day' vulnerability to hack NATO and Ukraine in a cyber espionage campaign.[42] The list of targets was not confined to Ukrainian sites. In January 2015, *CyberBerkut* claimed responsibility for a cyber attack on German Government sites, demanding that Germany end its support to the Ukrainian government.[43]

On the pro-Ukraine side, the *Ukrainian Cyber Troops* reportedly claimed to have hacked into Russian interior ministry servers and CCTV cameras in separatist-controlled eastern Ukraine.[44]

3.3.1 Legal Analysis

The International Committee of the Red Cross (ICRC) has characterised the situation in eastern Ukraine as a 'non-international armed conflict',[45] a situation in which hostilities occur between governmental armed forces and non-governmental organised armed groups, or between such organised armed groups. The two requirements are a certain degree of organisation of the non-governmental groups and the existence of 'protracted armed violence'.[46] The conflict in Eastern Ukraine does in fact reach a high level of violence over a longer period of time, and the separatists do in fact have a high degree of organisation.

Although Russia has consistently denied involvement, there continues to be widespread belief to the contrary, suggesting that Moscow actively supports the Donetsk and Luhansk separatists, including by sending Russian military forces as 'volunteers' to the area. If Russia actively participates or exercises 'overall control' over the separatists, the conflict could be considered an international armed conflict. To meet the criterion of 'overall control', a state must not only finance, train, equip, or provide operational support to local forces, but also have a role in organising, coordinating, and planning their operations.[47]

However, for the purpose of this chapter, the conflict in eastern Ukraine is considered to be a non-international armed conflict.

This analysis results in a situation where different legal regimes apply simultane-

---

41 Aarti Shahani. 'Report: To Aid Combat, Russia Wages Cyberwar Against Ukraine', *NPR*, 28 April 2015, http://www.npr.org/sections/alltechconsidered/2015/04/28/402678116/report-to-aid-combat-russia-wages-cyberwar-against-ukraine.

42 Ellen Nakashima. 'Russian hackers use 'zero-day' to hack NATO, Ukraine in cyber-spy campaign', *The Washington Post*, 13 October 2014, http://www.washingtonpost.com/world/national-security/russian-hackers-use-zero-day-to-hack-nato-ukraine-in-cyber-spy-campaign/2014/10/13/f2452976-52f9-11e4-892e-602188e70e9c_story.html.

43 Michelle Martin and Erik Kirschbaum. 'Pro-Russian group claims cyber attack on German government websites', *Reuters*, 7 January 2015, http://www.reuters.com/article/2015/01/07/us-germany-cyberattack-idUSKBN0KG15320150107.

44 'The Daily Beast: Ukraine's lonely cyber warrior,' *KyivPost*, 18 February 2015, http://www.kyivpost.com/content/ukraine-abroad/the-daily-beast-ukraines-lonely-cyber-warrior-381094.html, and Vitaly Shevchenko, 'Ukraine conflict: Hackers take sides in virtual war', BBC News, 20 December 2014, http://www.bbc.com/news/world-europe-30453069.

45 'Fighting in eastern Ukraine continues to take its toll on civilians, and we urge all sides to comply with international humanitarian law, otherwise known as the law of armed conflict', said Mr Stillhart. 'These rules and principles apply to all parties to the non-international armed conflict in Ukraine, and impose restrictions on the means and methods of warfare that they may use [in Ukraine]': ICRC calls on all sides to respect international humanitarian law, *ICRC News Release* 14/125, 23 July 2014. Non-international armed conflicts are 'armed conflicts not of an international character occurring in the territory of one of the High Contracting Parties', Geneva Conventions, Common Article 3.

46 The criterion 'protracted armed violence' stems from Tadić, Decision on the Defence Motion for Interlocutory Appeal, para 70, International Criminal Tribunal for the Former Yugoslavia, 2 October 1995.

47 'Overall control' is addressed in: Tadić, Appeals Chamber judgment, International Criminal Tribunal for the Former Yugoslavia, 15 July 1999, para 132, 137, 141, and 145. See also: *Tallinn Manual*, 79-82.

ously. The Law of Armed Conflict pursuant to international armed conflicts applies to the occupation of Crimea. Eastern Ukraine is a national issue in which the law pursuant to *non*-international armed conflicts applies. There is a crucial difference. During an international armed conflict, the Law of Armed Conflict applies to the full extent; during a non-international armed conflict, minimum rules apply.[48] An example is that in an international armed conflict, combatants captured by the enemy are entitled to Prisoner of War (PoW) status. In a non-international armed conflict, the combatant's status is unknown; belligerents have to be treated well, but the extensive rules that protect PoWs do not apply. However, many rules of international armed conflict are customary law and apply also in a non-international armed conflict, as we will see with respect to cyber operations.

4   LEGAL IMPLICATIONS FOR CYBER OPERATIONS IN UKRAINE

The conflict started as an internal matter, the protests at Maidan Square, to an unlawful intervention and occupation of Crimea, culminating in the non-international armed conflict in eastern Ukraine.

During the first phase, the *Euromaidan* protests, the cyber incidents were a law enforcement issue. For example, the defacement of websites and DDoS attacks restricting the use of internet services violated Ukrainian criminal law and could have been prosecuted in Ukrainian courts.[49] Malicious cross-border cyber activities, involving both Ukraine and other countries, would fall under the criminal jurisdiction of Ukraine and the affected countries.

During the occupation of Crimea and the armed conflict in eastern Ukraine, the Law of Armed Conflict applies. It regulates the conduct of all actors in the conflict, including the cyber actors. Hereafter, first the status of the different cyber actors will be discussed; after that the cyber operations we have seen in the Ukraine conflict will be evaluated from the perspective of the Law of Armed Conflict.

> *During the Euromaidan protests, cyber incidents were a law enforcement issue.*

4.1 Actors in Cyberspace
In an *international* armed conflict, belligerents that qualify as 'combatants' enjoy combatant immunity, meaning they cannot be prosecuted for taking part in hostilities (except

---

48   These 'minimum rules' are formulated in Common Article 3 of the Geneva Conventions, and in Additional Protocol II to the Geneva Conventions. The rules laid down in that protocol apply to a conflict within a state that is party to the Protocol between the armed forces of that state and dissident armed forces or organised armed groups that control sufficient territory so 'as to enable them to carry out sustained and concerted military operations', Protocol Additional to the Geneva Conventions of 12 August 1949, and relating to the Protection of Victims of Non-International Armed Conflicts (Protocol II), 8 June 1977, Article 1(1). Ukraine is party to Additional Protocol II, and the separatists do control significant territory.
49   Ukraine is Party to the Convention on Cybercrime (Budapest, 2001). The Convention aims to harmonise cybercrime legislation and facilitate information exchange and international cooperation in the area of prosecution of cybercrimes. States that are party to the convention are obliged to incorporate certain violations in their national laws: 'illegal access', 'illegal interception', 'data interference', 'system interference', and 'misuse of devices'.

for war crimes) and, on capture, have PoW status. These rules also apply during occupation, as in Crimea. Most cyber actors in Crimea were nominally non-state actors, for example the pro-Russian hacker group *CyberBerkut*. If such a group were an integrated part of Russia's military forces, they would be combatants. If not, they could nevertheless be considered combatants if they were part of an organised armed group, belonging to a party to the conflict, when they fulfil the following conditions: (a) being commanded by a person responsible for his subordinates; (b) having a fixed distinctive sign recognisable at a distance; (c) carrying arms openly; and (d) conducting their operations in accordance with the laws and customs of war.[50] These criteria are important to distinguish combatants from civilians. It is unlikely that non-state hacker groups, also those active in the Ukraine crisis, meet all these criteria, especially when they are only 'virtually' organised, only in contact through the internet.

Hackers or hacker groups who are non-combatants are to be regarded civilians. However, if they are 'directly participating in hostilities', they lose their protection as civilians and can be targeted by the opposing party. Three criteria have to be met to be regarded 'civilians directly participating in hostilities.'[51] First, there has to be a certain amount of 'harm'; the 'act must be likely to adversely affect the military operations or military capacity of [the adversary] or [...] to inflict death, injury or destruction on persons or objects protected against direct attack.'[52] Second, there has to be a 'causal connexion' between the acts and the harm inflicted. Third, there has to be a 'belligerent nexus', meaning that the operations must be intended to affect the adversary's military operations. Harm can also be inflicted by cyber operations, and does not necessarily have to include physical damage. In the case of *CyberBerkut* and other active hacker groups the effects probably did not reach the threshold of 'harm'.

In *non-international* armed conflicts, like in eastern Ukraine, 'combatant immunity' does not exist. Whether or not belligerents – especially non-state armed groups – have immunity, will be determined based on domestic law. Certain cyber operations will be illegal based on domestic law. Civilians have protected status, but as in international armed conflicts, when they are 'directly participating in hostilities' they lose that protected status.

4.2 Information Operations

During the conflict in Ukraine, cyber was mainly used for information warfare and intelligence gathering – not to damage cyber or critical infrastructure. Irrespective their effects, cyber operations are very often called 'cyber attack.' It is important to note that, in the context of international and non-international armed conflicts, 'attack' has a very specific meaning. 'Attacks means acts of violence against the adversary, whether in offence or in defence.'[53] Whether or not an operation qualifies as attack is crucial

---

50 Geneva Convention (III), 12 August 1949, Article 4, para A(2).
51 ICRC Interpretive guidance on the notion of Direct Participation in hostilities under international humanitarian law, May 2009.
52 ICRC Interpretive guidance, 47.
53 Protocol Additional to the Geneva Conventions of 12 August 1949, and relating to the Protection of Victims of International Armed Conflicts (Protocol I), 8 June 1977, Article 49(1).

because the law imposes prohibitions and restrictions with respect to attacks, for example the prohibition to attack civilians, civilian objects, and medical installations, and the requirement to take precautions before conducting an attack. Not every cyber operation that affects the adversary is an attack. A cyber operation that constitutes an act of violence however, *is* an attack. The *Tallinn Manual* defines a 'cyber attack' as 'a cyber operation, whether offensive or defensive, that is reasonably expected to cause injury or death to persons or damage or destruction to objects.'[54] This interpretation of the current law restricts 'cyber attacks' to acts that have physical consequences.

If the parties to the conflict in Ukraine would have used cyber to inflict physical damage, injuries, or death, or to support kinetic operations, those cyber operations would be '(cyber) attacks' and subject to the relevant prohibitions and restrictions. Most of the cyber activities in Ukraine however are information operations and do not meet the 'attack' threshold. Information operations, as such, are not directly addressed in the Law of Armed Conflict. Whether they would be in violation of the law basically depends on the content of the message. One example would be disseminating a threatening message with the purpose to spread terror among the civilian population.[55] The disruption

> *Information operations, as such, are not directly addressed in the Law of Armed Conflict.*

of elections, that took place in Ukraine, definitely violated domestic law, and when conducted or supported by another state, could also have been a breach of international law, but was not a violation of the Law of Armed Conflict.

4.3 Cyber Espionage

During the conflict in Ukraine, cyber means have been used to gather intelligence including *Snake*, *Blackenergy*, and *Sandworm*. Intelligence gathering and espionage are not forbidden by international law. Espionage, in the context of the Law of Armed Conflict, has a narrow scope: it refers to operations that are conducted clandestinely or under false pretences, taking place on territory controlled by the adversary; 'behind enemy lines.'[56] For instance, a close access cyber operation where an agent is gaining access to servers being used by the adversary by feigning a false identity and extracting information by using a thumb drive, could be espionage. An agent captured before reaching his own troops has no PoW status and can be tried as a spy. Gathering intelligence from a distance is not espionage in the meaning of the Law of Armed Conflict.

Snake, *Blackenergy*, and *Sandworm* reportedly have a Russian connection. If Russia – or another state – would be actively supporting the separatists in eastern Ukraine by providing intelligence, that would not necessarily 'internationalise' the conflict. Mere operational support does not meet the 'overall control' threshold.[57]

---

54 *Tallinn Manual*, 106.
55 Protocol I, Article 51(2), and Protocol II, Article 13(2).
56 *Tallinn Manual*, 192-193.
57 *Tallinn Manual*, 81.

5   CONCLUSIONS

International law applies to cyberspace. During armed conflict, the Law of Armed Conflict applies to any cyber operation conducted in association with the hostilities. Until now, we have not seen a case where cyber hostilities between parties *by themselves* constituted an armed conflict. Rather, they have remained as one part of a larger, traditional conflict. This dynamic has not changed during the conflict in Ukraine.

This chapter describes the international legal framework for the conflict in Ukraine and the cyber operations that have been conducted in association with that conflict. The 'legal situation' is somewhat unclear due to diverging views on various aspects of the crisis, such as the annexation of Crimea and the alleged involvement of Russian military forces in eastern Ukraine. Another aspect that complicates a legal evaluation is that cyber operations are often conducted by non-state actors, whose status and affiliation are not always clear.

The protests at Maidan Square turned violent, but they were not an 'armed conflict'; they were an internal law enforcement matter. The annexation of Crimea led to the peninsula's occupation by Russia, but Russia disputes that interpretation. During an occupation, the Law of Armed Conflict applies. Eastern Ukraine can today be considered a non-international armed conflict, where cyber operations must be conducted in accordance with the minimum safeguards the Law of Armed Conflict provides for such situations.

> *Cyber operations are often conducted by non-state actors, whose status and affiliation are not always clear.*

In the Ukraine conflict, the publicly known cyber operations have not generally been considered to be sophisticated – likely not corresponding to the real national capabilities of Russia and Ukraine. The prevailing assumption is that, with the exception of some advanced cyber espionage malware such as Snake, the known cyber attacks could have been conducted by non-state actors. These hackers or hacker groups, trying to affect the adversary's military activities, are participating in hostilities and have to conduct their operations in accordance with the Law of Armed Conflict.

At the end of the day, cyber operations in the Ukraine conflict have been used either to gather intelligence or as part of an ongoing 'information war' between the parties. They were not launched to inflict damage to infrastructure and other military capabilities. As a result, most of these cyber operations have not yet risen to the level of activities proscribed or even governed by the Law of Armed Conflict. That would be different when cyber would be more integrated in kinetic warfare operations.

CHAPTER 15

THE UKRAINE CRISIS AS A TEST FOR PROPOSED CYBER NORMS

HENRY RÕIGAS

NATO CCD COE

1   INTRODUCTION

In international forums, governments, academia, and the private sector have strenuously argued that states must agree on existing or develop a set of international norms for conflict in cyberspace. Our current environment is characterised by a steep rise in the development of offensive cyber tools and tactics – as well as a general disagreement on when and where it is appropriate to use them. The overall result is a popular perception of a weakened international security environment that threatens to devolve into an anarchic Hobbesian world of 'all against all'. Against this backdrop, there have been urgent calls for greater investment in cyber diplomacy.[1]

The term 'norm' has become somewhat of a buzzword in these discussions used to argue that states should adhere to certain rules of behaviour with regard

> *The term 'norm' has become somewhat of a buzzword.*

to conducting cyber operations. This chapter will thus first describe the nature of 'cyber norms' and then discuss the primary developments in the global arena. The author's focus will be on the *proposed* cyber norms of behaviour that would have a politically binding character, and will avoid discussing *existing* international law

---

1   See, for example, developments in the United Nations: http://www.un.org/disarmament/topics/informationsecurity/, and The Council of the European Union's conclusions on cyber diplomacy: http://data.consilium.europa.eu/doc/document/ST-6122-2015-INIT/en/pdf.

(legal norms)[2] as well as the challenges of practical implementation of the these norms.

Finally, this chapter will analyse the Ukraine crisis in light of these proposals, and attempt to assess their rationality and applicability. The Russo-Ukrainian conflict, in theory, offers a suitable case study in that there has been ample room for malicious state-sponsored cyber activities: first, nation-states perceived as having considerable cyber capabilities – not only Russia and Ukraine, but also surrounding nations and the member states of NATO – are involved, at least indirectly; and second, the crisis has both endured and evolved from the Euromaidan street protests to the Russian annexation of Crimea to open, armed conflict in eastern Ukraine.

2 PROPOSED 'POLITICAL' CYBER NORMS

In international relations, norms are often defined as 'collective expectations of proper behaviour for an actor with a given identity,'[3] which is broad enough that states (and other stakeholders) use the term to put forward a wide range of proposals in diplomatic forums. This chapter takes a simplified approach, limiting its scope to (1) legal and (2) political norms: the 'proper behaviour' of states is comprehensively regulated by international law (i.e. *legal* norms such as treaties, international customs, and general principles of international law)[4] and through cyber diplomacy in the form of *political* or non-legally binding agreements. The United Nations Group of Governmental Experts (UN GGE) has explained the nature of these politically binding instruments by stating that 'norms reflect the international community's expectations, set standards for responsible State behaviour and allow the international community to assess the activities and intentions of States'. The problem, of course, is that breaches of such political norms only give rise to political, non-legal consequences.[5]

> *Norms reflect the international community's expectations, set standards for responsible State behaviour.*

There has been some agreement between nation states on setting international 'cyber norms'. In 2013, the UN published an accord, written by a GGE including representatives from the US, UK, China, and Russia, expressing consensus on the

---

2   For a discussion on the role of legal cyber norms, see Michael N. Schmitt and Liis Vihul. 'The Nature of International Law Cyber Norms,' *Tallinn Papers*, no. 6 (2014), https://ccdcoe.org/sites/default/files/multimedia/pdf/Tallinn%20Paper%20No%20%205%20Schmitt%20and%20Vihul.pdf.

3   See Martha Finnemore and Kathryn Sikkink. 'International Norm Dynamics and Political Change,' *International Organization* 52, no. 4 (October 1, 1998): 887–917.

4   See sources of international law listed in the Statute of the International Court of Justice (ICJ), Article 38.

5   Some have also used the terms 'hard' and 'soft' law in this context, see Dinah Shelton. 'Normative Hierarchy in International Law', *The American Journal of International Law* 100, no. 2 (April 1, 2006): 291–323. For a concept listing policy responses to cyber incidents, see Tobias Feakin. 'Developing a Proportionate Response to a Cyber Incident' *Council on Foreign Relations*, August 2015, http://www.cfr.org/cybersecurity/developing-proportionate-response-to-cyber-incident/p36927.

basic notion that existing international law applies to cyberspace.[6] In 2015, the same forum published another report[7] which delved into greater detail, but the GGE has previously not elaborated on precisely how to apply existing laws (legal norms) to the nuanced field of cyber security. The reports did state, however, that the unique attributes of information and communications technology (ICTs) could demand the creation of altogether new norms.

The fairly general agreement expressed in the reports can be viewed both as the lowest common denominator between the world's key cyber powers and as a manifestation of a general lack of clarity in this new geopolitical arena. Meanwhile academia has to some degree filled the void, actively addressing the applicability of existing international law,[8] although work in the area of state practice and interpretation has been relatively limited. In the context of norms restraining state behaviour, existing international law such as the prohibition on the use of force and the law of armed conflict (LOAC) are highly relevant and indispensable, but it is likely that additional norms – political rather than legal – will be developed by the international community over time. Two somewhat opposing approaches to these new political norms will be addressed below.

One group of nations acting as 'norm entrepreneurs'[9] seems to aim for a treaty-level agreement to govern state activities in cyberspace. Member nations of the Shanghai Cooperation Organisation (SCO)[10] have proposed a Code of Conduct for International Information Security[11] to the UN. In parallel, Russia has developed (in 2011) a separate concept for a Convention on International Information Security[12] which covers, to a large extent, the same territory.

These proposed instruments do not apply the prefix 'cyber' when addressing ICT-related issues; instead, the focus is on preserving 'information security' which represents a broad conceptualisation of the threat environment and the scope of limited state activities.[13] According to SCO's own agreement on information security (the Yekaterinburg Agreement of 2009)[14] and the aforementioned Convention proposal by Russia (2011), 'information war' entails, in addition to damaging information systems and critical infrastructures (which is often the 'Western' scope of

---

6   United Nations, General Assembly, *Group of Governmental Experts on Developments in the Field of Information and Tele-communications in the Context of International Security*, A/69/723, 2013, http://www.un.org/ga/search/view_doc.asp?symbol=A/68/98.
7   United Nations, General Assembly, *Group of Governmental Experts on Developments in the Field of Information and Tele-communications in the Context of International Security*, A/70/174, 2015, http://daccess-dds-ny.un.org/doc/UNDOC/GEN/N15/228/35/PDF/N1522835.pdf?OpenElement.
8   See the Tallinn Manual process: https://ccdcoe.org/research.html.
9   See Finnemore and Sikkink. "International Norm Dynamics and Political Change," October 1, 1998.
10   Member States of the SCO are China, Kazakhstan, Kyrgyzstan, Russia, Tajikistan, and Uzbekistan.
11   United Nations, General Assembly, *Letter Dated 9 January 2015 from the Permanent Representatives of China, Kazakhstan, Kyrgyzstan, the Russian Federation, Tajikistan and Uzbekistan to the United Nations Addressed to the Secretary-General*, A/69/723, 2015, https://ccdcoe.org/sites/default/files/documents/UN-150113-CodeOfConduct.pdf.
12   The Ministry of Foreign Affairs of the Russian Federation. *Convention on International Information Security (Concept)*, 2011, http://www.mid.ru/bdomp/ns-osndoc.nsf/1e5f0de28fe77fdcc32575d900298676/7b17ead7244e2064c3257925003bcbc-c!OpenDocument.
13   See, for example, James A. Lewis. 'Liberty, Equality, Connectivity: Transatlantic Cybersecurity Norms,' Strategic Technologies Program (Center For Strategic and International Studies, 2014), 6.
14   Annex 1of SCO, *Agreement between the Governments of the Member States of the Shanghai Cooperation Organisation on Cooperation in the Field of International Information Security*.

actions when the term 'cyber security' is used), also 'psychologic brainwashing to destabilise society and state', signalling that for them the threat also stems from content and information itself.[15]

The Code of Conduct puts a strong emphasis on the principle of *information sovereignty*,[16] arguing that states should not use 'ICTs and information and communication networks to interfere in the internal affairs of other states or with the aim of undermining their political, economic and social stability'. It asks states to refrain from 'activities which run counter to the task of maintaining international peace and security' and highlights a state's responsibility to protect 'information space and critical information infrastructure against damage resulting from threats, interference, attack and sabotage'. Further, it includes a section that prohibits states from using 'dominant position in ICTs' to engage in the aforementioned activities. In terms of international cooperation, the Code seeks to curb 'the dissemination of information that incites terrorism, separatism or extremism'.

> *Documents demonstrate the ambition of SCO members to see a treaty-level agreement.*

These documents demonstrate the ambition of the SCO members to see an eventual treaty-level agreement. However, if the Code of Conduct would actually be adopted in the current form, it could not be considered as a source of international law (a legal instrument) since the norms are of a politically binding character due their 'aspirational' and non-compulsory nature.[17]

The Code of Conduct has not been put to a vote as adoption at the UN is highly unlikely due to opposition from many liberal democracies. An alternative strategy, promoted initially by the US, is to strengthen international cyber security through voluntary norms of behaviour that pertain during peacetime.[18] According to this logic, most cyber operations fall below the 'use of force' threshold, which means that most of the existing legal norms regulating interstate cyber operations are not sufficient.[19] During the height of the cyber incidents in Ukraine, the US promoted the fol-

> *An alternative strategy is to strengthen international cyber security through voluntary norms.*

---

15   See, for example, Keir Giles. 'Russia's Public Stance on Cyberspace Issues,' in *2012 4th International Conference on Cyber Conflict*, ed. Christian Czosseck, Rain Ottis, and Katharina Ziolkowski (NATO CCD COE Publication, 2012), http://www.ccdcoe.org/publications/2012proceedings/2_1_Giles_RussiasPublicStanceOnCyberInformationWarfare.pdf.

16   See the Chinese viewpoint in Lu Wei. 'Cyber Sovereignty Must Rule Global Internet,' *The Huffington Post*, December 15, 2014, http://www.huffingtonpost.com/lu-wei/china-cyber-sovereignty_b_6324060.html.

17   Schmitt and Vihul. 'The Nature of International Law Cyber Norms,' 4.

18   States supporting this view strongly emphasise the applicability of existing international law and see that these norms should be 'voluntary measures of self-restraint' during peacetime, see Christopher M. E. Painter. *Testimony of Christopher M. E. Painter, Coordinator for Cyber Issues, U.S. Department of State Before the Senate Foreign Relations Committee Subcommittee on East Asia, the Pacific, and International Cybersecurity Policy Hearing Titled: 'Cybersecurity: Setting the Rules for Responsible Global Behaviour,'* 2015, http://www.foreign.senate.gov/imo/media/doc/051415_Painter_Testimony.pdf.

19   *Ibid.*, 8–9. Also, see Tallinn Manual 2.0 process focusing on international law applicable to cyber operations that do not mount to an 'use of force' or do not take place during armed conflict, https://ccdcoe.org/research.html .

lowing four norms of which the first three were included in the recent UN GGE report:[20]

(1) states should not conduct or knowingly support online activity that damages or impairs critical infrastructure (norm 1);
(2) states should not conduct or knowingly support activity intended to prevent the national Computer Security Incidents Response Teams (CSIRTs or CERTs) from responding to cyber incidents, nor use CSIRTs to do harm (norm 2);
(3) states should cooperate with other states in investigating cybercrime by collecting electronic evidence and mitigating cyber activity emanating from its territory (norm 3); and
(4) states should not conduct or knowingly support cyber-enabled theft of commercially valuable intellectual property (norm 4).

Before we move on, it is important to note that these and other cyber norms have been analysed in academic circles[21] as well as in the private sector. For example, Microsoft has recommended six cybersecurity norms designed to limit the proliferation of cyber weapons and offensive operations in cyberspace.[22]

3   OBSERVATIONS FROM UKRAINE: HINTS OF STATE-SPONSORED OPERATIONS

The attribution of cyber attacks is notoriously difficult. In order to discover state-sponsored operations, one can only speculate based upon inconclusive indicators such as target, malware, motive, and complexity.

In Ukraine, some advanced cyber espionage tools such as Turla/Snake/Ourobours and Sandworm have not only been linked to the conflict, but also associated with an 'Advanced Persistent Threat' (APT) actor (i.e. nation-state), likely Russia.[23] At the same time, analysts have argued that *most* of the cyber attack methods in Ukraine such as DDoS attacks and defacements have been technically unsophisticated. Thus, on balance, the 'complexity criterion' appears unmet.

---

20   Painter. *Testimony of Christopher M. E. Painter, Coordinator for Cyber Issues, U.S. Department of State Before the Senate Foreign Relations Committee Subcommittee on East Asia, the Pacific, and International Cybersecurity Policy Hearing Titled: 'Cybersecurity: Setting the Rules for Responsible Global Behaviour.'*

21   For example, drawing parallels with state obligations during crises on the sea, a duty to assist victims of severe cyberattacks (an e-SOS) has been proposed by Duncan B. Hollis in 'An E-SOS for Cyberspace,' *Harvard International Law Journal* 52, no. 2 (2011), http://papers.ssrn.com/sol3/papers.cfm?abstract_id=1670330.

22   Angela McKay *et al.*, 'International Cybersecurity Norms. Reducing Conflict in an Internet-Dependent World' (Microsoft, 2015), http://download.microsoft.com/download/7/6/0/7605D861-C57A-4E23-B823-568CFC36FD44/International_Cybersecurity_%20Norms.pdf.

23   See, for example, 'Suspected Russian Spyware Turla Targets Europe, United States,' *Reuters*, March 7, 2014, http://www.reuters.com/article/2014/03/07/us-russia-cyberespionage-insight-idUSBREA260YI20140307; 'Zero Day Vulnerability CVE-2014-4114 Used in Cyber-Espionage,' *iSIGHT Partners*, October 21, 2014, http://www.isightpartners.com/2014/10/cve-2014-4114/.

*Actions attributed to hack-
tivist groups raise questions
regarding possible coordination with state entities.*

Actions attributed to hacktivist groups also raise questions regarding possible coordination with state entities. For example, Ukrainian officials reported that, even when the hacktivist group CyberBerkut failed to compromise Ukraine's online election system and only managed to present fake election results on the election's website for a very brief period, a Russian state-owned TV channel still displayed these results immediately.[24] In another incident, CyberBerkut allegedly leaked the recording of a phone call between Estonian Minster of Foreign Affairs Urmas Paet and European Union (EU) High Representative for Foreign Affairs and Security Policy Catherine Ashton, suggesting that Cyber Berkut either possesses sophisticated cyber capabilities or has links to Russian intelligence services.[25]

Here, we must remember SCO's focus on 'information security', as opposed to 'cyber security', and in fact many analysts believe that both Russia[26] and Ukraine[27] are conducting information operations within the context of the ongoing conflict in eastern Ukraine. The internet is a natural terrain for these operations;[28] the reported 'troll factories' in St. Petersburg creating pro-Russian comments for online new media serve as prominent examples.[29]

4   Which Norms of Behaviour Were Followed?

Thus, there are two dominant ongoing conversations relative to the creation of political cyber norms: (1) the information security norms proposed by the SCO, and (2) the voluntary norms of behaviour in peacetime (initially promoted by the US). This section will analyse the known cyber incidents in Ukraine in the context of these two normative frameworks.

---

24   Mark Clayton. 'Ukraine Election Narrowly Avoided 'Wanton Destruction' from Hackers,' *Christian Science Monitor*, June 17, 2014, http://www.csmonitor.com/World/Passcode/2014/0617/Ukraine-election-narrowly-avoided-wanton-destruc-tion-from-hackers-video.

25   Ewen MacAskill. 'Ukraine Crisis: Bugged Call Reveals Conspiracy Theory about Kiev Snipers,' *The Guardian*, March 5, 2014, http://www.theguardian.com/world/2014/mar/05/ukraine-bugged-call-catherine-ashton-urmas-paet; Trend Micro, 'Hacktiv-ist Group CyberBerkut Behind Attacks on German Official Websites,' *Security Intelligence Blog*, http://blog.trendmicro.com/trendlabs-security-intelligence/hacktivist-group-cyberberkut-behind-attacks-on-german-official-websites/.

26   NATO StratCom Centre of Excellence, *Analysis of Russia's Information Campaign Against Ukraine*, October 15, 2014, http://www.stratcomcoe.org/download/file/fid/1910.

27   Maksim Vikhrov. 'Ukraine Forms 'Ministry of Truth' to Regulate the Media,' *The Guardian*, December 19, 2014, http://www.theguardian.com/world/2014/dec/19/-sp-ukraine-new-ministry-truth-undermines-battle-for-democracy.

28   Maeve Shearlaw. 'From Britain to Beijing: How Governments Manipulate the Internet,' *The Guardian*, April 2, 2015, http://www.theguardian.com/world/2015/apr/02/russia-troll-factory-kremlin-cyber-army-comparisons.

29   Dmitry Volchek and Daisy Sindelar. 'One Professional Russian Troll Tells All,' *RadioFreeEurope/RadioLiberty*, March 25, 2015, sec. Russia, http://www.rferl.org/content/how-to-guide-russian-trolling-trolls/26919999.html; Shearlaw. 'From Britain to Bei-jing.'

4.1 The Information Security Norms Proposed by the SCO

In general, the state-sponsored conventional military operations in Ukraine are not in accordance with international norms;[30] therefore, it should come as no surprise that the reported cyber incidents also appear unorthodox. However, one important question, given that Russia is directly involved in the Ukraine conflict, is how these cyber incidents fit into the Code of Conduct framework whose primary focus is information sovereignty. In that regard, alleged Russian cyber operations would appear inconsistent with the norms it has hitherto proposed or supported. In fact, most of the cyber incidents reported by both sides in the conflict

Alleged Russian cyber operations appear inconsistent with the norms it has hitherto proposed.

seem to fall into the category of information operations, which could be interpreted as violating another state's information sovereignty. In the words of the Code of Conduct, ICTs were likely used in an effort to interfere 'in the internal affairs of other States [...] with the aim of undermining their political, economic and social stability'.

Since the norms supported by SCO and Russia focus on 'information' rather than strictly 'cyber' security, one can see that the non-cyber information operations via other media such as TV are also inconsistent with the stated principle of information sovereignty. The Code of Conduct also prohibits the abuse of a 'dominant position' in cyberspace; in this regard too, Russia may have violated its own principles by abusing its control over Russian-owned social media networks such as *Vkontakte* and *Odnoklassniki* which are also popular among Ukrainian users.[31]

Analysing the application of the SCO-proposed information security norms reveals an inherent weakness: quantifying the influence of highly subjective information content or identifying a breach of 'information sovereignty' is problematic, if not impossible.

4.2 The Voluntary Norms of Behaviour in Peacetime

The voluntary, politically binding norms advocated by the US (and partly recommended by the UN GGE) are intended to apply in peacetime. Nonetheless – and however one classifies the Ukraine conflict from a legal perspective[32] – we can still speculate relative to their application during a time of conflict.

In Ukraine, the most important observation so far is that no destructive cyber attacks on critical infrastructure (CI) have been reported by either side. To some degree, this offers hope that the norm of limiting cyber attacks against CI could

---

30 See collection of legal arguments related to the use of force in the Ukraine conflict, 'Debate Map: Ukraine Use of Force,' accessed August 17, 2015, http://opil.ouplaw.com/page/ukraine-use-of-force-debate-map.

31 Margarita Jaitner and Peter A. Mattsson. 'Russian Information Warfare of 2014,' in *2015 7th International Conference on Cyber Conflict*, ed. Markus Maybaum, Anna-Maria Osula, and Lauri Lindström (NATO CCD COE Publication, 2015), 39–52; 'Vkontakte Founder Flees Russia, Claims Persecution,' *The Moscow Times*, April 22, 2014, http://www.themoscowtimes.com/news/article/vkontakte-founder-flees-russia-claims-persecution/498715.html.

32 See Chapter 14 by Jan Stinissen.

> *This offers hope that the norm of limiting cyber attacks against CI could evolve into a standard of behaviour.*

evolve into a standard of behaviour.[33] A possible exception is the alleged sabotage of the Ukrainian election system, but even here, one might disagree over whether this was a simple information operation or a serious attack against CI.[34] The pertinent question here may relate to the proper definition of CI.

Historically, there have been some significant network intrusions,[35] but relatively few examples of effective cyber attacks against CI.[36] The few cases that are presented as destructive state-sponsored attacks – Stuxnet being the best-documented example[37] – can still be seen as outliers. With that in mind, even well-established norms are mere 'collective expectations of proper behaviour'[38], and it is unrealistic to assume that every actor (especially a nation at war) would always abide by them.

Assuming there have been no attacks against CI in Ukraine, can we say that this is another example of cyber powers restraining themselves?[39] First, this restraint may be strongly influenced by case-specific factors, as explained by Martin Libicki in Chapter 12. Second, one can identify more universal reasons stemming from classical realpolitik calculus of state actors. Is it possible that cyber does not give nation-states a revolutionary way to damage CI

> *Is it possible that cyber does not give nation-states a revolutionary way to damage CI for strategic gain?*

(or otherwise harm the citizens of an adversary state) for strategic gain?[40] Or does the case of Ukraine show that cyber operations are now universally employed, but less effective than feared?[41] In other words, the tactical opportunities that cyber is often seen as providing – the infinite reach, low cost of entry, and plausible deniability – may not easily translate to the strategic level.[42] This is also apparent as there

---

33 Limiting attacks against CI was also covered in the aforementioned SCO's Code of Conduct.
34 Clayton. 'Ukraine Election Narrowly Avoided 'Wanton Destruction' from Hackers (+video).'
35 See, for example, Trend Micro and Organization of American States. 'Report on Cybersecurity and Critical Infrastructure in the Americas,' 2015, http://www.trendmicro.com/us/security-intelligence/research-and-analysis/critical-infrastructures-security/index.html?cm_mmc=VURL:www.trendmicro.com-_-VURL-_-/oas/index.html-_-vanity; Jack Cloherty et al., "Trojan Horse' Bug Lurking in Vital US Computers,' *ABC News*, November 7, 2014, http://abcnews.go.com/US/trojan-horse-bug-lurking-vital-us-computers-2011/story?id=26737476; 'Havex Malware Strikes Industrial Sector via Watering Hole Attacks,' *SC Magazine*, June 25, 2014, http://www.scmagazine.com/havex-malware-strikes-industrial-sector-via-watering-hole-attacks/article/357875/.
36 Thomas Rid. *Cyber War Will Not Take Place* (Oxford ; New York: Oxford University Press, 2013); Brandon Valeriano and Ryan C. Maness. *Cyber War versus Cyber Realities: Cyber Conflict in the International System* (Oxford ; New York: Oxford University Press, 2015).
37 David E. Sanger. 'Obama Ordered Wave of Cyberattacks Against Iran,' *The New York Times*, June 1, 2012, http://www.nytimes.com/2012/06/01/world/middleeast/obama-ordered-wave-of-cyberattacks-against-iran.html.
38 Finnemore and Sikkink. "International Norm Dynamics and Political Change," October 1, 1998.
39 Valeriano and Maness. *Cyber War versus Cyber Realities*; Rid, *Cyber War Will Not Take Place*.
40 For a collection of authors challenging the cyber threat perception, see 'The Cyberskeptics,' *Cato Institute*, http://www.cato.org/research/cyberskeptics.
41 Rid. *Cyber War Will Not Take Place*; Valeriano and Maness. *Cyber War versus Cyber Realities*.
42 See similar remarks made by Jason Healey at Atlantic Council's panel on 'Waging Cyber Conflict', https://www.youtube.com/watch?v=aTKk4CSC9EM.

is still no shortage of 'cyber sceptics',[43] even if the vexing attribution problem were hypothetically to go away.[44]

The Ukraine case study, at least, suggests that cyber has not yet 'changed the game' in terms of state vs. state cyber attacks that destroy physical infrastructure. More likely, it can be understood as one additional weapon in a state's arsenal, and that existing norms – both legal and political – governing traditional state-to-state actions are still followed as if they were applying to other, more conventional attack methods.

As of October 2015, the examples of cyber incidents in the Ukraine crisis allow us to make tentative observations about the other proposed norms of behaviours (2, 3, and 4). In respect of norm number 2, there have been no reported allegations of interference with the work of the national CERTs. However, although some personal communications may have continued, there have been few official CERT to CERT discussions since the conflict began.[45] Against number 3, there have been no published reports of recent Russo-Ukrainian cybercrime investigations,[46] but that may be too much to hope for given that the two countries are currently in open conflict. However, the fact that Russia is unwilling to accede to the Budapest Convention on Cybercrime does not stand in its favour.

The final norm, number 4, which asks states not to steal intellectual property via cyber means, is also likely not followed, given the two countries' current state of hostilities and numerous reports of ongoing cyber espionage. Adopting the norm concerning cyber espionage is in any case fraught with challenges, as its primary norm entrepreneur, the US, has been heavily criticised by both allies and adversaries in the wake of the Snowden revelations. Further, it can be difficult – if not highly subjective – to determine whether any given attack was intended for political or economic gain. On a global level, cyber espionage appears to be a silently accepted norm. The latest UN GGE (2015), for example, did not mention it in its latest publication, signalling that the international community is currently not motivated to address the topic, and its global curtailment, at least in the short term, is unlikely.

5   Conclusion

The Ukraine case study suggests that, during this conflict, nation-states have not adhered to many of the proposed 'political' cyber norms covered in this chapter. Hence, it is doubtful that these rules will be globally accepted in the near future.

---

43   See, for example, note 40 on 'The Cyberskeptics', and discussion between Jarno Limnéll and Thomas Rid. 'Is Cyberwar Real?,' *Foreign Affairs*, March/April 2014, https://www.foreignaffairs.com/articles/global-commons/2014-02-12/cyberwar-real.

44   See, for example, Martin Libicki. 'Would Deterrence in Cyberspace Work Even with Attribution?,' *Georgetown Journal of International Affairs*, April 22, 2015, http://journal.georgetown.edu/would-deterrence-in-cyberspace-work-even-with-attribution/.

45   Conversations with Ukrainian cyber security experts.

46   Brian Ries. 'Gang of Cyber Criminals on the Run in Ukraine and Russia,' *Mashable*, June 3, 2014, http://mashable.com/2014/06/03/cyber-criminals-russia-ukraine-gameover-zeus/; Tom Brewster. 'Trouble with Russia, Trouble with the Law: Inside Europe's Digital Crime Unit' *The Guardian*, April 15, 2014, http://www.theguardian.com/technology/2014/apr/15/european-cyber-crime-unit-russia.

First, the known cyber operations appear contrary to the letter and spirit of the Code of Conduct as most of the incidents can be seen as part of the larger information war. Second, most of the norms advocated by the US were also breached as cyber espionage was widely reported, and international cooperation between the two nation's CERTs and law enforcement agencies has been absent.

As a positive sign for international security, there have been no reports of destructive cyber attacks against CI in Ukraine. This appears to go against what one could expect to see in a modern military conflict. Is this a sign that the norm of not using cyber to harm CI – as also recently advocated by the UN GGE – is likely to be globally accepted and followed in the future? Hopefully, as this potential norm is perhaps the most important in terms of strengthening international cyber security and stability. As of October 2015, the Ukraine conflict appears to indicate that cyber operations have not yet (contrary to popular belief) substantially challenged the existing norms governing state behaviour in conflict situations.

Cyber operations have not yet (contrary to popular belief) substantially challenged the existing norms governing state behaviour in conflict situations.

CHAPTER 16

Northern European Cyber Security in Light of the Ukraine War

Jarno Limnéll

Aalto University

1 Introduction

The Ukraine war is a game changer in the international security environment, and its ramifications in Northern Europe are profound. Numerous countries in the region feel that their national security is directly threatened, especially those bordering Russia. New NATO members Estonia, Latvia, Lithuania, and Poland are seeking concrete forms of reassurance from Washington and Brussels, while non-members like Sweden and Finland have reinforced their ties with the NATO Alliance. The Nordic and Baltic countries have sought a closer partnership during the Ukraine war, and this has created an opportunity to advance their regional cyber security dialogue.

Received wisdom states that small countries, especially those located next to a big country, are most at risk when international security breaks down, and that big states do what they want while small states do what they must. During the war in Ukraine, northern European countries have been forced to re-evaluate their relationship with NATO as well as their preparedness against Russia's 'hybrid warfare' which blends conventional and unconventional operations, regular and irregular tactics, information warfare, and cyber warfare. Cyber threats in particular have been an integral part of these ongoing discussions, as northern European countries have been subjected to various forms of cyber attack during the Ukraine war.

This chapter concentrates on two of Russia's neighbours that have always been in the 'realist' camp in term of their national security policy: Finland and Estonia. The response of each nation to the Ukraine crisis has been different, reflecting their traditional approaches to foreign and security policy as well as their existing ties to NATO. Yet these two nations have much in common: a fundamental interest in regional stability, Western unity, a norms-based view of international order, interdependence, and an essential need for cooperation in the field of foreign and security policy. These same principles drive both nations' prevailing views on both information security and cyber security – two issues which are sometimes distinct, and sometimes closely related.

2 Finland: Coming to Terms with Hybrid Warfare

'Is Finland really getting ready for war with Russia?' An American news channel posed this question in May 2015, when nearly a million Finnish military reservists received letters detailing their assigned duties in a crisis situation.[1] In fact, the correspondence was unrelated to Russia's annexation of Crimea or its ongoing war in Ukraine, but the media attention that this event generated speaks volumes about the age-old nature of the Russo-Finnish relationship.

Historically, Finland´s national security strategy has almost exclusively been focused on Russia, and Finns have been following the war in Ukraine extremely closely. From the beginning, Finland has condemned Russia´s activities in its largest European neighbour. Finnish President Sauli Niinistö summarised the current situation well: 'We have a long history with Russia — not that peaceful all the time. So everything the Russians are doing, surely the Finns notice and think very carefully about what that might mean.'[2] Defence Minister Carl Haglund was more direct in his choice of words: 'Russia says one thing but does another. I do not trust Russia at all.'[3]

The concept of 'cyber' is rather new in the Finnish language.[4] It was institutionalised in 2013, when Finland published its *National Cyber Security Strategy*, which described cyber security as 'the desired end state in which the cyber domain is reliable and in which its functioning is ensured'.[5] Public discussion of the importance of cyber security is a natural outgrowth of Finland being one of the most advanced information societies in the world, a country that relies heavily on the proper functioning of myriad electronic networks and services. For years, there has been an active societal debate in Finland on topics such as public-private partnerships in cyberspace, the need for better legislation, the development of cyber defence capabilities within the Finnish Defence Forces, and much more.

1   Holly Ellyatt. 'Is Finland really getting ready for war with Russia?' *CNBC*, May 25, 2015.
2   Griff Witte. 'Finland feeling vulnerable amid Russian provocations,' *The Washington Post*, November 23, 2014, 6.
3   Gerard O'Dwyer. 'Finland Brushes Off Russian Overtunes,' *DefenseNews*, February 15, 2015, http://www.defensenews.com/story/defense/international/2015/02/15/finland-russia-border-relationship/23301883/.
4   Jarno Limnéll. 'Kyber rantautui Suomeen,' *Aalto University Publication Series 12/2014*, Helsinki 2014. Concepts like information security or computer security have been used for decades in the Finnish language.
5   Secretariat of the Security Committee, *Finland´s Cyber Security Strategy*, Government Resolution 24.1.2013, 1.

In Finland, there has been intense analytical focus on Russia´s traditional warfare capabilities (including in Ukraine), but there has been limited discussion regarding Russia's cyber activities. Finnish analysts have noticed Russian cyber espionage in Ukraine, Distributed Denial-of-Service (DDoS) attacks against Ukraine, and the disruption by pro-Russian hackers of Ukrainian media and telecommunications networks.[6] However, most Finnish cyber experts have been surprised that cyber attacks have not played a greater role

It has not been necessary for Russia to use its more strategic cyber capabilities.

in the conflict, and frankly, we expected to see more. According to our analysis, the primary reason for this is likely that Ukraine is simply not a very cyber-dependent country; therefore, Russia could better fulfil its national security agenda by other means, as cyber attacks may not have the desired effect. As a consequence, it has not been necessary for Russia to use its more strategic cyber capabilities.

In Finland, one change has been a deeper appreciation of the seriousness of cyber espionage, and this is partly due to Russia´s cyber activity in Ukraine. For the first time, Finland has accused Russia of carrying out intelligence activities – both physical and cyber – within its territory. In the past, Finnish Security Police reports had only vaguely mentioned that some 'foreign countries' had engaged in espionage against Finland.

Cyber threats from Russia have been viewed in Finland primarily in the context of 'hybrid' warfare, which is understood in Finland to be a more intelligent or efficient way to wage war because it seeks to achieve political goals without the extensive use of traditional violence. Using a range of tools such as cyber attacks, economic pressure, information operations, and limited physical attacks to generate uncertainty in the mind of the general population, an aggressor may be able to achieve its desired political goals.

In Finland, it is understood that modern Russian warfare puts great emphasis on cyber and electronic warfare. In particular, Russian activities in Ukraine have spurred Finland to strengthen its military and societal defences. The new Finnish Government programme puts it this way: 'The Government will strengthen the comprehensive concept of security nationally, in the EU and in international cooperation. This applies, in particular, to new and large-scale threats, such as the defence against hybrid attacks, cyber attacks and terrorism'.[7]

From a Nordic perspective, one of the most alarming aspects of the Ukraine crisis has been Russian attempts to wage information warfare to influence public opinion. Finnish media – and even ordinary Finns – have discussed this dynamic in detail. Even the Finnish Prime Minister has openly stated that there is an ongoing

---

6   Jarno Limnéll. 'Ukraine crisis proves cyber conflict is a reality of modern warfare,' *The Telegraph*, April 19, 2014, http://www.telegraph.co.uk/technology/internet-security/10770275/Ukraine-crisis-proves-cyber-conflict-is-a-reality-of-modern-warfare.html.
7   Prime Minister´s Office, *Strategic Programme of Prime Minister Juha Sipilä's Government*, Government Publications 12/2015, May 29, 2015, 38.

information war in Ukraine. Finns have noted pro-Russian 'trolling', or the aggressive use of online arguments and false information toeing the Kremlin line. Such

One of the most alarming aspects of the Ukraine crisis has been Russian attempts to wage information warfare to influence public opinion.

tactics increased significantly as the Ukraine crisis escalated.[8] In the flood of Finnish, English and Russian troll messages, the same phrases are constantly repeated: Russia and President Vladimir Putin are idolised and the military operations of Russia in Ukraine are justified – or simply denied. The Russian Embassy in Helsinki has active Facebook and Twitter accounts; on Twitter, @russianembfinla has retweeted pro-Russia trolls and the (often anonymous) tweets of anti-Western voices, blocked Finnish journalists critical of Russia, distributed photos of Ukrainian civilian casualties, and altered the messages of Finnish tweeters.

There are numerous vexing challenges. For example, it is difficult to prepare countermeasures for an attack that is outsourced to hacker groups that lie outside normal state structures. In Ukraine, these are theoretically separatist groups in Crimea and eastern Ukraine. Cyberspace is the ideal place to wage anonymous – or at least plausibly deniable – operations.

For Finnish defence planning, the increased use of hybrid warfare does not mean forgetting more traditional military threats to our nation, but it does complicate matters – especially societal preparedness. Cyber attacks are now an integral part of all conflicts and wars, and they are blurring the line between peace and war. As Finland´s President Niinistö stated:

> *'With hybrid warfare, we are facing a substantial change in military operations. The boundary between actual war and other exercise of power is becoming blurred. Means of cyber war and information war are becoming increasingly important. It is now possible to fight a war without actually being at war. At the same time, conflict escalation is setting new speed records, as we saw for instance in the Crimea.'[9]*

3   ESTONIA: CYBER ATTACKS AND NATO ARTICLE 5

In 2007, Estonia became the first country in the world to be targeted by a coordinated international cyber attack which came in retaliation for Tallinn's decision to relocate a World War II monument from the centre of Tallinn to a military cemetery

---

8   Finland's national public-broadcasting company YLE gathered a large amount of information on pro-Russia trolling. 'Yle Kioski Investigated: This is How Pro-Russia Trolls Manipulate Finns Online – Check the List of Forums Favored by Propagandists,' last modified June 24, 2015. http://kioski.yle.fi/omat/troll-piece-2-english.

9   Speech by President of the Republic Sauli Niinistö at the ambassador seminar, August 26, 2014. http://www.presidentti.fi/public/default.aspx?contentid=311373&nodeid=44807&contentlan=2&culture=en-US.

on the outskirts of the city. Today, Estonia is considered to be a world leader in all things digital, including cyber security.[10] Estonia's current *Cyber Strategy* notes that the environment is growing more dangerous: 'The amount and activeness of states capable of cyber-attacks are increasing'.[11]

Estonia has been subjected to pressure from Moscow for years, but Russian cyber espionage in Estonia's government and commercial affairs is also getting worse. Therefore, when tensions began to rise in Ukraine, Estonia was one of the first nations to sound the alarm. In late 2014, Estonia´s Prime Minister Taavi Rõivas declared that '[w]e, in Estonia, fully understand that challenges may arise from other directions, including in the cyber domain'.[12]

Russian´s annexation of Crimea has raised fears in the Baltic states that they could be the next victims of Russian aggression. In all three countries, there are many people alive today who personally witnessed Russian tactics similar to those now on display in Ukraine. Both Latvia and Estonia have large Russian-speaking minorities living within their borders.

Estonia is different from Finland in one key regard – its NATO membership. Estonia´s President Toomas Hendrik Ilves is an active figure in NATO security and policy circles, particularly those that relate to cyber: 'Shutting down a country with a cyberattack would be very difficult but not impossible. If you did that, why wouldn't that be a case for Article 5 action?' Article 5 of the NATO Charter states that any attack on one member of the Alliance can be viewed as an attack on all. At the NATO Wales Summit in 2014, in part due to Ilves´s tireless work, NATO ministers ratified a policy stating that not only conventional and nuclear attacks, but also cyber attacks, may lead to an invocation of Article 5.[13,14]

In the past, a NATO ally under cyber attack could convene a group to consult on the attack, but not call on allies to respond in any way. With cyber attacks now falling under Article 5, NATO members now have the option of doing so. This is a major shift in policy, given that cyber warfare is still largely shrouded in mystery and secrecy. National cyber capabilities tend to be highly classified. Therefore, despite differing capabilities, viewpoints, and thresholds (after all, what Estonia might consider to be an intolerable assault on its sovereignty might not be seen the same way in Brussels or Washington) this was a significant event in that a public announcement that NATO might respond to a cyber attack as it would to a kinetic or traditional attack has tangible value in the realm of international military deterrence.

During the conflict in Ukraine, DDoS attacks against Estonia have been surprisingly few. In fact, despite expectations, the past year has been unusually calm

10   According to the global cyber security index of the International Telecommunication Union (ITU), Estonia is ranked fifth in the world in the field, and according to the recently published Business Software Alliance (BSA) report, Estonia, Austria and Netherlands are the most cyber-secure countries in Europe.

11   Ministry of Economic Affairs and Communications, *Cyber Security Strategy 2014-2017*, 2014, 5.

12   Ashish Kumar Sen. 'Estonia´s Prime Minister: NATO Presence Key to Counter Russia´s Provocations,' *Atlantic Council*, December 11, 2014.

13   NATO, 'Wales Summit Declaration,' September 5, 2014. http://www.nato.int/cps/en/natohq/official_texts_112964.htm.

14   E.g. Roger Boyes. 'NATO must respond to Russian cyber assault,' *The Times*, April 3, 2015.

compared to the previous year.[15] In 2013, the level was much higher: for example, the websites of the Ministry of Defence and the Estonian Defence Forces were both hit by DDoS, for which responsibility was claimed by 'Anonymous Ukraine'.[16] Also in 2013, the website of Estonian railway company *Elron* (which happens to be the most popular Google search term in Estonia) was defaced with messages claiming that passenger train traffic had been halted as a result of a NATO military exercise.[17] Earlier the same day, the website of the NATO Cooperative Cyber Defence Centre of Excellence (NATO CCD COE) came under DDoS attack (Anonymous Ukraine again claimed responsibility). At NATO Headquarters in Belgium, several websites have been targeted during the Ukraine war, as well as NATO's unclassified e-mail system. NATO officials have described these attacks as serious assaults, but also said that they did not pose any risk to NATO´s classified networks.[18]

The hacker group 'Cyber Berkut' said the attacks were carried out by patriotic Ukrainians angry over NATO interference in their country, and also stated that NATO CCD COE experts had been in Ukraine training 'cyber terrorists'. Although attribution of cyber attacks to specific actors and nations is difficult, technical analysis of the Cyber Berkut's domains as well as the nature of its propaganda strongly suggest ties to Russia.[19]

Since the beginning of 2014, however, Estonian cyberspace has been unusually calm. Like Finland, Estonia has seen espionage, pro-Russia trolling on Estonian web forums, and propaganda, but little in the way of malware or computer exploits. Estonians feel that the 'hostile information flow' from Russia is aimed at creating and widening rifts between native Estonians and ethnic Russians (Moscow does not see normal relations as beneficial to its current foreign policy). For example, on 4 March 2015, the television channel *Rossiya-1* (a key source of information for many ethnic Russians in the Baltic region) aired a satirical anti-Nazi video that was said to be 'proof' of Estonia's support for Nazism.[20] In response, Estonia will create its own Russian-language TV channel, to be launched in September 2015 by a state-financed public broadcaster, that will seek to empower the local ethnic Russian identity.[21]

A NATO member only since 2004, Estonia today occupies a highly visible position within the Alliance. Thus, the hybrid military campaign that Russia has launched in Crimea and in eastern Ukraine almost forces NATO to take proactive steps to guard against the use of such tactics in the Baltic states, if not to rethink some of its defence strategies altogether. As Estonia´s Defence Minister Sven Mikser stated, 'We have reason to believe that Russia views the Baltic region as one

15   Private conversations with Estonian officials.
16   CERT-EE kokkuvõte, 'Hajusad ummistusründed, võltsitud saatjaga e-kirjad ning näotustamised 1.-7. Novembril 2013, aka #OpIndependence,' https://www.ria.ee/public/CERT/opindependence.pdf.
17   E.g. Ronald Liive. 'Väide Regnumilt: NATO suurõppuse käigus rünnati ekslikult ehtsaid veebilehti,' *Forte*, November 13, 2013.
18   'NATO websites hit in cyber attack linked to Crimea tension,' *Reuters*, March 16, 2014.
19   Rodrigo, 'Cyber Berkut Graduates from DDoS Stunts to Purveyor of Cyber Attack Tools,' *Cyber Threat Intelligence*, June 8, 2015. https://www.recordedfuture.com/cyber-berkut-analysis/.
20   Ott Ummelas. 'Estonia Must Counter Hostile Russian Propaganda,' *Bloomberg Business*, March 25, 2015.
21   Silver Tambur. 'EER's new Russian-language TV channel will be called ETV+,' April 20, 2015.

of NATO's most vulnerable areas, a place where NATO's resolve and commitment could be tested'.[22]

Today, cyber security is increasingly seen as playing a vital role in national security affairs, both in and out of NATO. For its part, Estonia is already sharing its cyber security experience and expertise with Ukraine, including the organisation of large cyber security drills. And finally, Estonia has one major advantage on its side: it is home to the NATO CCD COE, whose symbolic importance to Estonia has grown rapidly.

4 CONCLUSION: DAVID VS. GOLIATH IN CYBERSPACE

Finland and Estonia both rank among the world's most connected and cyber security-savvy countries.[23] In both nations, there is a high degree of dependence on the internet, as well as a deep appreciation for the strategic nature of modern networks and the need to secure them. Therefore, both Finland and Estonia are at the forefront of the nations creating cyber norms in the world.[24]

The need to prepare defences against modern hybrid warfare forces governments, including those of Finland and Estonia, to take steps sooner rather than later. There will be conflicts in which the regular armed forces of a foreign state are not the most active participants. Some of the attacks may occur entirely in cyberspace, and the attackers might even remain anonymous. In the internet era, a wide range of national laws must be re-examined and contingencies rehearsed, so that decision-makers have the best possible tools to respond to the challenges of hybrid warfare in the future.

Russia is far larger and more populous than both Finland and Estonia, but traditional notions of size – especially in the globalised internet era – is not the only determining factor on the cyber battlefield. Smaller countries such as Finland and Estonia, with a strong heritage of technical capability and experience, may possess some advantages that not even great powers could dream of. In the near term, Finland will continue to strengthen its defences independently, while Estonia will continue to emphasise NATO´s Article 5. In the long term, Finland and Estonia will continue to punch above their weight in the cyber domain – especially relative to their size.

> *Smaller countries with a strong heritage of technical capability and experience may possess some advantages that not even great powers could dream of.*

---

22 Geoff Dyer. 'NATO shifts strategy in Europe to deal with Russia threat', *Financial Times*, June 23, 2015.
23 *Global Cybersecurity Index and Cyberwellness Profiles*. International Telecommunications Union, April 2015 http://www.itu.int/dms_pub/itu-d/opb/str/D-STR-SECU-2015-PDF-E.pdf.
24 See e.g. Jarno Limnéll. 'Can Finland Act As a Mediator on Cyber Norms?' *Council on Foreign Relations*, May 28, 2015, http://blogs.cfr.org/cyber/2015/05/28/can-finland-act-as-a-mediator-on-cyber-norms/.

CHAPTER 17

What's Next for Putin in Ukraine: Cyber Escalation?

Jason Healey
Michelle Cantos

Columbia University

1   Introduction

We may be facing the internet's most dangerous moment.

From the earliest days of cyber intelligence, a rule of thumb was that 'those with the capability to cause significant cyber disruption lack the intent; those with the intent lack the capability'.[1] Some governments, including the United States, Russia, and China, have always had the capability, but have lacked the motivation to bring down the internet. However, times change, and Vladimir Putin, now facing strong sanctions and a weak rouble, could choose to retaliate against the West in the form of 'little green bytes'. US and European economies may, in fact, be natural targets, carrying the implicit message: if you seriously affect Russia's financial health, you too will feel the pain.

> *We may be facing the internet's most dangerous moment.*

---

1   Matthew Devost. 'Risk of cyber terrorism raised at seminar,' *Massey University News*, September 12, 2002, http://www.massey.ac.nz/~wwpubafs/2002/news_release/13_09_02a.html.

Conflict in cyberspace offers adversaries many possibilities and Putin has numerous options. In the near term, there are four obvious scenarios: local instability, intimidation, frozen cyber conflict, and coercion.

The first option, local instability, would exclusively target Ukraine, causing cyber disruption in the hope of keeping the country prostrate while trying to avoid escalation with the West and a tightening of sanctions. In the second option, intimidation, Putin would use cyber capabilities against the West to mirror his existing recipe of strategic threats, military exercises, submarine deployments, nuclear threats and nuclear-capable bomber flights. A further escalation here could be a third option – a frozen cyber conflict, where techniques of hybrid warfare are used to try for medium-term disruption to the internet itself. The fourth option, coercion, would go beyond local disruption and provocations and would attempt to use cyber force to disrupt Western economic and military targets. This last scenario is the most dangerous of all, potentially signifying a calculation by Putin that Russia has little remaining stake in the global economic game. In that case, why not upend the table and ruin the party for everyone?

2   LOCAL INSTABILITY: FROZEN CONFLICT WITH A TOPPING OF CYBER

In the least aggressive scenario, Putin would escalate only within Ukraine in an attempt to further destabilise and delegitimise the existing government. The 'little green bytes' might deny service to Ukrainian government and media sites, or even target critical infrastructure. As in other post-Soviet frozen conflicts, the goal is not necessarily to prevail, but rather to keep Ukraine destabilised for years and unable to pose any challenge.

As noted elsewhere in this book, the Russians, due to their legacy from the Moscow-dominated Soviet Union, have an extensive knowledge of Ukrainian systems. Most of Ukraine's infrastructure is well understood – if not designed by – Russian enterprises, so exploiting them for cyber attack would be far easier than for a typical cyber campaign elsewhere. There may also be a sufficient number of insiders who are friendly to Russia, and who could either be bribed or blackmailed into leaking sensitive government materials, disseminating propaganda, installing malicious software, or even physically destroying key systems.

Russia has shown some of its digital arsenal. Cyber espionage campaigns such as 'Sandworm' have played a role in intelligence collection operations against the Ukrainian government and some NATO nations, even taking advantage of multiple zero-day exploits.[2]

The local instability cyber option could allow Putin to maintain pressure on Ukraine while avoiding an increase in tensions with the West. He might even be

---

2   'iSIGHT discovers zero-day vulnerability CVE-2014-4114 used in Russian cyber-espionage campaign,' *iSight*, October 14, 2014, http://www.isightpartners.com/2014/10/cve-2014-4114/.

able to accomplish this while claiming to be de-escalating the conflict. Russia, in this scenario, would only launch disruptive cyber attacks *within* Ukraine, not against other targets in the West, and attempting to limit the upper bound of escalation. The international community might be happy, however, to countenance a 'cyber war' in Ukraine if it caused little tangible damage to other countries, limited the body count, and generated fewer disturbing media images.

3   INTIMIDATION: CYBER PROVOCATIONS AND ESCALATION

A second option for Putin is to send a digital warning shot across the West's cyber bow, in effect saying that Russia has additional cards up its sleeve and may play them if necessary. Russia is already escalating all sorts of military operations against the West, from massive exercises and military flights to nuclear threats. 'Little green bytes' could therefore be just one additional form of provocation to add instability on the world stage.

Such attacks would be just-deniable-enough and might target defence and military systems and networks. Russia could target allies with weaker defences, or governments which Putin might calculate as being easier political prey, and more susceptible to Russian coercion.

This cyber escalation would simply be a natural extension of Putin's provocative behaviour in other military forces. In the last fifteen months, Russia has apparently sneaked submarines into Swedish and Finnish territorial waters, stating that Finland's growing ties with NATO were a 'special concern';[3] flown jet fighters and nuclear-capable bombers along the periphery of Europe; and buzzed NATO ships including the US guided-missile destroyer USS Ross as it sailed in international waters off the Russian-occupied Crimean peninsula.[4]

Apart from drilling his conventional forces, Putin in the spring of 2014 organised large-scale exercises designed to assess the preparedness level of his nuclear forces.[5] In the context of Russia's nuclear threats against Denmark, these appear to be calculated (if clumsy) efforts to intimidate the West.[6]

The Russian cyber assault on Estonia in 2007 was a blueprint for a geopolitically inspired and just-deniable-enough digital disruption. When

> *Estonia in 2007 was a blueprint for a geopolitically inspired and just-deniable-enough digital disruption.*

---

3   'Finnish military fires depth charges at suspected submarine,' *Reuters*, April 28, 2015, http://www.reuters.com/article/2015/04/28/us-finland-navy-idUSKBN0NJ0Y120150428.

4   Barbara Starr. 'Russian planes, U.S. warship have close encounter near Crimea,' *CNN*, June 1, 2015, http://www.cnn.com/2015/06/01/politics/russia-plane-navy-uss-ross/.

5   Bill Gertz. 'Russia Conducts Large-Scale Nuclear Attack Exercise,' *Washington Free Beacon*, May 8, 2014, http://freebeacon.com/national-security/russia-conducts-large-scale-nuclear-attack-exercise/.

6   Adam Withnall. 'Russia threatens Denmark with nuclear weapons if it tries to join NATO defence shield,' *The Independent*, March 22, 2015, http://www.independent.co.uk/news/world/europe/russia-threatens-denmark-with-nuclear-weapons-if-it-tries-to-join-nato-defence-shield-10125529.html.

the Estonian government decided to move a Soviet war memorial from the centre of its capital Tallinn to a military cemetery on the outskirts of town, Russia responded by encouraging 'patriotic hackers' to engage in a three week long Distributed Denial-Of-Service (DDoS) attack against numerous sectors of the Estonian economy including the government, media, and financial institutions.[7] This template relies on a combination of threats, cyber capabilities, the use of proxies, and plausible deniability.

Russia might alternately hold off on such disruptive attacks in favour of increasingly aggressive espionage. In fact, it seems an escalation in such intrusions is already underway.

Russian state-sponsored hackers are believed to have recently compromised the US Department of State, then used that access to penetrate the unclassified network of the Executive Office of the President.[8,9] Unlike during previous intrusions linked to Russia, on this occasion the digital spies did not back out of the system once they were discovered, but fought back in order to maintain their foothold in the network.[10] Investigators also believe that Russian spies were behind the recent intrusion into the unclassified email of the Joint Chiefs of Staff, an intrusion which forced the Pentagon to take the system down for several days.[11]

4   Freezing the Conflict in Cyberspace

Rather than, or in addition to, using cyber to help destabilise the Ukraine, Putin might try to make the internet itself a new zone of frozen conflict. This option is perhaps not as likely as the others, but might offer Putin an intriguing possibility: inflict on the internet, which delivers 'harmful' content in the form of unwanted truths to Russian citizens, just enough long-term disruption so that it is less useful, less trusted, and less an enabler to Western economies and societies.

In this option, Putin's forces would use cyber capabilities to periodically disrupt core internet infrastructure such as the domain name system, or frequently take down Western information providers. Each new week could see a large-scale denial-of-service attack.

This option differs from the previous 'intimidation' option in two ways. First, the attacks would be far more disruptive than mere shows of force. Compared to

---

7   Ian Traynor. 'Russia accused of unleashing cyberwar to disable Estonia,' *The Guardian*, May 16, 2007, http://www.theguardian.com/world/2007/may/17/topstories3.russia.

8   Evan Perez and Shimon Prokupecz. 'Sources: State Dept. hack the 'worst ever',' *CNN*, March 10, 2015, http://www.cnn.com/2015/03/10/politics/state-department-hack-worst-ever/index.html.

9   Ellen Nakashima. 'Hackers breach some White House computers,' *The Washington Post*, October 28, 2014, http://www.washingtonpost.com/world/national-security/hackers-breach-some-white-house-computers/2014/10/28/2ddf2fa0-5ef7-11e4-91f7-5d89b5e8c251_story.html.

10   Michael S. Schmidt and David E. Sanger. 'Russian Hackers Read Obama's Unclassified Emails, Officials Say,' *New York Times*, April 25, 2015, http://www.nytimes.com/2015/04/26/us/russian-hackers-read-obamas-unclassified-emails-officials-say.html

11   Nancy A. Youssef. 'Russians Hacked Joint Chiefs of Staff,' *The Daily Beast*, August 6, 2015, http://www.thedailybeast.com/cheats/2015/08/06/russians-hacked-joint-chiefs-of-staff.html.

the intimidation option where Russia threatens force to avoid a conflict, in this frozen-conflict option, Putin already accepts Western nations as adversaries. The goal is therefore not to get them to back down, but hopefully to destabilise the internet just enough to deny cyber benefits to his perceived enemies.

5   COERCION: ESCALATE TO DE-ESCALATE

The most aggressive option for Putin is to use cyber capabilities to disrupt the economies of the West. Imagine a massive, long-term and continuing attack against the West's financial system or power grids. What if, Sony-style, one bank a week were to be targeted for a disruptive and embarrassing attack?

> *What if, Sony-style, one bank a week were targeted for a disruptive and embarrassing attack?*

Russia in the past had, along with at least the United States and China, the capability to conduct such attacks, but lacked the intent. Russia had disagreements with the West but was not engaged in any real conflict. Further, to some extent, Russia needed healthy Western economies to itself thrive.

That situation has changed. Today, Putin may well see himself in a conflict with the West, perhaps even a shooting war, and feel the very survival of his regime could be at stake. In 2013, sanctions including asset freezes and export prohibitions pushed Russia to the brink of a recession, and the economy grew by only 1.3%.[12] By the end of 2015, the World Bank predicts that ongoing sanctions coupled with the decrease in oil prices will shrink the Russian economy by 3.8%.[13] Putin could calculate that Russia has few remaining stakes in the global economy and financial system.

Without international economic entanglement, it is far easier for Putin to use Russia's impressive cyber capabilities to try to directly coerce (rather than threaten) the West. By inflicting economic turmoil, he could turn Russia's lack of a stake in the global financial system from a liability into an asset. With nothing to lose and everything to gain, Putin might calculate that unleashing his just-deniable-enough 'little green bytes' against Western economies could be a win-win situation for Russia.

Russia is already pushing the idea that they may need to 'escalate to de-escalate' a brewing conflict with the West. In an extensive article in *Vox*, Max Fisher lays out the evidence that the world is ever closer to conflict, even a world war, and especially that Putin 'has enshrined, in Russia's official nuclear doctrine, a dangerous idea no Soviet leader ever adopted: that a nuclear war could be winnable'.[14]

---

12   'How far do EU-US sanctions on Russia go?' *BBC*, September 15, 2014, http://www.bbc.com/news/world-europe-28400218
13   Andrey Ostroukh. 'Russia's Economic Outlook Worse Than Thought, World Bank Says,' *The Wall Street Journal,* April 1, 2015, http://www.wsj.com/articles/russias-economic-outlook-worse-than-thought-world-bank-says-1427883522.
14   Max Fisher. 'How World War III Became Possible,' *Vox,* June 29, 2015, http://www.vox.com/2015/6/29/8845913/russia-war.

In that light, cyber weapons may offer an even more attractive opportunity given that cyber effects can be temporary and reversible. Russian Deputy Prime Minister Dmitry Rogozin has already declared that Russian tanks 'don't need visas' to cross international borders.[15] If Russia is willing to make nuclear threats and roll T-72s across borders, then how much more likely are attacks using faster, more deniable, electrons?

One obvious target would be Western financial firms that currently enforce the sanctions against Russia. Many analysts believe that Iran chose precisely this form of retaliation in 2012, in response to Stuxnet.[16] Other obvious targets could be the oil, gas, or electricity sectors, in order to raise the price of oil.

During our research for this chapter, several security analysts stated that Russia may be preparing for this contingency with its Havex and BlackEnergy cyber campaigns.[17] In both cases, Russian government hackers apparently targeted Western energy companies, not for espionage, but in order to prepare for a potential follow-on disruptive attack. It appears Russia has proved that it has the required capabilities already in place to disrupt Western energy systems, now it is just a matter of having the intent.

Or Putin could focus his cyber attack not against sectors, but against specific Western allies; those he felt would be most likely to submit to coercive pressure. His whispered promise might be something along the lines of 'Drop your support for sanctions and all these cyber failures you're experiencing can just go away.' Countries which might not have been fully committed to the sanctions in the first place might not need much convincing.

6   CONCLUSION

Cyberspace – and cyber attacks – offer many ways, especially for a capable nation-state, to target an adversary. In the current conflict, the most likely near-term options for Russia are perhaps local instability, intimidation and coercion. Of course, the scenarios discussed in this chapter are not mutually exclusive; Putin could jump between them or even employ them all simultaneously.

Fortunately to help analyse Russia's cyber current actions, it may be enough to analyse his actions in the physical world: Russian hostility in Europe is likely to be matched with Russian hostility online. If this process starts to get out of control, then Western leaders have to be at their highest level of concern.

If Putin believes he is approaching a use-it-or-lose-it situation for his autocratic regime and its stolen billions, he may just decide to take the internet down with him.

---

15   'Russian Official: 'Tanks Don't Need Visas', *Defense One/Agence France-Presse,* May 25, 2015, http://www.defensenews.com/story/defense/international/europe/2015/05/25/russian-official-tanks-need-visas/27924351/.

16   Siobhan Gorman and Julian Barnes. 'Iran Blamed for Cyberattacks,' *The Wall Street Journal*, October 12, 2012, http://www.wsj.com/articles/SB10000872396390444465780457805293155576700.

17   Blake Sobczak and Peter Behr. 'Secret meetings tackle back-to-back energy-sector cyberthreats,' *EnergyWire*, October 31, 2014, http://www.eenews.net/energywire/stories/1060008193.

CHAPTER 18

STRATEGIC DEFENCE IN CYBERSPACE: BEYOND TOOLS AND TACTICS

RICHARD BEJTLICH

The Brookings Institution

1   INTRODUCTION

The digitisation of information, which began during the Second World War, has significantly deepened the relationship between human beings (from the individual to the nation-state) and unstructured data, structured information (such as a databases), and intelligence (information of political or military value). Every part of society has benefited from information technology; however, as we have increasingly become data-reliant, our adversaries have sought to leverage information against us. Attackers and defenders now battle for access to, and control of, information in the political, economic, military, and social spheres. In military parlance, data has become a virtual 'high ground' from which the better-informed can influence an adversary.

The Ukrainian Government currently finds itself at a tactical disadvantage *vis-à-vis* Russia, both on the traditional field of battle as well as in cyberspace. However, cyber security, especially at the national level, is a strategic game, and Kyiv can make smart investments that will pay off over the long run. In Ukraine, as in every other nation-state, practitioners, academics, policy-makers, and the public are individually and collectively vexed by the question of how to defend data, information, and intelligence. Part of the problem is that adversaries do not have one or even several attack strategies at their disposal: they can steal, destroy, deny access to, or even alter information – as well as the systems that store, process, and display it to its ostensible owners.

Digitised information is a human product which resides in mechanical devices built by engineers and programmers, and so decision-makers naturally turn to the technical community for answers to these challenges. Technical proposals take many forms. Several frequently appear in policy-making circles: we could scrap the internet entirely and replace it with a 'more secure' alternative;[1] we might build software that is 'not hackable,' possibly through 'leap ahead' technologies that make defence easier than offense (which is today manifestly not the case);[2] or we can outsource our security to third-party vendors.[3] These are all technical ideas, but they are generally not feasible for a variety of reasons. More fundamentally, it is dangerous to rely solely on technology to mitigate core security problems.

2   The Limitations of Technology-driven Approaches

Technology plays an important role in defending data. Thoughtfully designed networks, higher quality software, and agile start-ups can frustrate opportunistic intruders seeking easy prey. Unfortunately, well-resourced, professional attackers sometimes have long-standing missions to compromise specific high-value targets, whether for information theft or data manipulation. They will not give up until their mission requirements change or until they succeed in their assignment.

Digital defenders may only get a glimpse of the intruder, and often this comes far too late in the game. Whereas the victim's perspective is usually narrow and incomplete, professional attackers are persistent and know exactly what they are targeting. According to the Mandiant 2015 *M-Trends* report, the median number of days in 2014 that a successful threat group was present on a victim's network before detection, was 205. In one case, an adversary had maintained unauthorised access for over 8 years.[4] Even after discovery, organisations can spend months trying to remove the intruder. In February 2015, the *Wall Street Journal* reported that the US State Department continued to be plagued by foreign hackers fully three months after the agency confirmed reports of an intrusion.[5]

A technology-centric worldview obsesses about a static, one-time exchange between attacker and defender.

This relationship between security and time is central to protecting digital

---

1   Thom Shanker. 'Cyberwar Chief Calls for Secure Computer Network,' *New York Times*, 23 September 2010, http://www.nytimes.com/2010/09/24/us/24cyber.html; John Markoff. 'Do We Need a New Internet?' *New York Times,* 14 February 2009, http://www.nytimes.com/2009/02/15/weekinreview/15markoff.html.

2   Jim Garamone. 'DARPA Director Discusses Cyber Security Challenges,' *DoD News,* 1 October 2014, http://www.defense.gov/news/newsarticle.aspx?id=123307.

3   Over 400 vendors demonstrated their products and services at the RSA Conference in San Francisco, California in April 2015. RSA Conference 2015 vendors, http://www.rsaconference.com/events/us15/expo-sponsors.

4   The median number for 2013 was 229 days. FireEye, *M-Trends 2015: A View from the Front Lines* (Milpitas, CA: FireEye Corporation 2015), https://www2.fireeye.com/rs/fireye/images/rpt-m-trends-2015.pdf.

5   Danny Yadron. 'Three Months Later, State Department Hasn't Rooted Out Hackers,' *Wall Street Journal,* 19 February 2015, http://www.wsj.com/articles/three-months-later-state-department-hasnt-rooted-out-hackers-1424391453.

resources. An analysis of time intervals is key to understanding the interaction between attackers and defenders, but in general the security community does not sufficiently understand or appreciate the nature and consequences of this relationship. A technology-centric worldview obsesses about a static, one-time exchange between attacker and defender. This is not an accurate description of the real world, which is populated, not with mindless code, but with rational and irrational human beings who are both intelligent and adaptive adversaries and who observe their targets, allocate resources, and make dynamic decisions in order to accomplish their goals.[6]

Digital defenders ignore these facts at their peril. The interactive and time-dependent nature of network attack and defence leads to the promotion of suboptimal approaches to security. The emphasis on 'cyber hygiene' is illustrative.[7] To defeat intruders, this method promotes knowing one's network, removing unauthorised systems, patching vulnerabilities, and improving configurations. All of these are certainly both requisite and commendable defensive steps. However, they are insufficient when confronting an attacker who has the time and resources to adapt to and overcome the target's defences. 'Washing cyber hands' is helpful when minimising the spread of mindless germs, but it is less effective when those germs are as smart as, or better-resourced and motivated than, the hand-washer.

3   STRATEGIC THOUGHT IN CYBER DEFENCE

To better address the dynamic challenge of continuous interaction between adaptive, intelligent adversaries, this chapter advocates the application of strategic military concepts to conflict in cyberspace. Armed conflict has long been characterised as a struggle between persistent adversaries over time. However, the advent of mass armies, modern weapons, and nation-state warfare in the late 18th and early 19th centuries took this concept to a higher level. During the 20th century, military strategists therefore had to think beyond the traditional dichotomy of strategy versus tactics. Over time, they codified multiple 'levels of warfare'.

Beginning in the 1980s, U.S. Army doctrine described three levels of war: strategic, operational, and tactical.[8] These built on previous writings and lessons learned, from Napoleonic battles to Soviet military planning. National goals and policy – sitting above the strategic level of war – were incorporated into doctrine, although this can be confusing given that the word 'strategic' often appeared in both the model's name and one of its primary elements.

---

6   John R. Boyd. 'The Essence of Winning and Losing,' unpublished PowerPoint presentation, 1985, http://www.danford.net/boyd/essence.htm.

7   Jonathan Trull. 'Practice Makes Perfect: Making Cyber Hygiene Part of Your Security Program,' *CSO Magazine,* 3 March 2014, http://www.csoonline.com/article/2891689/security0/practice-makes-perfect-making-cyber-hygiene-part-of-your-security-program.html.

8   United States Department of the Army, *Field Manual 100-5: Operations* (Washington, DC: US Army 1982), http://cgsc.contentdm.oclc.org/cdm/compoundobject/collection/p4013coll9/id/48/rec/10.

Policies and Goals

|

Strategies

|

Operations (including Campaigns)

|

Tactics

|

Tools

Figure 1-1 – Strategic Thought, Adapted for Digital Conflict

In this chapter, the author argues that decision-makers need to better understand the role of technology in strategic thought, and so it adds a new level below the tactical layer: 'tools'. Certainly in physical warfare one uses 'tools' to inflict kinetic damage. In the digital world, the model explicitly introduces tools in order to show practitioners where they fit in strategic thinking. Too many digital security professionals believe tools are the sole focus of defensive action. By placing tools at the bottom of the model, they appear, in the author's opinion, in their proper place. Furthermore, in this model, the term 'campaign' is included at the operational level. 'Campaigns' and 'operations' are sometimes interchanged, so both appear to reduce confusion.

> *Too many digital security professionals believe tools are the sole focus of defensive action.*

These five levels are depicted in Figure 1-1. Policies and goals are broad statements by organisational leadership that describe the desired purpose of the strategic programme. Strategies are concepts for employing organisational resources to accomplish the stated policies and goals. Operations (which in this schema are organised into campaigns) are sets of activities designed to implement strategies that are pursued over days, weeks, months, or even years. Tactics are actions taken within individual encounters with an adversary, and serve as the atomic elements of a campaign. Tools are the digital equipment with which an actor implements tactics.

All of these elements must be connected in order to achieve successful outcomes. Before explaining how these five levels can improve digital defence, it is important to recognise that I am not advocating the 'militarisation' of cyberspace – which is a valid concern of many analysts. For example, in 2013, Jason Healey wrote in *Foreign Affairs* that the military had 'prioritised one national security goal – more spying and attack capabilities – above all others'.[9] A *Forbes* journalist defined the problem as 'giv[ing] a military character to' it, 'equip[ping] [it] with military forces and defences' or 'adapt[ing] [it] for military use',[10] This author, while generally disagreeing with these premises, does not equate strategic thought with militarisation. The purpose of this chapter on strategic thought is to familiarise defenders with another strategy to protect information, one suited to the timescales and interactive nature of modern computer intrusions.

4   Traditional Security within the Strategic Model

Squaring traditional security concepts with the strategic model contributes to a rich discussion of digital defence. Typically, network defenders concentrate on tools and tactics, which are in turn dominated by the notions of security software, software security, and securing software. Security software consists of programs written by vendors, open source developers, and individual security teams that are designed to detect, frustrate, and remove adversaries. Software security refers to the process of writing computer programs that are free from coding, process, and logic flaws, optimally using a process such as the Building Security In Maturity Model (BSIMM).[11] Securing software is a process to enable the 'cyber hygiene' model, whereby defenders take various tactical steps to reduce the likelihood of compromise.

Beyond the security team, one finds multiple layers of management, including a chief security or information security officer (CSO or CISO), one or more chief technology or information officers (CTO or CIO), other members of the so-called 'C-suite' including the chief financial or operating officers (CFO, COO), and ultimately the chief executive officer (CEO) and board of directors. At the nation-state level, some governments have appointed cyber security coordinators reporting to the head of government. Recent examples include the United States, the United Kingdom, Germany, Russia, Japan, and France.[12] In China, President Xi Jinping personally leads the country's top information security group.[13] One would think

---

9   Jason Healey. 'How Emperor Alexander Militarized American Cyberspace,' *Foreign Policy*, 6 November 2013, http://foreignpolicy.com/2013/11/06/how-emperor-alexander-militarized-american-cyberspace/.
10 Sean Lawson. 'Is the United States Militarizing Cyberspace?' *Forbes*, 2 November 2012, http://www.forbes.com/sites/seanlawson/2012/11/02/is-the-united-states-militarizing-cyberspace/.
11 BSIMM, https://www.bsimm.com/.
12 French Ministry of Foreign Affairs and International Development, 'France and cyber security,' http://www.diplomatie.gouv.fr/en/french-foreign-policy/defence-security/cyber-security/.
13 Shannon Tiezzi. 'Xi Jinping Leads China's New Internet Security Group,' *The Diplomat*, 28 February 2014, http://thediplomat.com/2014/02/xi-jinping-leads-chinas-new-internet-security-group/.

that, with so much focus on cyber and information security at the upper levels of management, defence strategies would be clear. However, despite numerous recent high-profile breaches, security leaders continue to fret that their 'organisation's business leadership didn't provide them the support and space they need to secure their organisations properly'.[14]

Improving the dynamics of strategic thought according to the proven military model can help organisations and nation states move beyond a 'tools and tactics' focused approach. The latter is by far the prevailing paradigm. For example, one 2014 RSA Conference presentation encouraged attendees to 'exploit pet projects' and 'capitalise on timely events' by using the 'near-death experiences of others to justify security spend'.[15] One 2015 article written for security managers stressed the need for more capable software, stating that 'a CISO must successfully address many challenging elements when procuring a new security technology solution'.[16] In 2014, Symantec's Senior Vice President for Information Security said that only 45% of cyber attacks are prevented by anti-virus software, calling it a 'dead' technology.[17] Writing secure software, while a laudable goal, continues to be difficult, even for leading companies like Microsoft. Bill Gates accelerated the programme to find a secure development lifecycle in 2002, but the vendor continues to release patches for 'remote code execution' vulnerabilities in core Microsoft platforms on a monthly basis. In brief, we need more than tools and tactics to counter digital adversaries.

When trying to learn how to communicate with higher level managers and CISOs, agency leads, and policy-makers are bombarded with advice like the following:

> 'One of the most strategic skills a security chief can bring is the proficiency in translating security speak into the language of business risks and financial ROI [return on investment] terms... At the board level, the ability to show dollar return on security initiatives is critical to ensure continued executive support on security investments'.[18]

The problem with the focus on tools and tactics, and related topics of risk and ROI is that higher-level management and boards do not feel connected to the true defensive posture of their organisation. Because leaders have not been valued parts of the security program development process, they think security is mainly an issue to be solved by technical professionals. Their experience with the IT and security

14 George V. Hulme. 'The CSO's failure to lead,' *CSO Magazine*, 9 June 2014, http://www.csoonline.com/article/2360984/security-leadership/the-cso-s-failure-to-lead.html.

15 John B. Dickson. 'Getting Your Security Budget Approved without FUD,' RSA Conference 2014, http://www.rsaconference.com/writable/presentations/file_upload/ciso-w04a-getting-your-security-budget-approved-without-fud.pdf.

16 Craig Shumard. 'CISOs Face Tough Challenges When Procuring Security Technologies,' Tenable Network Security, 5 March 2015, http://www.tenable.com/blog/cisos-face-tough-challenges-when-procuring-security-technologies.

17 Danny Yadron. 'Symantec Develops New Attack on Cyberhacking,' *Wall Street Journal*, 4 May 2014, http://www.wsj.com/articles/SB10001424052702303417104579542140235850578.

18 Danelle Au. 'Getting the CISO a Seat,' *Security Week*, 16 July 2012, http://www.securityweek.com/getting-ciso-seat.

worlds has led them to approach security as an issue of approving budgets to purchase ever-more-costly security software. The *Christian Science Monitor* reported the following in February 2015:

> '*In a survey commissioned by defence contractor Raytheon of 1,006 chief information officers, chief information security officers, and other technology executives, 78 percent said their boards had not been briefed even once on their organisation's cybersecurity strategy over the past 12 months ... The findings are similar to those reported by Pricewaterhouse-Coopers in its Global State of Information Security Survey last year in which fewer that 42 percent of respondents said their board actively participates in overall security strategy*'.[19]

In light of these challenges, this chapter advocates making boards and higher-level managers integral aspects of the security process, by way of strategic thought.

> *This chapter advocates making boards and higher-level managers integral aspects of the security process.*

5   Cyber Security without Strategy

The following scenario will help the reader understand how the application of strategic cyber security principles can better protect digital assets. A private organisation suffers targeted attacks by both criminal and nation-state threat groups, which not only compromise the organisation but also steal intellectual property including trade secrets, sensitive commercial data, and other digital resources.

The traditional 'tools-and-tactics' security model is characterised by suboptimal communication and poor alignment between the management, board, and security team. The latter, led by the CISO, is determined to counter the adversary. Their first instinct will be to take some concrete action: to hire new personnel, to develop a new capability, to adopt a new tactic, or to purchase a new software tool. Next, they will attempt to translate their plan into 'business speak', and the CISO will develop an argument based on an ROI estimate that includes the cost of the initiative, the amount of money it should save (if all goes well), and a mathematical calculation of the overall risk to the enterprise.

If asked by the CEO or board to explain his or her rationale, the CISO will reply that a tools-and-tactics approach will save the enterprise money and reduce its level of risk. Finally, the management will give the proposal a green light, or send the CISO back to the drawing board.

---

19   Jaikumar Vijayan. 'After high-profile hacks, many companies still nonchalant about cybersecurity,' *Christian Science Monitor,* 19 February 2015, http://www.csmonitor.com/World/Passcode/2015/0219/After-high-profile-hacks-many-companies-still-nonchalant-about-cybersecurity.

This budget request cycle is repeated *ad nauseam*, until management gets wise to the fact that network security ROI seems to have an Alice-in-Wonderland quality about it: the more money they spend, the more money they are supposed to save. Eventually, management realises that security is a lot more about loss prevention than revenue generation, and they begin to feel disconnected (and disaffected) from the defence of their digital resources. Further, they recognise that their organisation is one of many whose boards are not briefed on real strategy, and who have in fact never participated in serious strategy formulation.

6   STRATEGIC CYBER SECURITY

A strategic cyber security programme, by contrast, does not begin with tools and tactics, but with an articulation of one or more programme goals. First, the strategy-minded CISO gets executive buy-in to those goals. To that end, the CISO must incorporate all levels of strategic thought, starting with the board and CEO – everyone must feel ownership and participation. The smart CISO recognises that security is a journey, not a destination, and that relationship building requires an ability to translate between technical and non-technical vocabularies.

The CISO ensures that the programme goals accurately govern the objectives of the enterprise's digital security programme. In our scenario, the CISO, board, and CEO all agree that, with respect to intellectual property, trade secrets, and sensitive data, the new policy goal is to minimise loss due to intrusion. This statement implies that everyone understands that stopping all adversaries and all attacks is simply not possible, especially when dealing with nation-state actors and some advanced criminal groups.

The primary objective of this exercise is to achieve consensus on a simply stated, non-technical programme goal. No in-depth technical discussion is needed to achieve consensus, although the CISO must ensure that all goals, policies, and strategies are technically feasible. With a mandate in hand, the CISO can confidently work with his or her security team to plan the necessary operations and campaigns and, if necessary, acquire new tools

> *The primary objective is to achieve consensus on a simply stated, non-technical programme goal.*

and tactics to facilitate them. Together, they decide to implement a network security monitoring (NSM) operation, defined as the collection and escalation of indications and warnings to detect and respond to intruders.[20] The security team begins the long-term, strategic process of hunting for hostile cyber attack campaigns, encompassing both known and unknown intrusion patterns.

---

20   Richard Bejtlich. *The Practice of Network Security Monitoring* (San Francisco, CA: No Starch 2013).

The CISO, board, and CEO all agree that a second programme goal is the rapid detection, response, and containment of cyber threats. This goal helps to ensure that when intruders breach the perimeter defences, the game is far from over. Defenders can still win, so long as they contain the threat before the attacker can accomplish his or her ultimate mission. Therefore, the security team will develop strategies to identify compromises quickly, determine their nature, give them some level of attribution, and above all develop a plan to stop the attacker from accomplishing his or her mission.

At the tactical level of individual engagements with the adversary – the equivalent of battles in war – the security team will have myriad decisions to make, including whether to dislodge the intruder immediately or whether to watch the intruder for a time in order to collect valuable intelligence. Some tactics govern how specific tools or techniques can be used, such as when Star Trek personnel switch their hand phasers between 'stun' and 'kill'. As always, the adversary gets a say in what happens, but from the enterprise's point of view, programme goals, policies, and guidelines should be written to govern this entire process.

7 The Relevance of Campaigns

Central to the concept, and success, of a strategic security program is the campaign, which functions at the operational level. In some sense, the maturity of a security programme can be derived from the attention shown by the CISO and his or her security team to campaign development, and the understanding of campaign progress and analysis by top management. Consider the following quote from a February 2015 Reuters report on defence contractor Lockheed Martin:

> '[Chief Executive Officer Marillyn] Hewson told the company's annual media day that Lockheed had faced 50 'coordinated, sophisticated campaign' attacks by hackers in 2014 alone, and she expected those threats to continue growing'.[21]

When Ms. Hewson spoke in terms of campaigns, she showed that her security team thinks and works at an advanced level. It is likely that Lockheed also aligns campaigns with specific threat actors and motives. Speaking about specific campaigns and ranking them in terms of sophistication and impact permits a vastly more meaningful discussion with other executives, the board, and other stakeholders. The CEO should be able to speak in detail about the threat actors behind the campaigns, including their means and motives, as well as illustrative examples of each campaign and how the security team detected and responded to them. The term 'campaign' also matches well with non-technology business operations such as marketing campaigns and sales campaigns.

---

21   Andrea Shalal. 'Lockheed sees double-digit growth in cyber business,' *Reuters*, 18 February 2015, http://www.reuters.com/article/2015/02/19/us-lockheed-cybersecurity-idUSKBN0LN03K20150219.

Contrast this approach with a recent briefing by Japan's National Institute of Information and Communications Technology, which appeared in the *Japan Times*:

> *'The number of computer attacks on government and other organisations detected in Japan doubled in 2014 from the previous year to a record 25.66 billion, a government agency said Tuesday'.*[22]

Discussing individual attacks has limited value, as discrete incidents include everything from a suspicious TCP packet, to an odd computer port, dubious SQL query, or 'phishy' email. On the other hand, how can anyone devise a credible programme goal to counter over 25 billion attacks? The sweet spot lies in the middle, in grouping the primary threats and threat actors into coherent and logical campaigns. This is the best way for the enterprise – or a nation state – to counter an interactive and adaptive adversary.

8 STRATEGIC CYBER DEFENCE IN UKRAINE

The government of Ukraine, which has tense relations with Russia and is embroiled in an ongoing war, is likely the target for many ongoing cyber attack campaigns. This author advises that the only way to counter an offensive campaign is with an equally determined defensive campaign.

> *The only way to counter an offensive campaign is with an equally determined defensive campaign.*

In April 2015, the security company Looking Glass exposed 'Operation Armageddon,' which it described as a cyber espionage campaign (active since 2013) designed to provide a 'military advantage' to Russia by targeting Ukrainian government, law enforcement, and military officials for information of intelligence value. The researchers found a 'direct correlation' between digital attacks and the ongoing war, including an 'alarming' blend of cyber espionage, physical warfare, and geopolitics.[23] Recent reports by security companies Trend Micro and FireEye describe other Russian campaigns, assigned the monikers 'Operation Pawn Storm' and 'APT28', respectively.[24] According to FireEye, APT28 appeared to target individuals affiliated with European security organisations, including the North Atlantic Treaty Organisation (NATO) and the Organisation for Secu-

---

22 'Cyberattacks detected in Japan doubled to 25.7 billion in 2014,' *Japan Times*, 17 February 2015, http://www.japantimes.co.jp/news/2015/02/17/national/crime-legal/cyberattacks-detected-in-japan-doubled-to-25-7-billion-in-2014/.

23 Looking Glass Security, *Operation Armageddon: Cyber Espionage as a Strategic Component of Russian Modern Warfare* (Bumpas, VA: Looking Glass Security Corporation 2015) https://lgscout.com/wp-content/uploads/2015/04/Operation_Armageddon_FINAL.pdf.

24 Loucif Kharouni, et al, *Operation Pawn Storm: Using Decoys to Evade Detection* (Trend Micro Incorporated: Irving, TX 2015) http://www.trendmicro.com/cloud-content/us/pdfs/security-intelligence/white-papers/wp-operation-pawn-storm.pdf   and APT28 https://www.fireeye.com/resources/pdfs/apt28.pdf.

rity and Cooperation in Europe (OSCE) which the Russian Government has long cited as existential threats.[25]

Similarly, Russian non-government groups such as CyberBerkut have been active against NATO and Ukrainian targets.[26] In March 2014, the group directed Distributed Denial of Service (DDoS) attacks against NATO's main website, the CCD COE website, and NATO's Parliamentary Assembly website.[27] In October 2014, on the eve of parliamentary elections in Ukraine, the website of the country's Central Election Commission suffered DDoS attacks.[28] The group has apparently also targeted US military contractors working in Ukraine, stealing and publishing documents about the movement of Western military equipment to Ukraine.[29]

Nation state security requirements are strategic in nature, and they do not frequently change. For what is seen to be a valid national security concern, states will devote enormous human and technological resources to achieve their objectives, and use a variety of methods and attack vectors. Neither does a state give up after one or even a hundred unsuccessful tactical engagements. Rather, it will adapt, and usually overcome defences eventually. The key factor that sets nation states apart from individuals and even hacker groups like Anonymous is *persistence*, and the ability to maintain persistence indefinitely.

Actors such as Russia also qualify as highly 'advanced'. Here is the author's working definition, published in 2009:

> *'Advanced means the adversary can operate in the full spectrum of computer intrusion. They can use the most pedestrian publicly available exploit against a well-known vulnerability, or they can elevate their game to research new vulnerabilities and develop custom exploits, depending on the target's posture'.[30]*

Recognising that any nation-state – in this case Russia – has the capability to adapt and overcome is one reason why threat attribution is so important, at all levels of strategic thought.[31] This means that any time the security team recognises a failed intrusion attempt as coming from an advanced persistent threat actor, they can be sure the foe will return with a new technique and perhaps even a new campaign.

---

25   *Ibid.*

26   'Berkut' is Ukrainian for 'special police force', although CyberBerkut is a pro-Russian group.

27   'Ukrainian CyberBerkut takes down NATO websites', *RT*, 16 March 2014, http://www.rt.com/news/nato-websites-ddos-ukraine-146/.

28   Vitaly Shevchenko. 'Ukraine conflict: Hackers take sides in virtual war', *BBC News*, 20 December 2014, http://www.bbc.com/news/world-europe-30453069.

29   Jack Smith IV, 'Pro-Russian Hackers Expose U.S. Military Contractor Activity in Ukraine', *Observer*, 2 March 2015, http://observer.com/2015/03/pro-russian-hackers-expose-u-s-military-contractor-activity-in-ukraine/.

30   Richard Bejtlich. 'What APT Is', *Information Security Magazine*, July 2010, http://www.academia.edu/6842130/What_APT_Is.

31   Richard Bejtlich. 'Five Reasons Attribution Matters', *TaoSecurity Blog*, 30 December 2014, http://taosecurity.blogspot.com/2014/12/five-reasons-attribution-matters.html.

9   CONCLUSION

The Ukrainian Government currently finds itself at a tactical disadvantage vis-à-vis Russia, both on the traditional field of battle and in cyberspace. However, cyber security, especially at the national level, is a strategic game, and Kyiv can make smart investments that will pay off over the long run.

Cyber security, especially at the national level, is a strategic game.

This chapter has argued for the need to apply strategic thought to digital defence. It began by advocating the utility of a military model in cyberspace, albeit without any desire for the militarisation of cyberspace. The author explained how the military mind set, based on conflict with dynamic, adaptive adversaries, is a more reliable strategy than the popular 'cyber hygiene' model. It then described the five levels of strategic thought, which link goals with policy, strategy, campaigns and operations, tactics, and tools. The author applied each level of strategic thought to a hypothetical network defence scenario. By integrating strategic thought into digital defence, this chapter demonstrated an alternative to technology-centric approaches that are not sufficient to defeat the adversary.

In a time of war, Ukraine is a natural target for many cyber threat actors and campaigns. The only way to counter them is to develop an equally determined defensive posture in cyber space.

Authors

Richard Bejtlich is FireEye's Chief Security Strategist; previously, he was Mandiant's Chief Security Officer. Richard is a nonresident senior fellow at the Brookings Institution, and an advisor to Threat Stack, Sqrrl, and Critical Stack. He is pursuing a Master/Doctor of Philosophy in War Studies at King's College London. He was Director of Incident Response for General Electric, where he built and led the 40-member GE Computer Incident Response Team (GE-CIRT). Richard served in the Air Force Computer Emergency Response Team (AFCERT), Air Force Information Warfare Center (AFIWC), and Air Intelligence Agency (AIA). He is a graduate of Harvard University and the United States Air Force Academy. His widely followed blog is at taosecurity.blogspot.com, and his fourth book is *The Practice of Network Security Monitoring*.

Michelle Cantos is the Cybersecurity Program Coordinator for Columbia University's Saltzman Institute of War and Peace Studies. Michelle is a graduate of Columbia's School of International and Public Affairs, where she studied international security policy with a focus on cyber defense. In the spring of 2015, she participated in The Atlantic Council's Cyber 9/12 Student Challenge, where her team competed against twenty teams and earned second place in the policy challenge. She has worked as a cybersecurity intern for the American Foreign Policy Council, and was a research assistant for Dr. Abraham Wagner.

Kenneth Geers (PhD, CISSP) is a NATO CCD COE Ambassador, a Non-Resident Senior Fellow at the Atlantic Council, and a Visiting Professor at the Taras Shevchenko National University of Kyiv in Ukraine. Dr. Geers spent twenty years in the U.S. Government (U.S. Army, NSA, NCIS, NATO), and was a Senior Global Threat Analyst at FireEye. He is the author of *Strategic Cyber Security*, Editor of *Cyber War in Perspective: Russian Aggression against Ukraine*, Editor of *The Virtual Battlefield: Perspectives on Cyber Warfare*, Technical Expert for the *Tallinn Manual on the International Law Applicable to Cyber Warfare*, and author of more than twenty articles and chapters on international conflict in cyberspace.

Keir Giles is an Associate Fellow of Chatham House's International Security Department and Russia and Eurasia Programme. He also works with the Conflict Studies Research Centre (CSRC), a group of subject matter experts in Eurasian security. After acquiring a wide range of experience in other fields in Europe and the former Soviet Union, Keir originally joined CSRC at the UK Defence Academy (UKDA) as a specialist in human factors influencing Russian military, defence and security issues. Keir now oversees the research and publications programme of the new, independent CSRC, while continuing to write and publish there and for Chatham House on his own specialist area of Russian approaches to conventional, cyber, and information warfare.

Jason Healey is a Senior Research Scholar at Columbia University's School for International and Public Affairs, specializing in cyber conflict, competition, and cooperation. He was the founding director of the Cyber Statecraft Initiative at the Atlantic Council, where he remains a Senior Fellow. Jason is the author of dozens of published articles and editor of the first history of conflict in cyberspace, *A Fierce Domain: Cyber Conflict, 1986 to 2012*. During his time in the White House, he was a director for cyber policy and helped advise the President and coordinate US efforts to secure US cyberspace and critical infrastructure. He has also been an executive director at Goldman Sachs in Hong Kong and New York, vice chairman of the FS-ISAC, and a US Air Force intelligence officer at the Pentagon and National Security Agency. Jason was a founding member (plankowner) of the first cyber command in the world, the Joint Task Force for Computer Network Defense, in 1998. He is president of the Cyber Conflict Studies Association.

Margarita Levin Jaitner researches Information Warfare in cyberspace within the Russia Project at the Swedish Defence University. Currently, she focuses on the Russian concept of "information superiority". Margarita holds an MA degree in Societal Risk Management from Karlstad University and a BA in Political Science from the Swedish National Defence College.

Nadiya Kostyuk is a doctoral student in a joint program of Political Science and Public Policy at the University of Michigan. Prior to her studies, Nadiya worked as a Program Coordinator for the EastWest Institute's Global Cooperation in Cyberspace Initiative, where she now serves as a Fellow. Nadiya's research interest is the relationship between cybercrime and international security, interdependence, cooperation, and state sovereignty. Currently, Nadiya is working on a project to map the relationship between kinetic and cyber operations in Eastern Ukraine.

Nikolay Koval is CEO of CyS Centrum LLC, in Kyiv, Ukraine. A graduate of the Kyiv Polytechnic Institute, Nikolay served at the State Service of Special Communication and Information Protection of Ukraine. He was responsible for the organization and coordination of Ukraine's computer emergency response team (CERT-UA) activities, including incident handling, technical analysis, and international engagement. His new company specializes in cyber threat prevention.

Elina Lange-Ionatamishvili is a Senior Expert at the NATO Strategic Communications Centre of Excellence (NATO StratCom COE) in Riga, Latvia, where she has analyzed Russia's ongoing information campaign against Ukraine. Previously, Elina was head of the Public Diplomacy Division at the Ministry of Defence of Latvia (2007-2009), worked on public diplomacy projects under the NATO Riga Summit Task Force (2006), managed the NATO Professional Development Programme in Georgia, and helped to found the international NGO *Baltic to Black Sea Alliance*, which has addressed media freedom and professionalism in EU Eastern Partnership countries. Elina has been awarded by the Latvian Minister of Defence, and received the Order of Honour from the President of Georgia.

James Andrew Lewis is a Senior Fellow at the Center for Strategic and International Studies, directs the CSIS Technology Program, and previously worked at the Departments of State and Commerce as a Foreign Service Officer and member of the Senior Executive Service. Lewis helped to develop the initial policies to secure and commercialize the Internet, led the U.S. delegation to the Wassenaar Arrangement Experts Group, and was Rapporteur for the UN Group of Government Experts on Information Security during their successful 2010, 2013, and 2015 sessions. Jim has authored numerous CSIS publications, and was Director for the *Commission on Cybersecurity for the 44th Presidency*, the best-selling report whose contributions to U.S. policy have been publicly recognized by the President. His current research examines sovereignty on the Internet, cybersecurity norms, warfare, and technological innovation. Lewis received his Ph.D. from the University of Chicago.

Martin Libicki (Ph.D., U.C. Berkeley 1978) has been a distinguished visiting professor at the U.S. Naval Academy and a senior management scientist at RAND since 1998, focusing on the impacts of information technology on domestic and national security. He wrote two commercially published books, *Conquest in Cyberspace: National Security and Information Warfare*, and *Information Technology Standards: Quest for the Common Byte*, as well as numerous RAND monographs, notably *Brandishing Cyberattack Capabilities, Crisis and Escalation in Cyberspace, Global Demographic Change and its Implications for Military Power*, and *Cyber-Deterrence and Cyber-War*. He co-authored *How Insurgencies End* and *How Terrorist Groups End*. Martin is currently writing a textbook (due out in Spring 2016) from which a Cyberwar class can be taught.

Jarno Limnéll is a Professor of Cybersecurity at Aalto University in Finland, and the Vice President of Cybersecurity at Insta Group plc. Professor Limnéll has been working with security issues for over 20 years. He holds a Doctor of Military Science degree in Strategy from the National Defense University in Finland; a Master of Social Science degree from Helsinki University; and an Officer's degree from the National Defense University. Limnéll served many years as an officer in the Finnish Defense Forces, and has worked as a Director of Cybersecurity at McAfee. His most recent book is *Cybersecurity for Decision Makers*.

Tim Maurer is the Director of the *Global Cybersecurity Norms and Resilience Project*, and Head of Research at New America's *Cybersecurity Initiative*. He is part of New America's *Future of War* project and serves as a member of the Research Advisory Network of the *Global Commission on Internet Governance*, the Freedom Online Coalition's cybersecurity working group "An Internet Free and Secure", and was co-chair of the Advisory Board for the Global Conference on Cyberspace. He holds a Master in Public Policy concentrating on international and global affairs from the Harvard Kennedy School.

Glib Pakharenko (CISA, CISSP) is an IT security specialist, board member for the OWASP and ISACA Kyiv chapters, forum moderator, and the conference organizer for the largest information security community of Ukraine, the Ukrainian Information Security Group. Glib has over 10 years of IT security experience in financial, telecom, media, and other industries. He actively supports the reform and modernization of Ukrainian national cyber security policies, and reviews technical and IT security translations into the Ukrainian language.

Liisa Past is a NATO CCD COE adviser and spokesperson, with academic interests in political communication, argumentation, and discourse analysis. Educated at Columbia University, the University of Oslo, and Tartu University, Liisa has taught at numerous institutions of higher education, and worked with companies, organizations, and a political party on strategic communication and public relations. As an activist, she has contributed to human rights causes and has worked with the International Debate Education Association, Estonian Debating Society, and Baltimore Urban Debate League.

Henry Rõigas is a researcher in the Law and Policy Branch at NATO CCD COE, studying policy matters such as state interest in global cyber diplomacy, international norm development, the role of international organisations, and the cyber security posture of small states. He is the Project Manager of the Ukraine case study book and the Centre's INCYDER (International Cyber Developments Review) database. Henry holds a Master's degree in International Relations from the University of Tartu.

Jan Stinissen is a military lawyer in the Netherlands Army with the rank of Lieutenant Colonel. He served as a military lawyer for more than 20 years in different positions in The Netherlands and in Germany. He was deployed as a Legal Advisor with NATO missions abroad. Most recently, Lt Col Stinissen worked as a Researcher with the Law and Policy Branch at the NATO CCD COE in Tallinn, Estonia. He holds a Master in Law degree from the University of Utrecht, The Netherlands.

Sanda Svetoka is a Senior Expert at the NATO Strategic Communications Centre of Excellence (NATO StratCom COE) in Riga, Latvia, where she is the project leader for StratCom's study on how social media are used as a weapon in hybrid warfare. From 2004-2005, she worked as a news reporter at the Latvian information agency LETA. In 2005, she joined the Latvian Ministry of Defence, where she coordinated Latvian cooperation with NATO partner countries. In 2010-2011, Ms Svetoka was Public Relations Advisor to the NATO Advisory Team in Kosovo. From 2011-2014, she served as a Press Officer at the Military Public Relations Department of the Latvian Ministry of Defence. Ms Svetoka holds an MA in Political Science from the University of Latvia.

Jen Weedon is a strategic threat intelligence analyst and cyber risk management consultant at FireEye. Jen played a key role in building out Mandiant's intelligence team and contributed to Mandiant's landmark APT1 report, linking a long-running cyber espionage effort to a Chinese military unit. She worked on the cyber espionage and hacktivist portfolios at iSIGHT Partners. Prior to that, Jen analyzed and briefed policymakers on Russia's intents and motivations in cyberspace for the U.S. defense community. She is a graduate of the Fletcher School of Law and Diplomacy (2008) and Smith College (2002), was awarded a Fulbright Fellowship in Ukraine (2002-2003), and is an inaugural fellow for Foreign Policy Interrupted (2015).

Professor **James J. Wirtz** is Dean, School of International Graduate Studies at the U.S. Naval Postgraduate School in Monterey, California. He is editor of the Palgrave Macmillan series, Initiatives in Strategic Studies: Issues and Policies, and a past president of the International Security and Arms Control Section of the American Political Science Association. In 2005, he was a Visiting Professor at the Center for International Security and Cooperation, Stanford University. Between 2009 and 2014 he served as the Director of the Global Center for Security Cooperation, Defense Security Cooperation Agency. His work on intelligence, deterrence, the Vietnam War, and military innovation and strategy has been widely published in academic journals. Professor Wirtz is a graduate of Columbia University (MPhil 1987, PhD 1989), the University of Delaware (MA 1983, BA 1980), and was a John M. Olin Pre-Doctoral Fellow at the Center for International Affairs, Harvard University.